Waltham Forest Libraries

ROYAL MARRIAGE SECRETS

CONSORTS & CONCUBINES, BIGAMISTS & BASTARDS

JOHN ASHDOWN-HILL

The History Press

In memory of my friend and colleague,
Dr Karen Tracy Yates-Sabren,
who read bits of it while I was working on it in Turkey,
and who had been looking forward to reading the whole thing.

✠ ✠ ✠

Oh, 'tis a glorious thing, I ween,
To be a regular Royal Queen!

W.S. Gilbert, *The Gondoliers*

✠ ✠ ✠

Such a lot of things are such rot.
History, for instance.
Why, it's quite different out of different books!

Agatha Christie, *The Moving Finger*

✠ ✠ ✠

Front cover image: The solemnisation of the marriage of Prince James
Francis Edward Stuart and Princess Maria Clementina Sobieska at
Montefiascone, 1 September 1719, Agostino Masucci. *National Galleries
of Scotland*

First published 2013

The History Press
The Mill, Brimscombe Port
Stroud, Gloucestershire, GL5 2QG
www.thehistorypress.co.uk

British Library Cataloguing in Publication Data.
A catalogue record for this book is available from the British Library.

ISBN 978 0 7524 8726 7

Typesetting and origination by The History Press
Printed in Great Britain

CONTENTS

ACKNOWLEDGEMENTS

I should like to thank Annette Carson and Dave Perry for reading and commenting upon draft versions of parts of the text. I am also grateful to Dr Alison Rowland for her advice on medieval love magic, and to Robert Galea-Naudi for his kind assistance with my researches in Malta.

AUTHOR'S NOTE

There are three practical points to draw to the attention of my readers concerning the way in which names have been written. First, in the days before her marriage to the Prince of Wales, it always struck me as a little bizarre when the media referred to HRH the Duchess of Cornwall by the surname of her first husband, rather than calling her by her birth surname – Camilla Shand. The practice of previous historians has often been inconsistent on this point. Some royal consorts, such as Elizabeth Woodville and Catherine Parr, are generally known by their maiden surnames, despite the fact that they had previous husbands. Others, such as Mrs Fitzherbert and Mrs Simpson, are generally called by their married surnames. But in genealogy and family history the normal practice is to refer to women by their maiden names. Therefore throughout this book women's maiden surnames are used consistently if these are known. Where their married surnames are more familiar, these are sometimes added in brackets in the text and they are cross-referenced in the index.

The second point is that in historical documents some first names occur in many variant spellings. 'Catherine', 'Catharine' and 'Katheryn' are good examples of this. Likewise 'Eleanor' in medieval documents is often 'Alianore'. I have tried to spell first names in one consistent way throughout. One exception is Isabel(le)/Isabella. Where this name refers to ladies of French origin the French spelling,

Isabelle is used; for Spanish ladies, the Spanish form, *Isabel*. *Isabella* is only used for English ladies who were baptised with that form of the name. Of course, my selections reflect my personal choice and my spellings may not be everyone's favourites.

Finally, sometimes royal names and/or numbers are given in square brackets – as for example George [IV]. This is simply to show that at the date in question the monarch had not yet succeeded to the throne.

INTRODUCTION

Some historians argue that personal relationships are of little or no real importance in the course of history. I believe that they are wrong. Private emotions certainly affect people and when they are the emotions of people in power they can change the course of events. Moreover, royal sexual activity and royal marriage have always exerted a certain popular fascination, and they continue to do so to the present day. The *ménage à trois* between the present Prince of Wales, his first wife Diana, and his mistress (later his second wife) Camilla, at times generated huge amounts of publicity. The marriage history of the prince's siblings – likewise that of his aunt, Princess Margaret – also engaged considerable media attention at key periods.

Modern media interest in royal marriages – particularly questionable royal marriages – is often perceived to date back to the 1930s, and the relationship of the then Prince of Wales (Edward VIII) with his American divorcee, Bessie Wallis Warfield (Mrs Simpson) – a drama which ended in marriage only after the king's abdication. However, eighteenth- and nineteenth-century press reports about George [IV]'s relationship with the Catholic widow, 'Princess Fitz' (Maria Smythe, Mrs Fitzherbert), and about 'Mrs Brown' (referring to Queen Victoria's reputed relationship with her highland ghillie, John Brown) show that there is a much longer history of public interest in such matters.

With only four or five (possible) exceptions[1] all English monarchs since the Norman Conquest in 1066 have married at some stage in their careers. Even those whose sexual proclivities may have led them to prefer partners of their own sex did usually marry – constrained to outward conformity by dynastic necessity.[2] Some kings married more than once. Many also had sexual partners outside their marriages. However, the number of English monarchs whose marriages have been a matter of dispute can be counted on two hands. Situations in which the identity of a sovereign's marriage partner was unknown or uncertain were normally ruled out by a natural concern for the succession to the throne.

Nevertheless, secret marriages have been reported or alleged in the case of eight English monarchs and one would-be monarch: Edward IV (reigned 1460–83), Henry VIII (reigned 1509–47), Elizabeth I (reigned 1558–1603), Charles II (reigned 1660–85), 'Charles III' (never quite a monarch, but a famous royal figure, and the Stuart pretender to the throne 1766–88), George III (reigned 1760–1820), George IV (reigned 1820–30), Queen Victoria (reigned 1837–1901) and George V (reigned 1910–36). In addition to these nine cases, there have also been allegations of secret royal marriage relating to two heirs to the throne who died before they could succeed. One of these allegations is linked with a celebrated case of serial murder. It relates to George V's elder brother, Albert Victor, Duke of Clarence. The other alleged secret marriage of an heir apparent relates to Edward III's son, the 'Black Prince'.

Although we shall focus chiefly on these eleven cases, alleged secret marriage within the royal family as a whole is a more widespread phenomenon. The secret marriages of princes and princesses will provide a background and context for our exploration.[3] Moreover, one case in the wider royal family – the alleged secret second marriage of the queen mother, Catherine of France (widow of Henry V) – is significant so it will be explored in some detail, focusing on possible new evidence.

In some of these allegations, religious issues are important. In particular the stories of the secret marriages of George [IV] and of Albert Victor, Duke of Clarence, to Catholic partners confront us with the discriminatory nature of the 1701 Act of Settlement. The provisions of this act still apply at the moment of writing. Recently it had seemed that things were about to change. In the Queen's Speech at the opening of Parliament in May 2012 it was announced that the prohibition which prevents British royalty from marrying Catholics would soon be lifted. However, it now seems that the coalition government of Britain has dropped its plans for repealing the Act of Settlement. But for this act, of course, and other legislation affecting the royal succession, one of our cases of disputed royal marriage – that of the Prince of Wales [George IV] with Maria Smythe (Mrs Fitzherbert) would undoubtedly have been legal. But this merely serves to reinforce the point that it is essential for us to be aware of precisely which marriage legislation was in force at the time when each of our disputed royal weddings is alleged to have taken place.

Six of the allegations against sovereigns involve the imputation of bigamy. This is most famously the case in respect of the future George IV. Another instance of bigamy can be detected (albeit heavily disguised by his own propaganda machine) involving Henry VIII. Further cases involving bigamy – largely overlooked by posterity – have been alleged in the cases of Edward IV, 'Charles III', George III and George V. These six instances of possible royal bigamy will all be examined and evaluated here.

We shall also consider the quite well-known secret royal marriage allegation involving Charles II. This was certainly not a case of bigamy, for Charles' two unions (whatever the nature of the first of them) did not overlap chronologically. Nevertheless, there are features which link his case with some of the bigamy allegations.

The remaining two cases of reigning monarchs that we shall explore involved two of England's queens regnant. These, like the case of Charles II, contain no element of bigamy as far as the monarch is concerned, though in the case of Elizabeth I the complicated story does involve the accusation of bigamy against at least one of the queen's alleged partners. It also impinges upon the true identity of William Shakespeare!

Of course, whole books have been written about each of these royal personages, and the stories of their alleged marriages have been recounted elsewhere. However, they have never previously been examined together to explore how the different cases can shed light on one another. This present study seeks to take an overview of the phenomenon of disputed English royal marriage as a whole, offering some new evidence, highlighting common features and points of contrast, and suggesting possible explanations.

In the case of Edward IV and Eleanor Talbot, the present writer himself has previously published a detailed exploration of the relevant surviving evidence.[4] It was interesting that subsequent discussion of this material and of its interpretation revealed that even some well-known historians apparently had little understanding of how marriage evolved over the past thousand years. Yet the changes in this key social institution have been enormous, and are ongoing. This serves to remind us that when we try to explore historical situations it is absolutely essential to try, as far as possible, to put ourselves back into the context of the period we are studying. Failure to do so is almost bound to lead to anachronisms and errors.

Before we can attempt to understand and interpret the evidence in our cases of disputed royal marriage, we must first try to understand the evolution of marriage practices in England.[5] Therefore we shall begin by tracing the overall development of English marriage practice in general over roughly the past one thousand years. We shall also consider the particular evidence relating to the history of royal marriages during this period.

Moreover, since the cases that we shall examine in detail relate to disputed *marriages*, we should consider what might have been the nature of these nine royal relationships if they were NOT marriages. This means that we shall also review background information relating to England's many illicit royal love affairs. And since it is important to define all our terms of reference as precisely as we can, as part of our background exploration we shall also consider the interesting question of what was, or is, a 'mistress'.

Even without reference to wider material on the history of marriage, the disputed royal marriage cases themselves, when considered together, highlight the important point that the form and nature of marriage has not been something fixed and immutable in English history. For example it is easy to see that the marriage legislation which impinged upon George IV made his matrimonial playing field very different from the one upon which Henry VIII had manoeuvred 250 years earlier.

Over the centuries there have been many changes in how marriage is perceived, and how it is carried out. Fifty years ago the majority of English marriages took place in churches. Now this is no longer the case – nor was it the case five hundred years ago. The wording of marriage vows has recently become somewhat flexible – as it was also in the distant past. Nowadays one essential component of any marriage is the marriage certificate. But, in general, prior to the sixteenth century no written records of marriages were kept. Even the history of wedding rings shows that what is now, in popular perception, a key feature of the wedding ceremony has witnessed changes. In the seventeenth century Puritans even attempted to ban wedding rings.

Some of the changes in practice and attitude have been quite huge. Modern rules about marriage are very clear, but in the medieval and early modern period marriage was a kind of minefield. It was only too easy to thoughtlessly utter the wrong words which, when coupled with subsequent sexual intercourse, might leave one tied up in an unintended but almost indissoluble bond. At the same time there is no doubt that this situation could be – and at times was – exploited by infatuated, cynical and powerful men to overcome the moral scruples of reluctant girlfriends. In another way, however, the situation was equally open to manipulation by clever women for their own advantage.

Looking at alleged secret royal marriages over nearly 700 years – from the case of the Black Prince in the mid-fourteenth century to that of George [V] in the late nineteenth century – will help us to understand the evolution of English marriage legislation in general, exposing the differences underlying the individual cases. At the same time, however, common features will be revealed. Hopefully both points will help us to understand each of the individual cases rather better.

Looking at the royal marriage disputes together is interesting in several respects. First, we shall see that in six of the nine cases the disputed marriage of the monarch was set in the wider context of other secret and disputed marriages within the royal family as a whole at the period in question. For example, the late fourteenth and fifteenth centuries had witnessed several unusual Plantagenet and Lancastrian royal marriages prior to the key Yorkist marriage case of Edward IV. The marital manoeuvres of Henry VIII and Elizabeth I occurred in the broader context of several *mésalliances* in the Tudor dynasty as a whole. For contemporaries, the alleged marriage of Charles [II] and Lucy Walter was set against the background of an acknowledged – but initially secret – non-royal marriage on the part of the king's younger brother, coupled with the alleged secret marriages of some of his cousins. And the stories of the marriages of George III and his beautiful Quaker, and of George [IV] and his Catholic widow – while each was exceptional in respect of the lady's religion – were both, in other ways, very similar to the independent and unauthorised matrimonial conduct of the younger brothers of the respective bridegrooms. In several of our cases we must also take account of the fact that it was an outside party who brought the alleged secret wedding into the public domain. An examination of the motivation behind this revelation will therefore form part of our assessment. Another important point, which we shall encounter in several instances, concerns the avowed religious or moral scruples of at least one of the female partners involved.

The purpose of this book is not, of course, to change the present reigning family! However, history has been very inconsistent in its handling of secret or questionable royal marriages. Had they been dealt with more consistently the order of succession might well have been different. Some of the cases have received a great deal of publicity, while others remain almost unknown to the general public. In the case of Henry VIII, the king's 'second marriage' (as popularly perceived) has passed more or less undisputed by historical writers – even though it was much disputed at the time. As a result, Anne Boleyn has usually been described by posterity as a Queen of England, despite the fact that Henry VIII himself officially deprived her of that title. In the case of George IV the existence of a secret marriage is generally accepted, though for legal reasons the status of the bride remains equivocal. In most of the other instances the idea of a secret marriage has been generally discounted by historians, sometimes on good evidence, but sometimes not. Thus, despite the fact that in 1484 Parliament officially enacted that Edward IV's true wife had been Eleanor Talbot, unlike Anne Boleyn, Eleanor has not generally been accorded royal status.

In several of the disputed cases, the disbelief of historical writers seems to be founded mainly on the lack of any *direct* proof of a marriage, coupled with the existence of what has been perceived to be an ulterior motive on someone's part in claiming that a secret marriage had existed. The logic of both of these arguments seems questionable, and in attempting to determine whether or not the disputed secret marriages really took place, we should ideally try to seek firmer ground. As we have already seen, prior to the sixteenth century there was rarely any formal written evidence of a marriage, so that for most, if not all, medieval marriages the available evidence is bound to be circumstantial. Moreover, lack of evidence that an event occurred can never be construed as proof that the event did *not* take place. If possible, clearer evidence against an alleged union should be sought before dismissing the allegation out of hand. Likewise, the fact that a third party may later have benefited from a secret marriage allegation does not, by itself, prove that allegation to be false.[6]

I hope that reviewing these nine cases of disputed royal marriage together, and setting them in the wider context of the contemporary marital activities of the royal family as a whole, will allow the individual cases to shed light on one another.

Thus we shall perceive some parallels between Henry VIII's relationships with Catherine of Aragon and Anne Boleyn, and Edward IV's relationships with Eleanor Talbot and Elizabeth Woodville in the preceding century. Reviewing the official position ultimately taken up by the establishment may, in some cases, also serve to highlight key similarities and differences. For example, in 1911 the case of George V was taken straight to court – presumably because it was considered that there was sufficient evidence for the king to win. Therefore in 1483–84, when Richard III took the disputed marriage of his late brother, Edward IV, to Parliament, perhaps that was for similar reasons. On the other hand, Henry VII's later suppression and destruction of Richard III's evidence tends to confirm that the evidence in Richard's case had been pretty convincing. My review of the case of George V, on the other hand, seems to reveal flaws in *that* king's evidence.

Some previous writers have chosen to make very firm judgements about our cases of disputed royal marriage. This will not be done here. Many of the cases are not black and white, and there may be no simple answer. In one sense Henry VIII was certainly married to Anne Boleyn – but in another sense he was not! George [IV] clearly had a wedding with Maria Smythe (Mrs Fitzherbert) – but was it legal? On the whole my preference will be to tell the stories, present the evidence (some of it new), draw some parallels, and then leave the final verdict in each case to my readers.

One

The Background

1

THE EVOLUTION
OF MARRIAGE

That the good purpose of marriage is better promoted by one husband with one
wife, than by a husband with several wives, is shown plainly enough by the very
first union of a married pair, which was made by the Divine Being Himself.

St Augustine, *On Marriage and Concupiscence*, Book 1, Chapter 10

O ne key word which will require careful consideration in this study
is *marriage*. This has been defined in many ways. The Oxford English
Dictionary describes it as 'the formal union of a man and a woman,
typically as recognised by law, by which they become husband and wife'.[1] An
alternative, slightly fuller dictionary definition states that marriage is 'the social
institution under which a man and woman establish their decision to live as husband and wife by legal commitments, religious ceremonies, etc'.[2]

Each of these definitions makes important basic points. At the same time they
both omit essential information.

Implicit in both definitions is the idea that marriage involves one partner of
either sex. In other words what is being defined here is *monogamous heterosexual*
marriage. Nowadays, of course, marriage is not universally heterosexual. However,
in the past history of English royal marriages heterosexuality always constituted
the normal and required pattern.

As for monogamy, as St Augustine's quote at the head of this chapter shows, in
the ancient past, that was not a universal norm, and even today monogamy is not
required in some cultures. In Christian contexts, however, monogamy has always
been accepted, so that when reviewing English royal marriages, monogamy is a
basic rule to which we should always expect those marriages to conform. Thus
if an English sovereign already had a spouse, (s)he could not acquire a second
married partner without first disposing in some way of the earlier commitment.
This point will prove significant in some of the cases which we shall examine.

From a historical perspective the most salient omission in the definitions of marriage quoted above is their failure to state that until five centuries ago the law involved in the recognition of marriage was not the law of the State, but the law of the Church. Prior to the sixteenth century the State generally had no say in matters of marriage, and played no role in the recording of marriages or in the adjudication of their validity.

The key point to remember is that marriage is not a static institution. In the course of history it has evolved a great deal. Until the middle of the sixteenth century Christian marriage throughout Europe was basically a matter of mutual consent between the two contracting parties – and also their families if titles or property were involved. The partners merely had to declare their intention to marry. This had to be followed by their physical union (sexual intercourse).

> The couple would promise verbally to each other that they would be married to each other; the presence of a priest or witnesses was not required. This promise was known as the *verbum*. If freely given and made in the present tense (e.g., 'I marry you'), it was unquestionably binding; if made in the future tense ('I will marry you'), it would constitute a betrothal.[3]

It is important to note that the promise was oral. There was no requirement for anything to be written down. Also the Church might or might not be directly involved, but there was certainly no question of any State involvement. And if subsequently any query arose about the validity of the marriage this would be adjudicated in a *Church* court, not a civil court.

On one level marriage has always been first and foremost a sexual union. But not all sexual unions are marriages. Implicit in marriage are concepts of commitment and authorisation. In the context of such a commitment a female partner is safe to surrender her virginity and risk pregnancy, because she has the supposed guaranteed support of a male partner, coupled with the approval of society. Sexual unions which were not marriages were much more risky. Even if they outlasted the initial phase of sexual attraction and became enduring long-term relationships, they still lacked official authorisation. The children produced by such unions were traditionally viewed – and treated – by European society as different in quality and inferior in importance to children produced within marriages. It is true that in the twenty-first century the concept of 'illegitimacy' has largely faded into insignificance, but historically the discrimination between 'official' and 'unofficial' offspring was extremely important.

The modern phenomenon of marriage may also be different in other ways from its historical counterpart. In twenty-first century England 55 per cent of marriages are celebrated in non-religious venues. The overwhelming majority of bridegrooms will wear a wedding ring.[4] Today, 93 per cent of the couples will have been living together prior to their marriage, and 88 per cent of the brides assume their husband's surname after marriage, but 3 per cent keep their maiden names. Other couples combine their two surnames.[5]

One hundred years ago the picture was different in many respects. Most marriages were then celebrated inside churches, and English husbands were rarely given wedding rings as part of the marriage ceremony. The modern move away from a religious venue for a wedding was initially regarded as somewhat revolutionary. However, marriages had not always been held in religious venues. Prior to the sixteenth century a wedding *inside* a church was by no means the norm. If they were formal, public events, weddings were often held in the open air, outside churches. But many marriages were made in private, by a simple exchange of promises, with no public present. Such simple, private exchanges of vows could take place anywhere – in a house, in a barn, in the open air. It is therefore clear that the history of marriage in England has witnessed many changes over the past 1,000 years, and the form and significance of marriage has by no means been fixed.

Royal marriages may always have been always something rather special, set apart a little from the general run of weddings – and in recent years, perhaps, a little conservative in nature. Thus twentieth-century royal partners did not usually live together before marriage, royal bridegrooms tend not to be given wedding rings in their marriage ceremonies, and royal marriages generally continue to be celebrated in large and significant churches.[6]

However, even royal marriages have undergone change and evolution. Fiona Macdonald, author of *Royal Weddings: A Very Peculiar History*, has claimed that recent royal weddings show a break with past tradition in respect of the choice of brides:

> Until the 19th Century and early in the 1900s, the pattern had been largely the same for the past 1,000 years. Royal weddings were usually arranged for political, dynastic and empire-building reasons, and the bride and groom were always of mutually royal rank. Marrying a commoner was exceptionally rare. The most famous example was Edward IV marrying Elizabeth Woodville in the 15th Century.[7]

Many people would probably intuitively agree with Macdonald's statement that 'the bride and groom were always of mutually royal rank', but in fact this is completely untrue. Appendix 1 (below) shows very clearly that, of the forty-nine listed English sovereigns and direct heirs since the Norman Conquest, less than half married consorts who were of royal birth. Royally born spouses have been particularly rare since the Hanoverian accession. Nevertheless, it is true that the most recent generations have certainly witnessed changes in the origin and social status of royal marriage partners by comparison with the immediately preceding centuries.

In other respects, prior to the twentieth century royal weddings varied very considerably. For example, in the past they were by no means automatically public affairs. Sometimes they were celebrated in the privacy of a chapel royal. Queen Victoria and Prince Albert were married on 10 February 1840, in the Chapel Royal of St James's Palace in London. More than three centuries earlier, on 11 June 1509, Henry VIII married Catherine of Aragon at an even more private ceremony at the Greenwich Greyfriars' Church – although Catherine had previously married Henry's elder brother, Arthur, much more publicly, at old St Paul's Cathedral.[8] Some royal weddings were celebrated outside England. The first marriage of Edward I and the marriage of Edward II are examples. A surviving illustration of the occasion implies that the wedding of Edward II may have been a public event, held in the open air, in front of (rather than inside) the shrine church of Our Lady of the Sea at Boulogne. The illustration, however, is not contemporary with the event (see below).

Sometimes royal bridegrooms did not even attend their own weddings. Some royal marriages were celebrated with only one of the two partners present. Thus Charles II married the Infanta of Portugal by proxy – and by Catholic rites, despite the fact that the Reformation had by this time taken place[9] – at a partly public, partly private ceremony in Lisbon on 23 April 1662.[10] Charles was 'present' on this occasion only in the guise of an oil painting. A month later, after the Infanta had reached England, repeat marriage ceremonies, both Catholic and Protestant, were conducted for them, at each of which both of the parties were physically present. The Protestant marriage ceremony was conducted by the Bishop of London. Nevertheless, that was a private, not a public event.

The legal situation in medieval and early modern Europe was similar to that which exists in some Moslem countries today – where religious (*sharia*) law either plays a significant role alongside civil law, or may even supersede it. In the same way in medieval and early modern Christian society Church law played an important role, and in some matters the religious law was entirely predominant. Thus, in the first part of the period we are considering, the laws relating to marriage were exclusively Church laws and had nothing to do with the State.

However, the medieval Church rules for marriage were in some ways imprecise. They included no provision for any written record, and generated no such document as a marriage certificate – an item which would be considered indispensable in any modern marriage. Curiously, perhaps, the Church marriage laws also required no specific ceremonial, no attendant priest,[11] no witnesses and no specific and authorised venue. A formal wedding ceremonial of the Church did certainly exist, and was sometimes used, but it was by no means an essential requirement.[12] Hence marriage promises could be, and were, exchanged anywhere. There was no compulsion for vows to be made in a church, or in any other legally established place. And since there was no formal requirement for a priest – or indeed anyone except the contracting couple – to attend, the verbal promises which comprised the first requirement for a wedding could be uttered with only the bride and groom present.

It has always been the Catholic Church's teaching that marriage is a self-conferring sacrament, which is basically effected by the free consent of the parties, confirmed by consummation. In the Middle Ages (when marriage had not yet become a civil contract) it was the logic of this argument which led to the practical conclusion that no formal, public ceremony was essential. 'Betrothal followed by intercourse was recognised by the Church as a binding marriage contract'.[13] In fact, either a promise exchanged *per verba de presenti*[14] alone (i.e. without subsequent sexual intercourse), or alternatively a promise *per verba de futura*[15] followed by sexual intercourse, constituted a valid marriage.

Vows followed by intercourse had been formally and explicitly acknowledged as constituting valid marriages by decretals of Pope Alexander III.[16] Consequently, as we have seen, the official position of the Church was that no special ceremony, no specific venue, no priest and no witness was essential for a valid marriage. One unfortunate result of this prevailing informality was that the promise of marriage could easily be employed by any unprincipled man as a seduction technique.[17] As a result, it does seem to have been widely regarded as a wise and useful precaution to have a witness present at any exchange of vows – in case of subsequent disputes.

Actually, although private and informal marriages were recognised, they were not greatly favoured by the Church. The ecclesiastical *magisterium* had been struggling for some time to impose a more orderly situation, and the medieval Church did already strongly recommend public marriage ceremonies, preferably preceded by the reading of banns,[18] precisely in order to avoid the kind of marriage disputes which were wont to arise from clandestine exchanges of promises. As early as 1215 the Fourth Lateran Council had sought to generalise throughout Europe the system of publication of banns before marriage.[19] Nevertheless, for several centuries the Church's attempts to impose a more ordered situation largely fell on deaf ears, and informal and private marriages continued to be practised, as the surviving records of litigation in the English Church courts clearly demonstrate.

In time, however, this situation was set to change.

> The failure of the medieval church to impose ... its own religious ceremony as the one binding ritual to legitimate a sexual union [makes] the medieval approach to marriage and sex very different from that of seventeenth century England. The introduction of registers of births, marriages and deaths in 1538 was evidence of a tightening of both lay and clerical controls over the private lives of the population.[20]

Thus, both within the Catholic Church and outside it, from the sixteenth century onwards more formal regulations surrounding marriage were imposed. But such regulations cannot be applied retrospectively when judging the validity of *medieval* marriages.

Leytonstone Library
Tel : 020 8496 5241
24 Hour Renewal 0333 370 4700

Item Title	Due Date
really	31/01/2019

R

Th

M

In general the marriage rules which applied to medieval English monarchs – including Edward IV (reigned 1460–83) – still applied in the case of the early Tudor monarchs such as Edward IV's grandson, Henry VIII (reigned 1509–47). These were the rules of the pre-Tridentine Catholic Church. In fact it was Henry VIII's own conduct which was to considerably alter the situation in England. When England ceased to be part of Catholic Christendom, changes, impelled in the first instance by Henry VIII's own specific matrimonial needs, began to be introduced into English Church law. Moreover, the fact that the head of State was now also the head of the Church introduced a degree of confusion as to where Church law ended and civil law began. Henry VIII abrogated the teaching of canon law at the English universities and thereafter lawyers who practised in the ecclesiastical courts had to be trained in civil law. As a result, slowly but surely marriage legislation ceased to be a matter for the Church. Of course, Church rules remained in force for the faithful, but in general marriage became increasingly a matter for civil legislation.

However, the historical picture is complex. While Henry VIII introduced notable changes – including a legal requirement for the registration of marriages – he was not acting completely in isolation, or without precedent. The dichotomy between Church legislation and the law of the State had begun to manifest itself much earlier. We shall see shortly that William the Conqueror defied the papacy in the matter of his marriage – and ultimately got his own way. Later the future King John also entered into conflict with the Church over the question of his marriage – in his case unsuccessfully.

The remarriage of widowed English queens was subject to State laws as early as the twelfth century, and these laws were extended by specific and explicit parliamentary legislation in the fifteenth century. Marriages within the royal family generally were subject to the sovereign's approval from a very early stage, and this particular feature of royal marriages would be progressively reinforced later in history (notably from the sixteenth to the eighteenth centuries).

The fifteenth century shows evidence of increasing State involvement in marriage disputes in several respects. Thus it seems to have been Parliament which took the lead in the moves to dissolve the marriage of Henry VI's uncle, the Duke of Gloucester, to Eleanor Cobham (see below), although of course the actual annulment decision had to be taken by the Church. Likewise it was Parliament which adjudicated the disputed marriage of Edward IV at the end of the fifteenth century. Thus when Henry VIII used civil law in the matter of his own disputed marriages, and instituted a law requiring marriage registration, he was not being revolutionary. Rather he was following (and developing) existing precedents.

The result of this historical process is that the marriage laws affecting later rulers – for example the Stuart king, Charles II (reigned 1660–85) – were not the same as those that had impinged upon Edward IV and Henry VIII. And, as we shall see, by the lifetime of George IV (born 1762, reigned 1820–30) specific new complications had been introduced, in the form of the Royal Marriages Act and other legislation.

The evolution of marriage law has led to some significant changes, and if attempts were made to apply the modern rules retrospectively to historical cases this might produce bizarre results. For example, the canon law of the Anglican Church – which arose as an independent ecclesial body from the dispute over Henry VIII's petition for nullity in respect of his marriage to his late brother's widow, Catherine of Aragon – now *permits* marriage to a deceased brother's wife without requiring any dispensation.[21] Thus under modern *Anglican* canon law Henry's marriage to Catherine would unquestionably be regarded as valid. On the other hand, despite the fact that Catherine of Aragon, in the sixteenth century, considered the question of whether her first marriage had or had not been consummated as a key issue, modern *Catholic* canon law now specifically decrees that 'affinity arises from a valid marriage, even if not consummated'.[22]

In modern Catholic law it is also now the case that if a marriage is declared null and void, any children born of the annulled marriage are regarded as legitimate.[23] Had this rule also applied automatically in the fifteenth and sixteenth centuries then Parliament might have thought twice about offering the throne to Richard III, and Henry VIII could not have declared his daughters Mary and Elizabeth to be bastards. However, the key point to remember is that at those periods the rules were different. From this we can see how important it is for historians to understand precisely *which* marriage laws were in force during the period about which they are writing.

2

MEDIEVAL

MARRIAGE PRACTICE

GROOM: I ... take thee ... for fairer or fouler ...
BRIDE: I ... take thee ... to be bonny and buxom at bed and at board ...

Extracts from late medieval marriage vows

Throughout the medieval period, then, marriage in England (and indeed in the whole of Western Europe) was a sacrament of the Catholic Church. This sacrament was self-conferring – that is to say all that was required was the free consent of a man and a woman to live together as husband and wife, mutually expressed firstly in the form of a vow or promise and secondly in the form of sexual intercourse. A formal wedding service did exist, which could be conducted by a priest, with witnesses and other guests present. Possibly there would be musical accompaniment to the ceremony, together with the offering of gifts to the marrying couple. However, this ceremony was not obligatory – though the Church certainly preferred it and increasingly encouraged its use.

Of course, the man and woman had to be free to marry. Most importantly this meant that they could not already be married to someone else, although there were also other rules governing the degree of kinship which was permitted (see below). They had to be old enough to be able to express their free consent in words. No actual age of consent for marriage was specified, and in practice children as young as four took the vows on occasions. However, they were not permitted to proceed to the second stage – sexual intercourse – until they reached the age of puberty. 'Sixteen was the normal age for the consumption of a marriage in which one (or both) of the contracting parties had been a minor'.[1]

The requirement of being 'free to marry' also comprised rules governing the degree of blood (or other) relationship which might exist between the couple, and these rules were very precisely laid down by the ecclesiastical authorities. A couple was not free to marry if the two parties were related within the

TODLERS AND LITLE CHILDREN PERMITED OR NOT, CAN NOT PHYSICALLY HAVE SEXUAL INTERCOURSE.

so-called 'prohibited degrees'. At the fourth Lateran Council, in 1215, Pope Innocent III limited this prohibition to the fourth degree of kinship. Broadly speaking, this refers to third cousins – individuals who share at least one great-great-grandparent – and closer relatives. Previously – dating back to the time of the Norman Conquest of England – the prohibition had been stricter, extending to the seventh degree of kinship: this earlier and wider prohibition having been formally established by Pope Alexander II (1061–73).[2]

In practice, of course, the royalty and nobility of medieval Europe – and also the medieval peasants living in a small village – were probably quite often related within the prohibited degrees. Therefore this rule of prohibition was not absolute. The Church could grant a dispensation, allowing a marriage within the prohibited degrees, and this practice was not uncommon. At times, however, the granting of such a dispensation could give rise to problems, as we shall see later. It was also the case that sometimes the bride and groom were either genuinely unaware that they were related within the prohibited degrees, or they chose to pretend not to know. Occasionally it subsequently suited one of the two parties to 'discover' a relationship of which they had previously pretended to be unaware, in order to end a marriage which was no longer viable (see below: annulment).

Although there was no formal requirement for marriage vows to be witnessed, in practice a witness was certainly a good idea, because there were many cases of disputed marriage, as the records of the medieval English Church courts testify. If the formal Church wedding service was used, the ceremony would probably be celebrated at the west door of a church, in the open air, with guests present as witnesses. It was probably in the late fifteenth century that marriages began to move *inside* churches. Ms Royal 14E. IV, f. 284 depicts the wedding of Richard II's cousin, Philippa (i) of Lancaster (the daughter of Richard's uncle, John of Gaunt), to King John I of Portugal. The wedding took place in 1387, but the illustration was painted about 100 years later, probably in the Low Countries. It shows the wedding taking place inside a church, before the high altar, so by about 1490 this must have been a normal venue for a wedding. However, Ms Royal 20E.VI, f. 9v depicts the 1420 wedding of Henry V and Catherine of France as taking place in a church porch. This picture was painted in 1487. Ms Royal 15E. IV, f. 295v shows the 1308 wedding of Edward II and Isabella of France taking place outside a church. This picture was painted in about 1475.

The earlier tradition of marriage in the open air may have had an impact on the question of whether or not a bridal veil was worn, and this point is considered in more detail below. Probably every couple would wear nice clothes if possible, but of course in the case of the medieval bridegroom this would have been neither a suit nor a military uniform. Likewise the modern white wedding dress was virtually unknown in the Middle Ages, and a dress of any colour might be worn by the bride.

The first recorded instance of a member of the English royal family wearing a white wedding dress was at the wedding of Philippa (ii) of Lancaster, daughter of Henry IV, at Lund, in 1406. Philippa married Eric, King of Denmark, Sweden and Norway, and for the occasion she wore white silk trimmed with squirrel fur and ermine. Curiously, the late fifteenth-century depiction of the wedding of her aunt, Philippa (i) (see above), while not contemporary with the event, also depicts *that* bride wearing a white dress trimmed with brown fur over a yellow under-dress trimmed with ermine. Possibly the painting was influenced by descriptions of the wedding dress of Philippa (ii). About sixty years after this picture was painted, in 1559, Mary Queen of Scots wore white for her marriage to the Dauphin of France, because it was her favourite colour. Her choice was remembered because white was the traditional mourning garb for French queens, and Mary's husband proved short-lived, giving rise to the notion that maybe his bride had made an unlucky choice of colour.

Only in the eighteenth century did white begin to become normal for a wedding dress. In the royal family, Princess Charlotte, daughter and heiress of George IV, wore a white wedding dress in 1816, for her marriage to Leopold of Saxe-Coburg-Gotha (later King Leopold I of Belgium). Queen Victoria wore a white wedding dress in 1840, and during the nineteenth century this custom gradually became more or less universal. Queen Victoria also introduced the custom of having her bridesmaids carry her train.

An old wedding rhyme still survives in England, which recommends for a woman at her wedding:

> Something old, something new,
> Something borrowed, something blue,
> And a silver sixpence in her shoe.

It is not known for certain when this rhyme was composed, and some sources suggest that it is Victorian. However, the traditions which it represents are probably much older. A silver coin worth six pennies was first minted in 1551, so the rhyme as it stands today cannot date back as far as the Middle Ages. But the last silver sixpences were minted in Britain in 1946, so the rhyme must be earlier than that.[3] The tradition of the coin in the bride's shoe may have its origin in an old Scottish custom, whereby the *bridegroom* put a silver coin in his left shoe for good luck. If so then the verse as it now stands may well date from the nineteenth century, when things Scottish were cultivated and popularised by the royal family.

However, the reference to 'something blue' for the bride is almost certainly ancient in origin. Western Christian tradition sees blue as the colour worn by the Virgin Mary and this may explain the preference for a blue garment of some kind to be worn at a wedding. This custom was perpetuated for centuries in England, as a second traditional wedding rhyme clearly shows.

> Marry in blue.
> Lover be true!

Possibly, blue clothing, through its association with the Blessed Virgin, was thought to symbolise the bride's virginity in medieval Christian society – just as the white wedding dress came to do later.

Even so, a blue *dress* was by no means compulsory for weddings in the Middle Ages. In the surviving coloured illustrations of English medieval royal and private weddings we can see an assortment of colours worn by the brides. Edward III's daughter is shown wearing a pink dress. Eleanor of Provence is portrayed in a green mantle. One surviving version of the wedding of Henry V and Catherine of France shows both bride and groom in gold robes – though this picture was painted many years after the event (see above).

However, blue clothing is shown at the wedding of Edward II. The king and his bride, Isabelle of France, were both depicted wearing very splendid robes of cloth of gold, trimmed with ermine, while the artist gave Edward a fashionable fifteenth-century pair of pointed red shoes. Isabelle's robe is of blue cloth of gold, and she is also holding up her robe to reveal a beautiful under-dress of royal blue and gold.[4]

Another point to consider is the question of the bridal veil. A bride who was to become a queen, and who arrived at her wedding a virgin, would not wear a bridal veil, though she did wear an open crown.[5] Princesses might also wear crowns to their weddings, as Edward IV's sister, Margaret of York, did in 1468.[6] But there is some evidence that a royal princess who was not marrying a king might have her hair covered.[7] In medieval Christian society, as in modern Moslem society, it was considered a sign of modesty for a woman to cover her hair in public. However, young girls and queens were both exempt from this veiling of the head, so that it may have been considered appropriate – and a further sign of the bride's virginity – for her head to be *uncovered* at her wedding. Nevertheless, it was traditional for women to cover their heads inside churches. Thus, in the medieval period, when weddings (if the public ceremony was being used) normally took place outside the church door, a prospective queen would have had no need of a bridal veil. Later, however, when weddings moved inside churches, a head covering for the royal bride would have become essential.

During a formal wedding ceremony, vows were exchanged by the bride and groom. Then the groom would place a ring on the bride's hand – probably in most cases on the ring finger of the right hand. The placing of the ring could be carried out in a little ceremony in which the groom said 'In the name of the Father' (touching the ring to the tip of the bride's thumb), 'and of the Son' (touching the ring to the tip of the bride's index finger), 'and of the Holy Spirit' (touching the ring to the tip of the bride's middle finger), 'Amen' (pushing the ring onto the bride's ring finger). The ring may have been made of metal – possibly a precious metal – but there were no rules about this. There is no evidence that a ring was given by the bride to the groom in England in the medieval period. No formal documents (such as marriage certificates) existed, or were signed, as part of the medieval church wedding. After the exchange of vows and the giving of the ring the couple would repair to their marital home or some other lay venue, accompanied by the guests, for a wedding celebration which culminated in the formal (and public) bedding of bride and groom.

Of course in cases where the formal religious ceremony was not employed, the situation was even more free and easy. A man and woman who were attracted to one another might simply make up their minds to promise to be husband and wife when they were alone together, maybe in a barn, where they could follow up the verbal promise immediately by making love to one another in the hay. Such an informal marriage might have no witness present at the exchange of vows. We know this because the lack of witnesses sometimes caused trouble later, if the marriage became a matter of dispute. Just like the formal church ceremony, an informal marriage had no accompanying paperwork to document it. The informal bride may not have been given a ring, or if she did receive one it might be merely a piece of hay or straw woven into a ring for the occasion: an ephemeral ring which would fall to pieces and be lost after a short time. Even metal wedding rings do not seem to have been worn permanently. Portraits of English queens consort rarely depict anything which can be clearly recognised as a wedding ring on either of the royal hands.

The Catholic Church has never countenanced divorce, so in the Middle Ages marriages which did not work, or which proved in some way inconvenient, could not be terminated in that way. The only means by which a marriage could be ended was either for one of the parties to die, or for the Church courts to rule that for some reason the marriage had never really taken place. The latter process is known as annulment. An annulment could be granted if one or both parties claimed that the marriage had never been consummated (i.e. sexual intercourse had never taken place). Alternatively the Church courts could set aside a medieval marriage on the grounds that the couple had not been free to marry. This might be because it was discovered that the man and woman were related within the prohibited degrees and had not obtained a dispensation for their marriage; because one of the two parties had previously married a person who was still living at the time when the second marriage was contracted, or because there had been constraints of some kind, forcing one of the parties to agree to the marriage. The Church's laws on these points relating to the validity or otherwise of a marriage will prove to be extremely important in our investigation of the disputed royal marriages of Edward IV and his grandson, Henry VIII.

But before reviewing the evidence about any specific case of disputed English royal marriage, it will be helpful to examine other areas of background information. First, it is essential to understand something of the history of royal marriages in general, and to see what this can teach us. Second, we need to know what were the general expectations relating to the status of the marriage partner, both in terms of birth and social status, and also in terms of marital background. For example, were royal brides always expected to be princesses? Was it essential that they be virgins? We must also review the history of irregular royal sexual partnerships – involving mistresses, lovers and royal bastards – because of course, if any one of the cases of disputed royal marriage we shall explore here is judged *not* to have been a genuine marriage, it might belong instead in this category of irregular partnerships.

We shall now begin to assemble these key elements of background information by briefly reviewing the history of the marriages of English monarchs from the Norman Conquest up to the fourteenth century. This will help us to form an initial overview of English royal marriage practice. It will also allow us to observe whether marriage practice was consistent over these four centuries, and if not, in what ways the practice might have varied. In subsequent chapters we shall go on to review expectations concerning royal marriage partners, and the history of illicit royal love affairs.

ROYAL MARRIAGES
1050–1330

Dammit sir, it's your duty to get married. You can't be always living for pleasure.

Oscar Wilde

Question marks over English royal marriages since the Norman Conquest are by no means rare. We might easily assume that royal weddings were always grand public occasions, and that the formal church ceremony was always used, but in fact this was not so. For example, in the case of the parents of William I, 'the Conqueror', no marriage ever took place. William the Conqueror is also known by the less complimentary name of 'William the Bastard', because his father, Robert, Duke of Normandy, had no legitimate children – only a son (and possibly also a daughter) by his mistress, Herleva, daughter of Fulbert of Falaise, a tanner.

Actually Robert was a usurper. He had seized the duchy of Normandy on the death of his elder brother – a death in which rumour suggests that Robert himself may have taken a hand. Robert's seizure of the power and the title was at the expense of his young nephew, the legitimate heir to the dukedom, whom Robert forced to enter a monastery. But having seized Normandy, Robert proved incapable of providing a new legitimate heir to the ducal title. Thus even before it came to England the house of Normandy was familiar with the problem of a disputed and questionable inheritance.

Robert's son, William the Conqueror, married his wife, Matilda of Flanders, before he became King of England, but the precise date of their marriage is a matter of interpretation. Negotiations for their union took place in 1049, but in October of that year, at the Council of Rheims, Pope Leo IX forbade the marriage contract. The wedding went ahead, nevertheless, in defiance of papal authority, in the early 1050s – probably in 1053. However, it was not until 1059 that papal approval for the marriage was finally granted. Thus the first five children of William and Matilda – including the future King William II – were all born in a kind of matrimonial limbo.

Their third son, the future King Henry I, was more fortunate than his elder brothers, Robert, Duke of Normandy and King William II. Henry's birth date of 1068 means that his parents were undoubtedly married by the time he was conceived. Following the childless death of his brother, William II, Henry seized control of the English royal treasury and assumed the Crown. At that time he was still unmarried, and one of his first priorities once he became king was to find a suitable consort. He chose Matilda (also known as Edith) of Scotland – a descendant of the pre-Norman English royal house of Wessex. By this means he strengthened his claim to the English throne. But this marriage also ran into some initial problems, for it was claimed that Matilda (Edith) was a nun, and thus unable to marry. The case was carefully investigated by the ecclesiastical authorities, but they finally concluded (as she herself had already stated categorically) that Matilda (Edith) had never taken vows as a nun, and that therefore the couple was free to marry. The marriage was celebrated at Westminster Abbey on 11 November 1100, by Archbishop Anselm of Canterbury, the wedding being followed by Matilda's coronation as queen consort. The wedding probably took place outside the west door, after which the couple would have processed into the church for the new queen's coronation.

The questions raised about the marriages of William I and Henry I are instructive. Both cases clearly show that the authority to judge the validity of the marriage rested entirely in the hands of the Church. And at this period 'the Church' in western Europe meant the Catholic Church, for there was then no other Church in existence in Europe apart from the Orthodox Church in the east.[1]

As we have seen, for the Catholic Church marriage was (and is) a sacrament. It is a union which reflects the oneness between God and his Church. At this early period marriage was not a civil contract, and the secular authorities had no jurisdiction whatever in matters of matrimonial dispute. The only *legal* element associated with matrimony was not the marriage contract itself but, in the case of families which owned property, peripheral issues relating to such matters as the bride's dowry and jointure.[2]

Since no mass media existed at this early period, the only 'public opinion' which could express itself about a royal marriage comprised the very limited views of the court or the immediate entourage of the royal couple. Thus the context of a royal marriage was very different a thousand years ago than it is today. Although in the modern age the Church (nowadays, in England, the Anglican Church) may still play some role in deciding contentious issues affecting royal marriage – as it did, for example, in the case of the marriage of HRH the Prince of Wales to Camilla Shand – the Church is no longer the sole authority. Both the law of the State and public opinion have become its powerful rivals.

FAMILY TREE 1 - HOUSE OF NORMANDY

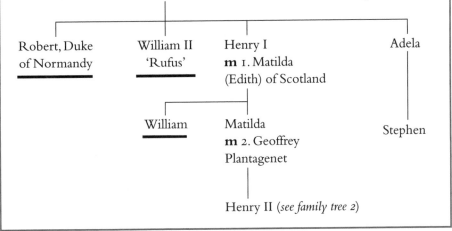

Robert, Duke of Normandy **x** Herleva of Falaise (mistress)

Matilda of Flanders **m** William I 'The Bastard'/'The Conqueror'

| Robert, Duke of Normandy | William II 'Rufus' | Henry I **m** 1. Matilda (Edith) of Scotland | Adela |

| William | Matilda **m** 2. Geoffrey Plantagenet | Stephen |

Henry II (*see family tree 2*)

Incidentally, the historical situation raises, perhaps, the interesting question of whether the civil authorities really need to have any involvement or jurisdiction in marriage, even today. For except in so far as it concerns ownership of property, care of children, and shared financial rights and obligations, marriage is arguably a purely private affair between two individuals: a matter in which government interference is neither required nor appropriate!

Following the unfortunate death of their son, William,[3] the only surviving legitimate heir of Henry I and Matilda (Edith) of Scotland was a daughter, also called Matilda. Although she eventually secured control of the duchy of Normandy, Matilda was never crowned Queen of England, and spent the whole of her 'reign' involved in a civil war against her cousin, Stephen. In her struggle for the throne, Matilda was ably assisted and supported by her illegitimate half-brother, Robert, Earl of Gloucester.

The existence of this powerful bastard half-brother reminds us of another significant aspect of the royal matrimonial situation – the fact that kings not infrequently had extra-marital relationships and illegitimate children. These irregular partnerships, and the families which sometimes resulted from them, are an important part of the context within which the phenomenon of disputed and questionable royal marriages must be understood. We shall explore the history of royal mistresses more fully in Chapter 5.

Henry I's daughter, Matilda, married twice. Her first marriage, at the age of 11, was to the Holy Roman Emperor Henry V, and took place in Mainz on 7 January 1114. Matilda may have borne a son to the emperor, but if so the boy died very young, and Emperor Henry V himself died on 23 May 1125, leaving Matilda a childless widow. She then returned to her father's court in England. Henry I subsequently arranged a second marriage for her, with Geoffrey Plantagenet, the future Count of Anjou. The wedding between the 26-year-old Matilda and the 14-year-old Geoffrey took place in Rouen, on 17 June 1128. It was a troubled union – not surprisingly, perhaps, given the age gap between the couple – but it did produce three sons, the eldest of whom, Henry, known as 'Fitzempress' (born at Le Mans on 5 March 1133), ultimately succeeded to the English Crown as Henry II.[4]

Henry Fitzempress married at the age of 19. It was the death of his father, the Count of Anjou, in 1151, which seems to have encouraged him to give serious thought to his own marriage, and to the provision of heirs. His eyes were focused upon Eleanor of Aquitaine. Unfortunately, at that time Eleanor was Queen of France, having married King Louis VII at Bordeaux Cathedral on 25 July 1137. The marriage of Eleanor and Louis had not proved a success, however, despite considerable early enthusiasm on the part of the bridegroom. The marriage had failed to produce any male heirs and the couple had gradually drifted apart.[5] Eleanor herself had sought to have the marriage annulled by the pope, initially without success. But an annulment was finally granted on 11 March 1152, on the grounds of consanguinity (the couple being related in the fourth degree). Interestingly the annulment specifically declared that the daughters of the marriage were legitimate, and custody of these little girls was granted to their father.

Eight weeks after the annulment, on 18 May 1152, Henry Fitzempress married Eleanor of Aquitaine. Their wedding was private, and without ceremony. Ironically, Eleanor was more closely related to Henry than she had been to Louis VII, so the validity of the new marriage could easily have been questioned. It certainly caused ill feeling and conflict between Henry and King Louis!

On 25 October 1154, Eleanor's new husband succeeded to the English throne, making Eleanor a queen for the second time. Her coronation as Queen of England, on 19 December 1154, made up for her quiet and private wedding to Henry. The couple eventually had a total of eight children, including five sons, but Henry was by no means faithful to Eleanor, and their marriage was tumultuous. After major conflicts, Henry II would ultimately find it necessary to imprison his wife.

The next English king, Richard I, was only the third son of Henry II and Eleanor of Aquitaine (see Family Tree 2), and he was not at first expected to succeed to the throne.[6] The heir in England should have been his elder brother, Henry, 'the young king'. On 2 November 1160 the young Henry was married to Margaret, one of the daughters of Louis VII of France by his second wife. At this time the plan was that Richard would marry one of the daughters of Count Ramon Berengar IV of Barcelona. However, that marriage never took place and subsequently Richard was betrothed to Alys of France, another daughter of Louis VII. However, this second proposed marriage also never took place, having been ruled out chiefly by the fact that Richard's father, Henry II, reputedly took Alys as his mistress, thereby creating a problem of consanguinity (among other things!)

Meanwhile, however, 'the young king' Henry died childless in 1183, moving Richard up in the order of succession, with the ultimate result that when his father died at Chinon on 6 July 1189, it was Richard who succeeded Henry II as King of England. Richard spent little time in his new kingdom, but while in Cyprus he finally married, his chosen bride being not Alys of France (to whom he was still officially betrothed) but Berengaria of Navarre. The wedding was a grand occasion, with great public celebrations. As part of the ceremonial following the wedding itself, Richard was crowned King of Cyprus, while his bride was crowned Queen of Cyprus and England.

Curiously, Richard seems to have had little hope or expectation of producing a son with his new bride, for while he was in Cyprus he also formally recognised his nephew, Arthur of Brittany (son of Richard's deceased younger brother, Geoffrey) as heir to the English throne. Perhaps this measure was some kind of tacit admission of Richard's sexual predilections (see above).[7] At all events, no children were ever born to the royal couple, despite the fact that Berengaria subsequently accompanied Richard throughout his crusade. In fact she never visited England until after her husband's death, because Richard himself spent so little time in his northern kingdom, which he reportedly characterised as cold and wet.

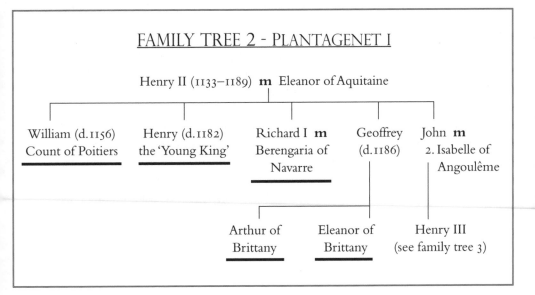

FAMILY TREE 2 - PLANTAGENET I

Henry II (1133–1189) **m** Eleanor of Aquitaine

William (d.1156) Count of Poitiers	Henry (d.1182) the 'Young King'	Richard I **m** Berengaria of Navarre	Geoffrey (d.1186)	John **m** 2. Isabelle of Angoulême

		Arthur of Brittany	Eleanor of Brittany	Henry III (see family tree 3)

Prince John, the youngest son of Henry II and Eleanor of Aquitaine, married much earlier than his brother Richard. On 28 September 1176 he wedded his cousin, Isabel of Gloucester, at Marlborough Castle, Wiltshire.[8] However, this marriage fell within the prohibited degrees of kinship, and no papal dispensation for it had been granted, so it was declared null and void by the Archbishop of Canterbury, who placed the lands of the couple under interdict. Subsequently the pope did grant a dispensation permitting the marriage – but only on the rather curious condition that the couple refrain from sexual intercourse. Not surprisingly, perhaps, when he ascended the throne, King John therefore chose to have the marriage formally annulled by three French bishops. A year later he married the beautiful 12-year-old Isabelle of Angoulême. This second marriage was celebrated in Bordeaux, after which Isabelle of Angoulême was given a splendid coronation at Westminster. After King John died, in 1216, Isabelle married again. Her second husband was Hugh de Lusignan. Isabelle married Hugh without waiting for the necessary permission of the royal council. As a result her lands were confiscated and her pension stopped for a time, until eventually an agreement was reached with the royal council.

King John had succeeded to the English Crown in April 1199, on the death of his brother Richard. Actually, as we saw earlier, in Cyprus, Richard had formally acknowledged as his heir his nephew, Prince Arthur, Duke of Brittany. Arthur (born 1187, died 1203?) was the posthumous son of Richard's younger (and John's elder) brother, Geoffrey (died 1186). However, on his deathbed Richard apparently decided that Arthur was too young for the responsibility of the English Crown, and he set the boy aside in favour of his own youngest brother, John.

John subsequently seized Arthur, and the boy disappeared mysteriously while he was in his uncle's custody. It is said that John, inflamed by strong drink and by the haughty attitude of his nephew, murdered the lad with his own hands. There are several contemporary sources for Arthur's murder – but they give different accounts. They are the *Margam Annals* (from Margam Abbey, Wales), the *Chronicon Anglicanum* of Ralph of Coggeshall, and the *Gesta* of William the Breton. The *Margam Annals* give the following version:

> After King John had captured Arthur and kept him alive in prison for some time, at length, in the castle of Rouen, after dinner on the Thursday before Easter, when he was drunk and possessed by the devil, he slew him with his own hand, and tying a heavy stone to the body cast it into the Seine. It was discovered by a fisherman in his net, and being dragged to the bank and recognized, was taken for secret burial, in fear of the tyrant, to the priory of Bec called Notre Dame de Pres.[9]

A medieval Breton folk song about the murder tells a similar story:

> *Arthur Plantagenest*
> To the Englysshe kynge yclept Lackelande
> Haþ Arþure ynto ambusshe yfallen.
> Yslayn bye þe Englysshe kynges sworde
> Is Arþur ynto the Seyne ycasten.
> Alas! Alas! Playe ye Mvsickers,
> All Brettanie is mvrnynge hedaye
> ffor here ydrouned Prynssë
> Arþure, in hys sixtenþe yere off lyffue.
> Þe Seyne is redde wiþ hys blvde.
> Soe maye Gvde damne warre.[10]

Arthur's elder sister, Eleanor, was undoubtedly kept in prison for her entire life at Corfe Castle, Dorset. This unfortunate princess, whose claim to the English throne was arguably better than that of King John and his descendants, finally died at Corfe in 1241.

John's own son and heir by Isabelle of Angoulême was Henry III, who came to the English throne on the death of his father. It was twenty years before Henry took a wife, Eleanor of Provence, in January 1236. The marriage was celebrated at Canterbury Cathedral – but probably not *inside* the church, rather at the great west door. We must remember that it was not the norm at this period for marriages to be celebrated *inside* churches.[11] The chronicler and artist, Matthew Paris (*c.*1200–59), Benedictine monk of St Alban's Abbey, has left us a representation of this royal wedding, which shows only the bride and groom (*see Plate 1*).[12] Eleanor is wearing a crown but no wedding veil (see above), and Henry is giving her a wedding ring. He appears to be touching the ring to the index finger of Eleanor's right hand. Presumably he is enacting the traditional ceremony which was described earlier, whereby the ring is touched to the fingertips as the groom says 'In the name of the Father/and of the Son/and of the Holy Spirit/Amen'. The ring is touched in turn to the tip of the thumb, the index finger, and the middle finger as the three persons of the Trinity are named. Finally it is slid onto the fourth (ring) finger at the word 'Amen'.[13]

Eleanor's wedding ring seems to have been a plain circle of gold, similar to a modern wedding ring. This may have been the normal kind of ring for weddings of royalty and members of the aristocracy. However, later in the Middle Ages *fede* ('faith') rings, showing hands clasping one another, seem to have been popular, and it is thought that these may have been used for weddings or betrothals. *Fede* rings were often made of silver gilt, or plain silver, and solid gold can hardly have been in normal use for all social classes. Economic factors will have militated against this, and later there were also legal restrictions upon the wearing of gold,[14] though it is known that the sumptuary laws were not always rigorously enforced in England.

At Henry and Eleanor's wedding there appears to have been no wedding ring for the bridegroom. Only a single ring for the bride is depicted.[15] It is also interesting that the ring is being placed on the *right* hand. This is still the practice in some countries, and it was the traditional Catholic practice in England until the eighteenth century. However, the norm in England today is for a wedding ring to be worn on the *left* hand.

Henry and Eleanor's eldest son, Edward [I], then aged 14, married his first wife, the Infanta Eleanor of Castile, on 1 November 1254 at the Abbey Church of Santa María la Real de las Huelgas in Castile.[16] This marriage seems to have been very successful and happy, and it lasted for thirty-six years. But Eleanor died in 1290, and at the age of 60 the widowed Edward married for the second time, his second wife being Margaret of France, the 17-year-old daughter of King Philip III. Edward's second marriage, like that of his parents, was celebrated at Canterbury Cathedral. It took place on 8 September 1299.

It was Edward I's son and heir by his first wife, Eleanor, who ultimately succeeded to the throne as Edward II. Edward II and his bride, Isabelle of France, were married on 25 January 1308 at the pilgrimage church of Notre Dame, Boulogne-sur-Mer. This church, dating from 1100, housed the shrine and miraculous image of Our Lady of the Sea.[17] The marriage was not a happy one. Edward was reputed to have male lovers (including Piers Gaveston, and later Hugh Despenser). Perhaps not surprisingly, Isabelle did likewise, her lover being Roger Mortimer. In the end Isabelle and Mortimer deposed and imprisoned Edward II, who is reputed to have been murdered in a particularly gruesome manner.

The new king, Edward III, was only a boy when he succeeded his deposed father. Plans for his marriage to Philippa of Hainaut began in 1323, when the Bishop of Exeter visited Hainaut to broker this match. Edward was first married to Philippa by proxy in Valenciennes (the second most important city in the county of Hainaut) in October 1327. The Bishop of Coventry acted as Edward's proxy on that occasion.[18] The marriage was ceremonially re-enacted – this time with both partners present – at York Minster on 24 January 1328.

The subsequent marriages of Edward III's children show changes from the royal marriage pattern which we have traced so far. We shall consider these changes – and most particularly the marital histories of the eldest son, and heir to the throne, Edward, the Black Prince, and of his younger brother, John of Gaunt, Duke of Lancaster, in Chapter 7. The general history of royal marriages from the fifteenth century onwards will then be considered progressively, as the background and context for the disputed royal marriages which comprise our main theme.

Meanwhile, let us briefly summarise the picture of English royal marriage practice that has emerged so far. Of the thirteen post-Conquest royal marriages we have considered, the majority (nine) were celebrated in public, and in some cases it is recorded that they were celebrated with considerable pomp.

However, in the other four cases the marriages seem to have been celebrated privately with little or no public ceremonial. The majority of the marriages (eight – or nine if we include the initial wedding by proxy of Edward III) took place *outside* the realm of England – though whether it would always be appropriate in those cases to use the modern term 'abroad' is open to question. The venue for most of the weddings was a church. However, a depiction of the marriage of Edward II and Isabelle of France show their wedding taking place in the open air, outside the west door of the church, and that was probably the norm. In one case (the marriage of Henry III) we have evidence that the bride received a wedding ring. In the next chapter we shall review this early period of English royal marriages again, this time in quest of the requirements expected of a suitable royal marriage partner.

4

SUITABLE STATUS

… Oh, if a virgin,
And your affection not gone forth, I'll make you
The queen of Naples.

Shakespeare, *The Tempest*, Act 1, Scene 2

Earlier we noted Fiona Macdonald's opinion that in royal weddings the 'bride and groom were always of mutually royal rank'.[1] Of course, Macdonald had England in mind, because outside Europe no such 'rule' ever applied. Japanese emperors did not habitually marry the daughters of Chinese emperors or vice versa. For Asian and Native American potentates, marriage with subjects was the norm. Having now examined a number of English royal marriages, we begin to see that Macdonald's statement also appears questionable in a medieval English context.

The future William I married Matilda of Flanders, the daughter of a ruling aristocrat, but not of a king. The first wife of Henry I was a Scottish princess, but his second wife was noble by birth, not royal. King Stephen's wife was also aristocratic rather than royal. The first husband of Henry I's daughter, Matilda, was the Emperor, but her second husband – the progenitor of the Plantagenet dynasty – was a count, and their son, the first Plantagenet King of England, married a duke's daughter. In fact of the thirteen English monarchs between William I and Edward III, less than half married foreign royalty.[2] One king (William II) failed to marry. One attempt at a royal marriage (the first marriage of King John) was within the English royal family. The other seven marriages of sovereigns or would-be sovereigns in this period were aristocratic but non-royal.[3]

Implicit in Macdonald's view that English royal marriages were traditionally with other royalty is the notion that the royal brides usually tended to be foreign – since the opportunities for English royalty to marry other English royalty would obviously be somewhat limited. And in fact we can see that, while all the marriages considered in the last chapter were with Europeans, only one attempt at marriage – the first marriage attempt of King John – could be described as English. Thus it is true that in terms of modern notions of nationality, most early medieval royal marriage partners certainly were foreign.

Here, however, we must beware of anachronism. Few, if any, of the English monarchs whose marriages were discussed in the last chapter would have regarded English as their native language.[4] Most of them did not choose to be buried in England. William I was entombed in Normandy. So too was his consort, Matilda of Flanders. Adeliza of Louvain, the second wife of Henry I, retired to the Abbey of Affligem (Brabant), where she died and was buried.[5] The Empress Matilda was buried in Normandy.[6] Henry II, Eleanor of Aquitaine, Richard I and Isabelle of Angoulême are all interred at the Abbey of Fontevrault, in France. Berengaria of Navarre is also buried in France, in the chapter house of the Abbaye de l'Epau at Le Mans. Only William II, Henry I and Matilda (Edith) of Scotland were buried in England. William II lies in Winchester Cathedral; Matilda (Edith), in Westminster Abbey. Henry I was buried at Reading Abbey.[7]

We should also remember that some of these monarchs spent very little time in their island kingdom while they were alive. Until the reign of King John all of them ruled territory on the European mainland in addition to the kingdom of England. In fact when John lost this mainland territory he was branded with the pejorative nickname of 'Lackland' – which indicates very clearly which parts of his territory had been considered the most important.

If the King of England is regarded chiefly, not as 'English', but rather as the Duke of Normandy, or as the Count of Anjou, or the Duke of Aquitaine, then marriage with the daughter of a neighbouring aristocrat who ruled Angoulême, or Provence, might well appear much less 'foreign'. The same would probably seem true of a marriage with a daughter of the King of France. Even noblewomen from the Low Countries, or daughters of the neighbouring kings of Navarre or Castile would probably not have felt very exotic at a period when modern notions of nationality did not yet exist, and when the whole of Western Europe was united by the Catholic Church and by a history which, to a very large extent, was shared.[8]

At this early period, therefore, Macdonald's bold assertion of the equality of status in traditional royal weddings – with the concomitant implication that royal weddings were normally with foreign royalty – represents a huge error. The class equality was rarely a perfect balance. Sometimes English royal personages married above them. Thus Henry I's daughter Matilda married the Emperor. Henry I may have considered that in Matilda (Edith) of Scotland he was acquiring a wife who was something of a bargain, for in some ways the daughter of a King of Scotland, who was a descendant of the former English royal house of Wessex, could also be regarded as superior in social status to a younger son of a *parvenu* English ruling dynasty of bastard origin. Likewise the 'Daughters of France' who married Henry the Young King, Edward I, Edward II, and later also Richard II and Henry V, may well have been regarded – at least by their fathers – as superior in status to their English royal husbands. On the other hand non-royal brides like Eleanor of Aquitaine may well have been seen, at the time of their marriages, as more or less the equals of their English royal husbands.

Another intriguing aspect of the medieval matrimonial situation is the rather curious phenomenon whereby English royal bastard brides were occasionally considered suitable consorts to be offered to foreign royalty. During the period we have already reviewed we can find two examples of this. The first was the marriage of Henry I's illegitimate daughter, Sybilla de Normandy, with Alexander I of Scotland. The second instance was when Joan, an illegitimate daughter of King John, was married to the Welsh Prince, Llewellyn the Great.[9] In the fifteenth century there would be further examples of this phenomenon. Thus, on the Feast of Candlemas (2 February) 1424, Joan Beaufort, half-niece of King Henry IV, was married to James I of Scotland. While Joan herself was not illegitimate, we shall have more to say about the questionable legitimacy of the Beaufort family later.[10] And in 1484–85, we find Richard III negotiating the marriage of his niece, Elizabeth of York, who was then officially designated as illegitimate, to a Portuguese prince (the future King Manuel I).[11] This was part of a royal marriage pact which also comprised Richard's own intended marriage to the Infanta Joana of Portugal.[12] Of course, these planned Portuguese royal marriages never actually took place, because of Richard III's defeat and death at the battle of Bosworth, in August 1485: however, the plans were undoubtedly serious.

✣ ✣ ✣

There seems to be a popular perception to the effect that English royal brides are expected to be virgins at the time of their marriage, and recent history may offer some justification for this. However, a closer examination reveals that this 'rule' has also not been applied invariably. We have already seen that at the time of her marriage to Henry II, Eleanor of Aquitaine was not a virgin. She had been married for almost 15 years to Louis VII of France, by whom she had given birth to two daughters. In later periods divorce would be seen as an obstacle to a royal marriage, but in Eleanor's case this issue did not arise. The Catholic Church did not admit of divorce, either in the Middle Ages or later. Eleanor's union with the King of France was therefore terminated not by a divorce but by an annulment. This was a formal ruling by the ecclesiastical authorities that no valid marriage between Eleanor and Louis had ever existed. Therefore strictly speaking it could not be claimed that at the time of her marriage to Henry Plantagenet Eleanor had already been married. Nevertheless the fact remained that she had been living with Louis VII for more than fourteen years, and she had borne him two children.

Eleanor's marriage to Henry II after the termination of her marriage to Louis VII leads us on to the wider question of how royalty were generally expected to behave when they were widowed. Not surprisingly, perhaps, the rules varied somewhat in the case of men and in the case of women. For kings, the prime consideration was the need for an heir to the throne. If a first marriage did not produce one, then a second marriage would be expected. In the case of Henry VIII this consideration was to become something of an obsession. For widowed queens consort, however, remarriage to produce an heir was not possible, since consorts held their Crown only by right of marriage and not by right of blood. Even so, some widowed queens did remarry.

One example of a medieval widowed king is Henry I. We have seen that when he became king, in 1100, and at the fairly advanced age of about 32, Henry I had sought a suitable royal bride. He had chosen Matilda (Edith) of Scotland. When Henry was left a widower in 1118, at the age of about 50, he did not immediately remarry. At that time he still had a living legitimate son and heir, William Adelin, who was married in the following year to a daughter of the count of Anjou in order to ensure the future of Henry's royal line. It was only when William Adelin died without heirs in 1120 that Henry I was compelled to review his own matrimonial status. His second marriage, to Adeliza of Louvain, then followed very quickly.[13] Henry I remarried – and was probably expected to remarry – because he needed to try to beget an heir. However, in the event, his second marriage remained childless.

Another example of a widowed English king of the Middle Ages is Edward I. Edward had less need than Henry I to remarry after the death of his first wife, Eleanor of Castile, as he had a living heir.[14] Nevertheless, political considerations made an alliance with France desirable, and so Edward negotiated to marry Blanche of France. When Blanche was married instead to Rudolf of Habsburg, Edward was angry at first, and declared war. But subsequently he was reconciled to the French king, and married Blanche's younger sister, Margaret. Despite the considerable age gap between the king and his new queen, this second marriage proved a success. However, Margaret was never crowned Queen of England.[15] She was destined to outlive Edward I by more than ten years, but she never remarried. She lived quietly in retirement at Marlborough Castle. Although she maintained a good relationship with her half-niece and successor, Queen Isabelle, Margaret did not frequent her stepson's court. She became a patron of the Franciscan Order, and after her death she was entombed in the Greyfriars' Church at Newgate.

As for Henry I's daughter, the Empress Matilda, she is a curious example of medieval widowed royalty. She was a queen who must to all intents and purposes be regarded as a king, because she was no mere consort. Had her civil war been more successful, she would have become England's first queen regnant, for she had blood rights to the Crown, which she could transmit. Therefore like her father, Henry I, before her, she needed heirs. When her marriage to the Holy Roman Emperor left her a childless widow, a second marriage was more or less inevitable.

Henry I's second wife, Queen Adeliza, offers us one example of the remarriage of a widowed consort. When Henry I's death left Adeliza a widow in 1135, she at first retired to Wilton Abbey, near Salisbury. However, she was only 32 years old, and in due course she set a precedent for future widowed consorts by marrying a second husband: William d'Aubigny, Earl of Arundel (born 1109, died 1176). William acquired Arundel Castle and his title as a result of his marriage to Adeliza, the castle having been part of the queen's jointure. By William, Adeliza had a number of children, becoming an ancestress of the subsequent d'Aubigny and Fitzalan earls of Arundel, and through them, of the Mowbray and Howard dukes of Norfolk[16] – and thus an ancestress also of Anne Boleyn and Lucy Walter, key figures whom we shall meet in later chapters.[17] Unlike some later second marriages of widowed royal consorts, that of Adeliza seems to have been approved by the royal family. Both King Stephen and his rival the Empress Matilda remained on good terms with her, and Henry II subsequently confirmed d'Aubigny's tenure of the lands and property which he had acquired as a result of his marriage to Adeliza.

Adeliza of Louvain was far from being the only medieval queen to remarry after being widowed. King John's wife, Isabelle of Angoulême, was only 28 years old when her husband left her a widow. After arranging the coronation of her young son, she left England, to rule her native Angoulême. There, less than four years after King John's death, she married Hugh X of Lusignan. In this case the widowed queen's remarriage had not received the approval of the royal council in England – who, indeed, had not even been asked. The wedding therefore caused a good deal of trouble. Initially Isabelle's dower lands were confiscated by the council, and payment of her pension was suspended. Isabelle and her new husband retaliated by refusing to hand over Isabelle's royal daughter, the Princess Joan, then betrothed to the Scottish king. Eventually, however, peace was made. Subsequently Isabelle's numerous children by her second marriage made their way to their half-brother's court in England.

Widowed queens and the question of their possible remarriage remained a problematic issue throughout the Middle Ages and beyond. Even in modern times this has had an echo – in the case of the divorced Diana, Princess of Wales. However, our last example of a medieval widowed queen in this chapter is Isabelle of France, the consort of Edward II. In some ways Isabelle's marriage to Edward seems to have been far from happy (but see below), and from 1325 (possibly even earlier) Isabelle was involved in a love affair with Roger Mortimer, Earl of March. Mortimer, however, had a wife of his own, and he and Isabelle were never married. Nevertheless, together they overthrew – and possibly murdered – Isabelle's husband. Later Mortimer was executed by Isabelle's son, Edward III. Isabelle, however, had a long life. Following her aunt and predecessor, Margaret of France (the widow of Edward I) Isabelle developed an interest in the Franciscan Order. She ultimately joined this order just before she died. Her body was carried to London, where Isabelle was buried close to her aunt Margaret (widow of Edward I), at the Greyfriars' Church, Newgate. Interestingly, Isabelle asked to be buried in her wedding dress, and she had the heart of her royal husband, King Edward II, placed in the same grave with her.

5

IRREGULAR
ROYAL AFFAIRS

Ce n'est plus une ardeur dans mes veines cachée:
C'est Vénus toute entière à sa proie attachée.

No longer a passion concealed from the light of day,
But Venus in all her power, grasping her prey.

Racine, *Phèdre*, act 1 (translation: J. Ashdown-Hill)

So far we have looked at the royal marriages from the Norman Conquest to the reign of Edward III, and we have identified the royal consorts during these four centuries. In most cases we have also noted where their weddings were celebrated, and in a few cases we have found a little evidence to show how certain parts of the marriage ceremony were conducted – though in that respect there are also many gaps in our knowledge.

We have also considered what the chosen consorts have to teach us in respect of the underlying criteria by which English sovereigns of these centuries appear to have selected their marriage partners. This information has to be deduced, because there is no surviving document which sets out the criteria explicitly. From the examples, however, we have been able to conclude that social status roughly equal to that of the English monarch was generally expected of a prospective marriage partner. However, this did not invariably mean that the marriage partner had to be of royal blood. At a time when the English sovereigns were feudal dependents of the French Crown, daughters of other French tenants-in-chief were seen as acceptable consorts. So too were the daughters of other European rulers who might have less than royal status.

In general, the queens consort chosen for England during these approximately 300 years were expected to be virgins at the time of their marriages. However, there was no absolute rule on this point, and women with a previous matrimonial history were definitely not ruled out, particularly if the king had strong personal reasons for preferring them – as the example of Eleanor of Aquitaine clearly shows.

The case of Eleanor of Aquitaine also indicates that sometimes personal attraction played a significant part in the choice of a bride. But the same case also shows that such attraction was no guarantee, either of marital fidelity, or of lasting happiness. In fact the outcomes of the royal marriages we have reviewed so far were variable. Some marriages seem to have been very happy, but this could prove to be the case even when the partner was initially selected for political rather than personal reasons – as the two marriages of Edward I, for example, both clearly demonstrate.

Let us now consider the irregular royal partnerships of the same period. First, what word should we use to describe the woman or women with whom a king conducted an extra-marital affair? The common practice is to use the word 'mistress' for *all* such sexual encounters. However, this word was certainly not in use with that meaning in the Middle Ages. The word 'mistress' can be found in texts from the sixteenth century onwards, but in the sixteenth century its meaning was different. At that time it could mean 'wife'! Thus the word 'mistress' needs to be regarded with some caution, particularly when it appears in ancient source material.

Also, if we want to use the word 'mistress' to refer to the extra-marital sexual partner of a king, we may need to define precisely what we mean by it. Dictionaries offer the following modern definitions:

> a woman (other than the man's wife) having a sexual relationship with a married man.[1]

> a woman who has a continuing extramarital sexual relationship with a man.[2]

The first of these would cover *any* extra-marital sexual relationship, but the second definition would confine the use of the word to an ongoing, long-term relationship, more or less akin to a marriage. It is with this second meaning that the term 'mistress' will generally be employed here.

We should also note that, at least during the first century or two after the Norman Conquest of England, the concept of the concubine was still very much alive, and this further complicates the issue. A concubine was a woman who had a semi-official and ongoing relationship with a man, usually of higher social status than herself. She was less than a wife, but rather more than a mistress, and her children were entitled to a kind of recognition. Hence one author suggests that 'it is probable that royal bastards of the tenth and thirteenth centuries, if not somewhat later, were considered as *nothi* (as they were under Roman law) that is children born in concubinage and thereby entitled to the support of their fathers but with no right of inheritance from them'.[3]

⊕ ⊕ ⊕

By no means all English monarchs of the early Middle Ages are known to have had mistresses in the sense of long-term partners outside of their marriages. No such partners seem to be recorded in the cases of William I, William II, King Stephen, Richard I, Henry III, Edward I and Edward II. Of course, in respect of William II, Richard I and Edward II a preference for members of their own sex is assumed, and this predilection may suffice to account for the lack of extra-marital female partners.[4] In the case of Edward II, the existence of male lovers has certainly been alleged, and two such lovers have been named. But curiously Edward II also had a bastard son, Adam Fitzroy, so he must have had a sexual relationship with a woman other than his wife on at least one occasion. Adam seems to have been born in about 1205, at a time when Edward was a teenager, still unmarried, and still heir to the throne.[5] However, there is no reason to suppose that Adam Fitzroy's mother was Edward's 'mistress' in terms of the definition we are using here. Adam may have been the fruit of a mere passing fancy.

Of the eleven kings between William I and Edward III, seven had no known long-term female partners outside of marriage. Does this mean that these seven kings were all faithful to their marriage partners? Not exactly, because William II had no wife, and Edward II was apparently unfaithful to Isabelle of France after their marriage – albeit with male partners rather than female. The precise conduct of Richard I is unclear. Nevertheless, of the ten married English kings in this period, 50 per cent may have been faithful husbands.

The others certainly seem to have made up for this! Henry I had sexual relations with at least six women other than his wives, and he is reputed to have fathered twenty illegitimate children. Henry II had at least five similar relationships, resulting in several bastards. King John had several sexual partners outside his marriages, and Edward III had one, or possibly two, such relationships.

Henry I's affairs were with Gieva de Tracy, Ansfride ... Sybil (or Adela or Lucia) Corbet, Edith Fitzforne,[6] Nest ferch Rhys ap Tewdwr and Isabel de Beaumont. Henry had chosen his first wife, Matilda (Edith) of Scotland, for largely political reasons, so it might not seem surprising if he felt little personal affection for her. In fact, however, the ages of Henry's bastards show that his relationship with most of their mothers dated from a period well *before* his marriage, and prior to his accession to the throne. Thus most of Henry's illicit relationships tell us nothing about the happiness or otherwise of his marriage, or about the king's marital fidelity.

Only the last two of Henry's six illicit partners had sexual relationships with the king *coeval* with his marriages. Interestingly, perhaps, these last two women were both of much higher social status than their predecessors (most of whom seem to have been of middling rank at best). Nevertheless, these last two relationships do not necessarily prove that Henry was unhappily married. Perhaps by this time his long bachelorhood had simply accustomed him to a somewhat free and easy lifestyle.

Henry I – our first instance of a post-Conquest English king who had known female partners outside marriage, and who fathered illegitimate children by them – is also the first such king to display clearly a pattern which was to recur subsequently in the context of later royal relationships. We find that while Henry was a prince, not even in the direct line of inheritance, and not yet married, he engaged in illicit relationships which resulted in bastard children. Later, however, he married, and settled down to a more regular lifestyle.[7] King Henry I recognised his bastards, which is how we come to know about them.

Some entered the Church, but for those who did not various provisions were made. One, as we have seen, was even married to the King of Scotland.[8] Others had less magnificent marriages found for them. Probably the most prominent of Henry I's illegitimate children in terms of English history was Robert Fitzroy,[9] Earl of Gloucester (?1090–1147). Incidentally, Robert Fitzroy had many descendants, and has been described by one author as the 'father of England'.[10] It is probable that Robert had a well-born mother (maybe Nest of South Wales), though his mother is not named in any surviving source. When his father died leaving no legitimate son and heir, Robert, who was a very intelligent and able man, even seems to have been considered a potential candidate for the throne. However:

> when he was advised, as the story went, to claim the throne on his father's death, deterred by sounder advice he by no means assented, saying it was fairer to yield it to his sister's son [the future Henry II] than presumptuously to arrogate it to himself.[11]

Given that his grandfather, William the Conqueror, had been a bastard, the fact that Robert's illegitimacy was ultimately seen as excluding him from the Crown is interesting. This established an important precedent, which has been followed in all subsequent periods.[12]

Like those of his grandfather, the extra-marital partners of Henry II seem to have covered a broad social spectrum, ranging from the royal, through the noble, to the plebeian. His reputed royal lover was Princess Alys of France, the fiancée of his own son, Richard (see above).[13] By Alys Henry II is rumoured to have had a child, though no details are available, and the evidence is uncertain.[14] Henry II's aristocratic partners were Ida de Tosny, later Countess of Norfolk, and her relative, Rosamund de Clifford.[15] Ida was the mother of Henry's best-known bastard son, William Longspee, Earl of Salisbury (1176–1226), but the celebrated Rosamund de Clifford – despite being probably the most famous of Henry's women – is not known for certain to have borne the king a single child.

Henry II may have had other affairs, with women whose names are lost.[16] However, the names of two partners of lower birth are recorded. One was the wife of Ralph Bloet. Her first name is in doubt but it may perhaps have been Nest. The other was a woman called Ykenai (or Hikenai) who was described by one hostile contemporary source as a prostitute. Between them these two women bore Henry three children, all of whom found their futures in the Church.[17]

In the case of Henry II the pattern noted earlier for Henry I's relationships applies again – at least in part. Whereas Henry I had most of his affairs, and fathered most of his illegitimate offspring, prior to his marriage, Henry II seems to have been less faithful to his consort. Of course, the marriage of Henry II and Eleanor of Aquitaine is known to have been turbulent, and ultimately Henry imprisoned his wife.

But Henry II's bastard son Geoffrey, Archbishop of York (1152–1226) was certainly born *before* the king's eldest legitimate child, Henry the Young King (1155–83), so that Henry's relationship with Geoffrey's mother presumably predated his royal marriage to Queen Eleanor (in May 1152). On the other hand, the birth of William Longspee occurred at a time when Henry II was already married to Eleanor of Aquitaine – but at a time when the sexual relationship between the king and queen had most probably come to an end. Henry's relationship with Rosamund de Clifford (a relation of William Longspee's mother) probably also post-dated the period of Henry's active sexual relationship with Eleanor of Aquitaine.[18]

In the case of King John the chronology of his relationships is not entirely clear, but he too may have been following, at least in part, the pattern established by his ancestor, Henry I. Certainly his relationship with Clemence d'Arcy dated from the 1190s (prior to his accession, and prior to his marriage to Isabelle of Angoulême). However, the overall pattern in John's case is not entirely clear, and the picture is complicated by his first (and subsequently annulled) marriage to his cousin. It is true that the king had at least five children with mistresses while he was supposed to be married to Isabel of Gloucester, but of course, as we have already seen, that first marriage was very peculiar, because John was not allowed to have sex with his wife. John's later behaviour (following his marriage to Isabelle of Angoulême) shows no sign of adultery. However, contemporary writers did complain that John's mistresses during the earlier period were married ladies of aristocratic status, which was thought to be improper.

There is no evidence of extramarital activity on the parts of Henry III and Edward I, and we have seen already that Edward II had no known relationships with other women during his reign as king. His relationships with Piers Gaveston, and later with Sir Hugh Despenser the Younger, seem to have been the key factors in his adult life.[19] Nevertheless, the fact that he fathered one illegitimate son during his teens, at a time when he was still heir to the throne, and still unmarried, has been noted. This reflects a pattern of conduct akin to that found in the cases of Henry I and Henry II. His relationship with Adam Fitzroy's unnamed mother was probably very brief, and it would therefore be inappropriate to describe her as Edward's 'mistress'. In terms of relationships with other *women*, it seems clear that Edward II was not unfaithful to his wife once he and Isabelle were married.

Edward III (reigned 1327–77) was born in November 1312. He was therefore only 11 years old when negotiations for his marriage to Philippa of Hainaut began. It was around the king's fifteenth birthday that his marriage was finally celebrated (in October 1327, by proxy, and at York Minster on 24 January 1328, in person). His bride was some two years his junior, and she would not have been considered old enough at the time of their wedding for the marriage to be consummated at once. However, it must have been consummated within a year or so, because their first child, Edward Prince of Wales ('the Black Prince') was born in 1330. Further children followed at regular intervals until 1348, after which a gap of about seven years intervened before the birth of the couple's last child, Thomas of Woodstock. Queen Philippa seems to have suffered from ill-health towards the end of her life, and she died in 1369.

Given this chronology, Edward III had little opportunity to follow the precedent established by his ancestor, Henry I, by engaging in love affairs and the fathering of bastards prior to his marriage. And in fact the pattern of Edward III's relationships does indeed seem to have been quite different. His marriage with Philippa was considered a success in all respects, and it was not until 1363, eight years after the birth of his last legitimate child, and just six years before the queen's death, that the king seems to have entered into any kind of long-term extra-marital relationship.

The woman in question was Alice Salisbury, and she was reportedly serving as a lady-in-waiting to Queen Philippa when she attracted the king's attention. Alice is better known under the surname Perrers, and indeed, until recently this was thought to have been her maiden name. However, research has now proved that her birth surname was not Perrers but Salisbury, and that Janyn Perrers was her first (and previously unknown) husband, whom she married prior to 1360.[20] Janyn must have died shortly after 1360, and Alice later married again, her second husband being Sir William Windsor.

Alice was hitherto thought to belong by birth to a gentry family from Hertfordshire, but this view must now be dismissed. The fact that she was in the service of the queen is not, in itself, sufficient to prove that Alice was of gentle birth, since the queen's ladies have been shown to come from quite varied backgrounds. Alice had a brother called John Salisbury and it is this fact which has recently established Alice's maiden name.

Her own reluctance to name or rely on any of her relatives means that it is ultimately impossible definitively to prove Alice's family origins. However, the Cobham petition links John Salisbury to a series of manors around Wantage (Berkshire) and gives some justification to Thomas of Walsingham's claim that Alice came from 'Henneye' (West and East Hanney, Berkshire). Further evidence of Alice's connections with a family named Salesby and with John Southbury, the previous holder of one of her East Hanney manors, generates the hypothesis that Perrers's origins lay in a family of petty landholders and traders operating in this corner of Berkshire.[21]

Another possibility is that Alice was a Londoner by birth, coming from one of the 'Salisbury' merchant families resident in the capital. A third possibility is that Alice was of quite low birth. In fact Thomas of Walsingham (who clearly despised the king's mistress) described her as a harlot, and the daughter of a thatcher!

Alice bore the king a son and two daughters.[22] Her relationship with Edward was regarded by contemporaries as scandalous.[23] Indeed, the degree of popular hostility to Alice was unusual in the history of English royal mistresses.[24] There was a widespread feeling of affront when she was given some of the queen's jewellery. Also, she profited financially from her situation. She grew wealthy as the king's mistress – although this seems to have been due in large measure to her own intelligence and business acumen.[25] Most importantly, however, her hold over the king was so strong, and the use Alice made of this situation was so evident, that it caused her influence to be feared. She was known – or at least widely believed – to exert her command of the king's ear in an unjust way in order to achieve her own ends, and it was seen as virtually impossible to oppose her will.

Alice's behaviour was certainly extraordinary at times, for 'this woman felt no embarrassment at taking her place on the bench of judges at Westminster; and she was not afraid to speak there, either on her own behalf or on that of her friends, or even on behalf of the king'.[26] Unsurprisingly, perhaps, under the circumstances, the judges were thought to be intimidated by her domineering influence.

The king's love for Alice was regarded by contemporaries as abnormal on the grounds of Edward III's age at the time, since it was considered that while the sin of lechery might be natural in youth, in old age such behaviour could only be a kind of insanity.[27] There could only be one possible explanation. Clearly Alice must have employed the black arts to achieve her wicked ends. Spells and potions were not necessarily required for this. Merely touching a man's hand intimately was sometimes taken as a kind of sorcery, capable of compelling desire![28] However, Alice was known to be associated with a Dominican friar, trained in the arts of healing. He was popularly reported to be 'an evil magician, dedicated to evildoing, and it was by his magical devices that Alice had enticed the king into an illicit love affair with her'.[29] Here we have one of the first recorded instances of sorcery being alleged in order to account for what was popularly perceived as an otherwise inexplicable royal love affair. Alice's Blackfriar friend was thought to have made love philtres for her, with which she had ensnared the king. 'He was accused of using spells and potions along with images of Alice and the king, suffused with herbs and other plants picked at the full moon, to work his magic'.[30]

Rightly or wrongly, similar allegations of sorcery were to resurface on several occasions in the fourteenth, fifteenth and sixteenth centuries to account for strange, inconvenient or otherwise inexplicable royal love affairs. But the allegations against Alice and her friend the friar provide one of the first indications that in England, as elsewhere in Europe, witchcraft was beginning to be taken more seriously. Hitherto there had been a tendency to regard sorcery as fairly harmless, but the climate was changing. Early in the following century Johannes Nider would publish his *Formicarius* ('*The Ant Hill*') in Augsburg – one of the earliest works to explore how witches could be hunted down and persecuted. Witchcraft was becoming a serious and potentially dangerous allegation, almost bound to lead to trouble, as it did for Alice. Although she was safe enough while her royal lover lived, after Edward III's death Alice was brought to trial, banished for a time, and her goods confiscated. However, she survived, and later she was even able to return to England and reclaim some of her property. Some subsequent royal consorts and lovers who were subjected to accusations of sorcery were to prove less fortunate.

There have been rumours that Edward III also had an affair in the 1340s with Catherine Montacute (or Montagu), Countess of Salisbury. It was said to have been in honour of this countess that the king founded the Order of the Garter. However, the story of this relationship is very confused and uncertain. Some sources have suggested that the Order of the Garter was founded not in Catherine's honour but in honour of her daughter-in-law, Joan of Kent, the future bride of the Prince of Wales (see below).[31] Thus it is not certain that Edward ever really had an affair with Catherine. If he did, it must have been a brief, one-off exception to his general marital fidelity at that period.

The pattern of Edward III's relationships seems, therefore, to have been one of early marriage, followed by faithfulness to his wife until she began to age and to lose her health. Then the king found himself one new, young and pretty sexual partner, to whom he subsequently appears to have remained faithful until his death. And unlike his predecessors, whose love affairs in later life seem to have been with ladies of some status, Edward III's late love was for a woman of moderate, or possibly even quite low birth.

6

SUMMARY OF THE BACKGROUND INFORMATION

So far we have been examining the medieval history of marriage in general, and of medieval English royal marriage in particular. We have not yet begun exploring *contentious* royal marriages, or seeking for new or detailed evidence of particular cases. Rather we have been trying to get an overview of the broad picture. What have we found out? Let us summarise the evidence.

First, medieval marriage had nothing whatever to do with the State, or with civil law. It was primarily a private matter between two consenting individuals. However, it was also a religious matter: a sacrament of the Church, in respect of which the ecclesiastical authorities had established certain rules and regulations. These were chiefly concerned with whom one was or was not allowed to marry. They were not, at this period, greatly concerned with *how* one should get married.

Thus, although provision existed for formal church wedding services, these were not compulsory, and the Church gave full recognition to private – and even secret – exchanges of marriage vows. The only essentials for a valid marriage at this time were mutual consent of two individuals who were free to marry each other, followed by sexual intercourse. Medieval marriage was, in some respects, a very simple matter!

Of course, if you were wise, you would probably arrange to have your marriage vows witnessed – just in case any subsequent dispute should arise. And in fact, the majority of people did opt for the Church's public wedding service – something which the Church itself was increasingly eager to promote and encourage.

If you did get married by means of such a church service, then a priest would officiate, and you would probably wear your best clothes for the occasion, and invite your family and friends. For the groom, 'best clothes' would not, of course, resemble a modern suit, however. Nor did medieval brides wear white – though wearing something blue may already have been quite a popular notion at this period, because of the colour's links with the Blessed Virgin Mary.

There would probably be music at the wedding ceremony – though this would more likely be supplied by the local waites, with their viols and shawms, than by a church organ. This was partly because the wedding ceremony would probably not be celebrated *inside* a church, but *outside* the building in the open air – usually near the west door.

During a public wedding ceremony the groom would probably give the bride a ring, placing this on the ring finger of her *right* hand. However he would not himself receive a ring from her in exchange. The ring he gave might be made of metal, although more ephemeral materials were also permissible since the ring was only required for the wedding ceremony. We have seen evidence suggesting that on at least one occasion a plain gold wedding ring was used at a medieval English royal wedding.

On the occasion of a publicly celebrated wedding, friends and family probably already gave presents to the happy couple, even at this early period.

As for royal marriages, these are traditionally imagined to have been with brides of equal (i.e. foreign royal) status. But in fact this was by no means always the case. Nevertheless, aristocratic status was normal for royal brides, since medieval English kings did not marry peasants.

There is also a traditional tendency to imagine that a virgin bride was an essential requirement, but again we have found that in fact this was not so. Some royal brides had been married previously, and already had children. As for royal bridegrooms, they were often sexually experienced – the experience having been gained with girls or women from lower social classes prior to their marriages. Kings and princes did sometimes acquire mistresses of aristocratic status, but if they did so this was usually later in their careers – when they had already been married and had produced the required heirs to the throne.

As for the bastards who were engendered as a result of royal extra-marital activities, these were variously treated by their fathers. The children of low-class mothers were quite often recognised, but they were not generally granted noble status. Yet sometimes careers were found for them in the Church, and such ecclesiastical careers were likely to bring the children preferment – for example as bishops or as abbesses. As for royal bastards who were born to higher-class mothers, these children might well be awarded noble titles in their own right, and one or two of them even grew up to make royal or princely marriages.

Two

Secret And Bigamous Medieval Royal Marriages

7

THE LOVE-MATCHES OF EDWARD III'S CHILDREN

… my dearest and truest sweetheart and beloved companion.

The Black Prince to Joan of Kent, 1367

In this chapter we shall begin to look at secret marriage in the English royal family by exploring the marriage pattern of Edward III's children. So far we have considered only the partnerships, marital and otherwise, of English *sovereigns*. Roughly half of the thirteen rulers from William I to Edward III married consorts of royal birth (children or grandchildren of other monarchs). However, the wider picture of marital and other relationships within the royal family as a whole has not yet been explored in any detail. We have merely noted in passing that in the case of at least one younger son (Henry I) no marriage was apparently arranged for him prior to his accession. Later, for Henry II's sons, marriages with the daughters of foreign royalty and aristocracy seem generally to have been planned. These were what may be described as typical royal marriages for that period – even though in the event some of these arranged marriages never materialised.

Only in the case of Prince (later King) John – the youngest son of Henry II, who was initially perceived as being very remote from any prospect of succession to the throne – was no such foreign marriage planned. The result was that initially John married a cousin from within the English illegitimate royal and aristocratic circle. Later, of course, when he had succeeded to the throne, John opted instead for a different marriage; one with a foreign heiress, which perhaps more closely approximated to the normal English kingly pattern – though his bride was of lower status than those of his elder brothers, Henry and Richard. However, we shall see that in the long run John's first marriage attempt, with Isabel of Gloucester, was probably more typical of the marriage pattern for younger royal sons.

By considering the marriages of those royal children of Henry III, Edward I and Edward II who were not in the immediate line of succession we can form an overall idea of what had been considered normal in the wider royal family during the hundred years or so prior to the marriages of Edward III's children. The picture that emerges is somewhat mixed, but in general younger sons married the daughters of either English or foreign aristocrats, while royal daughters either married foreign royalty or English aristocrats. However, for political reasons, during this period the eldest son – the heir to his father's throne – always married the daughter of a foreign ruler – though the bride's father might be of less than royal status.

By comparison the marriages of the children of Edward III (reigned 1327–77) present a curiously diverse and irregular picture. Thus, Edward III's eldest son and heir, the Black Prince, did not marry a foreign princess. Instead his chosen consort was an English bride who was certainly not a virgin when he married her. Indeed, she was a lady with a somewhat questionable marital history. We shall look at the Black Prince's marriage and its implications in more detail presently.

Most of the Black Prince's younger brothers initially married into the English aristocracy. Only Edmund of Langley, Duke of York, found a foreign royal bride as his first marriage partner – though Edmund's elder brother, John of Gaunt, Duke of Lancaster, also married a foreign princess as his *second* wife. In the end, however, it was to be Gaunt's choice of a *third* wife which would prove utterly astonishing, causing contemporary consternation both at court and in the country at large. This marriage will also be discussed in detail shortly.

Of Edward III's four daughters, two married at home, and two would have married abroad, had not one of them succumbed to the plague at Bayonne while on her way to marry Pedro of Castile. However, Isabel, the eldest daughter, married a man who was of lower rank than might normally have been expected. Like the marriage of her eldest brother, the Black Prince, and the third marriage of her fourth brother, John of Gaunt, Princess Isabel's choice of a spouse may have raised some eyebrows.

✠ ✠ ✠

In the next chapter we are going to trace how the surprising phenomenon of the secret marriage quietly but firmly established itself as a background feature of the English royal wedding scene during the course of the fifteenth century. But the first move in this direction actually occurred in the mid-*fourteenth* century, and this unexpected development arose out of the relationship between Edward Prince of Wales (the Black Prince) and his cousin, Joan, Countess of Kent.

Joan was a daughter of Edmund of Woodstock – one of the younger sons of Edward I, borne to him by his second wife, Margaret of France. Joan was thus of English royal blood in a cadet line. The male members of such junior branches of English royalty might marry daughters of the reigning monarch, but in the entire period since the Norman Conquest there was absolutely no precedent for the marriage of a bride from such a background with the heir apparent to the English throne. Normally the prospective bride of the heir apparent – or 'Prince of Wales', as he had been called since the reign of Edward I – was expected to be the daughter of a foreign ruler. The family backgrounds of Queen Philippa (the Black Prince's mother) and of Isabelle of France and of Eleanor of Castile (his grandmother and great grandmother respectively) all fitted this pattern. On the other hand, the family origins of Joan of Kent did not at all conform to this norm. However, what made Joan completely extraordinary and exceptional as a consort for the heir to the throne – and the future king, as far as anyone then knew[1]– was her previous marital history.

For although she was sometimes (and perhaps sarcastically) known as 'the Virgin of Kent', in actual fact Joan was by no means a virgin. In 1340, at the very young age of 12, she had contracted a clandestine marriage with a nobody. Thomas Holland was the son of a gentry family from Lancashire. He was probably also some years older than his royal child bride. The marriage between Joan and Thomas was clandestine, and was contracted without either requesting or receiving royal consent. Very soon afterward Thomas Holland, who was a soldier, departed for the Crusades, leaving his child bride behind in England.

Joan did nothing to reveal her marriage at that stage. However, her family evidently had some suspicions that their daughter might be involved with a man of questionable suitability. They therefore compelled Joan to contract a second (and bigamous) marriage, with William Montacute, son of the Earl of Salisbury and the heir to his title (to which William succeeded in 1344). William Montacute was about the same age as his bride, and the couple cohabited for several years, but possibly without the marriage being consummated. At all events, Joan bore William no children.

Joan's marriage with William Montacute was annulled by Pope Clement VI in 1349, on the petition of her true husband. Thomas Holland had returned from the Crusades a wealthy man, and had confessed to the king the truth about his marriage to Joan. Initially William Montacute contested the annulment of his marriage, and even imprisoned Joan for a time. Eventually, however, she was able to join her real husband, with whom she then lived until his death in 1360, bearing him four (or possibly five) children. In 1352, on the death of Joan's brother, John, she and Thomas succeeded to the titles of Countess and Earl of Kent.

After Thomas Holland's death, the Black Prince began to show an interest in his cousin, giving her presents, including a silver cup. However, Edward III and Queen Philippa viewed this new situation askance. The king and queen had many reservations about their son's relationship with Joan. Perhaps not surprisingly the royal couple seems to have felt that the girl's reputation left a good deal to be desired. Her lack of foreign ruling parents, coupled with her pre-existing bevy of children, meant that as a prospective daughter-in-law she was deficient in some respects and rather too well-endowed in others. The king and queen were also concerned about the fact that Joan and the prince were first cousins once removed, and therefore well within the prohibited degrees. Given their close blood relationship they would only be able to wed validly with a papal dispensation.

The Black Prince, unconcerned apparently at these ecclesiastical niceties, is reputed to have contracted a secret marriage with Joan in 1360. This was Joan's second secret marriage! However, the lack of any Papal dispensation at this stage rendered this secret royal marriage of questionable validity. Nevertheless the couple persisted in their intention, and on 10 October 1461 they were properly and officially married at Windsor Castle by the Archbishop of Canterbury, duly armed with the necessary permission from Rome, and with the king and queen in attendance.

Joan bore her royal husband two sons, the younger of whom ultimately succeeded to the throne as King Richard II. But after all the initial anxieties which had greeted her relationship with the Prince of Wales, in the end Joan – like a more recent Princess of Wales who similarly gave the establishment some cause for concern – never became Queen of England. In 1376 the Black Prince predeceased his father. Mercifully, perhaps, the much-married Joan showed no signs of seeking another husband. As Princess Dowager of Wales she seems generally to have been a popular figure during the reign of her son, and when she died in 1385 she left instructions that she should be buried not at Canterbury Cathedral with the Black Prince, but with her first husband, Thomas Holland, at the more modest venue of the Franciscan Priory (Greyfriars) at Stamford in Lincolnshire.

In the end, and on the whole, Joan's royal marriage should probably be regarded as a success. However, it had certainly shattered the traditional mould. Moreover, Joan's marital history did allow scope for a degree of undesirable gossip about her. Thus Adam of Usk, in his *Chronicle*, referred to rumours that Richard II was illegitimate, commenting in explanation that his mother had been 'given to slippery ways'.[2]

Generally, the subsequent two marriages of Joan's son, Richard II, and the marriages of his successors, the three Lancastrian kings, would seek to return to the usual pattern. Nevertheless, a curious and important precedent had now been established in the royal family, which allowed the king or his heir apparent to marry an English noblewoman with English royal ancestry. This precedent also permitted the King or Prince of Wales to contract a clandestine marriage with such a bride, while at the same time linking the secret marriage with hints of bigamy. This very strange new precedent would find echoes in the royal marital history of the fifteenth century and beyond, as we shall see.

Incidentally, we should note, perhaps, that despite the Black Prince's very unconventional marriage, in other respects Edward III's eldest son conformed to the usual royal sexual pattern of his day. Thus he fathered three illegitimate sons, all of whom were born prior to his marriage to Joan of Kent.[3]

❖ ❖ ❖

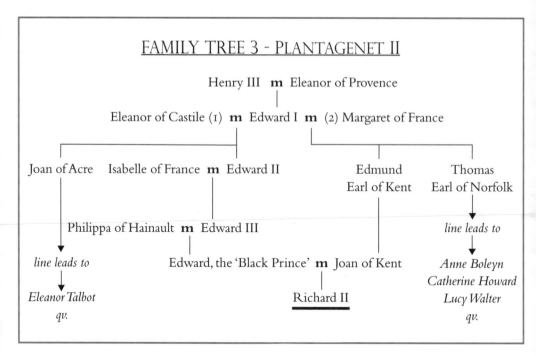

FAMILY TREE 3 - PLANTAGENET II

Henry III **m** Eleanor of Provence

Eleanor of Castile (1) **m** Edward I **m** (2) Margaret of France

Joan of Acre   Isabelle of France **m** Edward II   Edmund   Thomas
                                                              Earl of Kent   Earl of Norfolk

Philippa of Hainault **m** Edward III   *line leads to*

line leads to   Edward, the 'Black Prince' **m** Joan of Kent   *Anne Boleyn*
                                                                                   Catherine Howard
Eleanor Talbot   Richard II   *Lucy Walter*
qv.   *qv.*

A younger brother of the Black Prince, and the third surviving son of Edward III, was John of Gaunt, Duke of Lancaster (1340–99). John of Gaunt's marital history – like that of his elder brother – was to create something of a stir in the fourteenth century. However, John's story began in a fairly conventional way. Like his elder brother, before he was first married he had a mistress, by whom he fathered an illegitimate child called Blanche. Blanche was born in 1359 and later served as a lady-in-waiting to John's mother, Queen Philippa.[4]

Curiously, this illegitimate daughter was apparently named after John of Gaunt's first wife, his cousin, Blanche of Lancaster (1345–68), whom he married in the same year as the little girl was born. Blanche of Lancaster was the daughter, and ultimately the heiress of the first Duke of Lancaster – who was a direct descendant in an all-male line of Edmund Crouchback, a younger brother of Edward I.[5] Thus John of Gaunt's first marriage to an English royal descendant in a cadet line (rather like his fathering of a pre-marital bastard child) conformed to what seems by this period to have been regarded as the usual pattern for a younger son of the English monarch.

John's first wife, Blanche of Lancaster, died in September 1368, having given her husband several legitimate children. John then married Constance of Castile (1354–94), the elder daughter – and according to some points of view, the heiress – of King Pedro the Cruel.[6] In addition, Constance's younger sister, Isabel, married John's younger brother, Edmund of Langley (Duke of York). Through Constance (*iure uxoris*) John subsequently claimed the Castilian Crown – unsuccessfully, as things turned out.

From the point of view of English royal matrimonial history, John of Gaunt's second marriage to a foreign princess also fell within normal parameters. However, the marriage to Constance seems to have been a purely diplomatic arrangement, without any great degree of personal feeling behind it. Nevertheless, Constance gave her husband one more legitimate child – a daughter. This daughter, Catherine of Lancaster subsequently married the rival claimant to the Castilian throne, thus uniting the two Castilian royal lines.[7]

However, during the years in which John of Gaunt was married to Constance of Castile, the real focus of his love was centred elsewhere – on Catherine de Roët.[8] Catherine was the third daughter of a knight from the Low Countries who was possibly a connection of John of Gaunt's mother, Philippa of Hainaut (the consort of Edward III). If so, then Catherine de Roët may have been some kind of distant cousin of her lover and later husband.

Catherine entered the service of John of Gaunt's first wife, Blanche of Lancaster, and in about 1363–65 she married Sir Hugh Swynford, one of John of Gaunt's tenants.[9] Subsequently she became governess to John's children by Blanche of Lancaster,[10] and by 1371 she was also her employer's mistress. By that time Catherine's first husband and John of Gaunt's first wife were both dead.[11]

Between 1373 and 1377 Catherine bore John of Gaunt four children, who were given the surname 'Beaufort'.[12] The couple's relationship was seen as insulting to John of Gaunt's second wife, Constance of Castile, and some historians interpret the surviving evidence to mean that in 1381 Gaunt was forced by public opinion to distance himself from Catherine, who then retired both from her post as governess, and from Gaunt's household.[13] However, even if they officially parted for a time it is nevertheless likely that their relationship continued in secret.

When Constance of Castile died, John of Gaunt caused even greater general astonishment – and not a little disapproval – by marrying Catherine. The marriage was not secret but, not surprisingly, it was regarded in some quarters as a *mésalliance*. However, the marriage led to the legitimisation of the couple's Beaufort children.[14] Ironically it is through the Beaufort family that the Plantagenet royal dynasty now has its only living descendants in an all-male line – albeit via a double illegitimacy. These modern male descendants do not bear either the surname 'Plantagenet' or the surname 'Beaufort', however. They are the Somerset family, whose head is the Duke of Beaufort.

Through the marriage of John of Gaunt and Catherine de Roët, and the consequent legitimisation of the bastard Beauforts, one of the key elements leading to the ultimate establishment of the later royal house known as the 'Tudors' was set in place. It was through their descent from the legitimised Beauforts that these Tudors would derive their highly questionable claim to the English Crown. The second key factor in the creation of the royal Tudors came about as a result of another dubious royal relationship in the following century. This is one of the stories which we shall explore in our next chapter.

Meanwhile it is worth noting that, although it was at first regarded askance, the marriage of Catherine to John of Gaunt eventually became almost universally accepted. Catherine de Roët seems to have handled her potentially tricky situation with an impressive degree of skill and tact. Indeed, after his accession King Henry IV (whose father was John of Gaunt, but whose mother had been Blanche of Lancaster, not Catherine de Roët) treated Catherine with great respect. He even referred to her in writing as 'the king's mother'.

8

Secret Weddings and Witchcraft in the House of Lancaster

There was a Beldame called the wytch of Ey,
Old mother Madge her neyghbours did hir name
Which wrought wonders in countryes by heresaye
Both feendes and fayries her charmyng would obay
And dead corpsis from grave she could uprere
Suche an inchauntresse, as that tyme had no peere.[1]

William Baldwin & George Ferrers,
The Mirror for Magistrates, ed. L.B. Campbell

Novel features observed in relationships and marriages at the court of Edward III were to recur in the fifteenth century. The first such feature was the accusation of witchcraft levelled at the king's mistress, Alice Salisbury. In the course of the fifteenth century similar accusations were to be levelled at four powerful court ladies, not to mention one other royal mistress.[2] The second feature was the penchant for secret royal marriages, which we observed among some of Edward III's children.

During the fifteenth century several more clandestine marriages took place in the Lancastrian royal family, which ruled England from 1399 until 1460.[3] This was despite the fact that the three Lancastrian kings all had classic royal consorts – the daughters of foreign monarchs. On several occasions in fifteenth- and sixteenth-century royal history, the two features of clandestine marriage coupled with the accusation of witchcraft would appear in conjunction, as we shall see in this and the following two chapters. The process reached a kind of climax towards the end of the fifteenth century, when the problem inherent in the secret marriage was to make itself felt with a vengeance, causing major disruptions for the royal house of York.[4] First, however, we shall review the witchcraft accusations and the secret marriage allegations relating to the Lancastrian dynasty.

✤ ✤ ✤

The concept and image of a witch have varied considerably over the last six hundred years or so. The supposed 'traditional picture' was of an ugly woman with black robes and a tall black hat, riding on a broomstick. But recent iconography has included much less threatening depictions such as that of the attractive Elizabeth Montgomery in the twentieth-century American television series *Bewitched*.

Medieval depictions lay somewhere between the two. For much of the medieval period witches were the local wise women who had some knowledge of herbs and of healing. Surviving late medieval woodcuts depict such women in a fairly non-threatening way. In Plate 2, for example, two witches are shown adding herbs and other ingredients to a cauldron to produce a potion.

However, throughout Europe, from the fourteenth century onwards the picture seems to have been changing, as the Church began to produce anti-witch propaganda in an attempt to stamp out the phenomenon. We should also remember that, while every period has tended to associate witchcraft chiefly with the female of the species, there has also been a belief in male equivalents – such as the Dominican friar whom we have already encountered, who was accused of aiding Alice Salisbury.

As we have already seen, by the second half of the fourteenth century, an accusation of witchcraft could be a useful tool in the hands of enemies. It offered an effective means of attacking a person who was otherwise in a powerful position. It is possible that the witchcraft accusation laid against Alice Salisbury was nothing more than a clever way of attacking a powerful woman. At the same time, however, one should not rule out the possibility that, on some occasions at least, a woman in a powerful but insecure position may genuinely have sought to make use of witchcraft for her own ends, in an attempt to protect herself or to make herself more secure.

Both in the Middle Ages and today, one encounters varying attitudes to witchcraft. While many people may view the phenomenon as a myth, there are certainly believers, and such believers – whether they were opponents or supporters of witchcraft – were probably more numerous in the past. Thus some accusations of witchcraft were probably made in the genuine belief that the black arts were being practiced. Moreover, in at least some historical instances there is clear evidence that this was indeed the case.

The most interesting and best documented example of an authentic case of witchcraft involved a royal mistress – Athénais de Montespan – at the French court during the reign of Louis XIV. Actually there had been much earlier accusations of witchcraft at the French court. In the late fourteenth century Queen Isabeau of Bavaria accused her sister-in-law, Valentina Visconti, of causing the madness of Isabeau's husband, King Charles VI, by witchcraft. Subsequently, in the early sixteenth century, accusations of witchcraft were levelled against the queen mother, Catherine de Medici. In Valentina's case the accusation may merely have been part of a power struggle, but in Catherine's case there was certainly a real – and probably justified – suspicion that she made use of potions and poisons. Both of these earlier French royal reputed witches were Italian foreigners, which may have helped to prejudice French opinion against them!

Later, however, Mme de Montespan undoubtedly took part in black masses and used a number of revolting potions on her royal lover in an attempt to retain his favour. Her involvement – and the cause of the king's repeated headaches – was revealed in 1677 when her associate, a witch called La Voisin, was arrested and prosecuted. The black masses in which Mme de Montespan participated involved child sacrifice. They were celebrated on the naked body of a woman – perhaps Mme de Montespan herself. At the solemn moment of consecration a child's throat was cut, and its blood was drained into the chalice, while a prayer to Ashtaroth and Asmodea was said, asking that the king's love for Mme de Montespan should continue. Mme de Montespan herself escaped any severe punishment for her involvement in these practices, but La Voisin was burned at the stake for her activities.

At the English court, too, accusations of witchcraft were made on several occasions. In fact in the late medieval and early modern period such accusations surfaced more frequently in England than in France. We have already noted the case of Edward III's mistress, Alice Salisbury, in the late fourteenth century. In the fifteenth century similar accusations were made against two royal duchesses, Eleanor, Duchess of Gloucester and Jacquette, Duchess of Bedford, and against two English queens consort, Joanna of Navarre and Elizabeth Woodville. English queens could wear their hair down, and exposed, at a time when most respectable women were required to cover their heads. It is interesting, therefore, to note that one feature of medieval witchcraft was that sorceresses also tradition-ally 'let their hair down' (literally) while making incantations.[5] The accusations continued into the sixteenth century, when charges of witchcraft were levelled at Queen Anne Boleyn. We shall review the cases against Queen Joanna and the Duchess of Gloucester presently. The evidence against the Duchess of Bedford, Elizabeth Woodville and Anne Boleyn will emerge in later chapters.

Not all the English royal cases of alleged witchcraft are as well documented as the one at the court of Louis XIV, and it is sometimes difficult now to assess whether the women concerned were genuinely suspected of using the black arts, or whether this was just a convenient means of trying to bring them down. It is even more difficult to be sure whether the women themselves really had engaged in any activities which could have been described as witchcraft or whether they were totally innocent. In some of the cases, however, as we shall see, there do seem to be grounds for believing that, like Mme de Montespan, the English royal ladies really did resort to the use of spells and potions.

✤ ✤ ✤

The nature of the activities in which witches were supposed to be involved varied considerably. We have already seen that close physical contact could be interpreted as a kind of love spell. However, the use of potions and incantations was also a common feature. Details of some medieval European love spells do survive. Often potions involved the use of ingredients such as honey or mead (for sweetness), combined with herbs such as vervain or mandrake root, and sometimes rose petals. Such ingredients would be pleasant enough to the taste. However, sometimes body parts of the person seeking love were included. Pubic hair was especially favoured for this purpose.[6] The sexual organs of animals were sometimes incorporated in love potions, while menstrual blood seems to have been a popular ingredient for women who were attempting to win the affections of a man. Surviving records of sixteenth-century Venetian witch trials are revealing. 'In 1588 the courtesan Paolina de Rossi was accused of having asked her servant to put her menstrual blood into the wine of Gian Battista Giustiniani, in order to gain his passion. She mixed it with sage to make the drink more powerful'. Likewise 'Veronica Cattanea mixed her menstrual blood with leaves of belladonna to arouse love in a man'.[7] Belladonna (deadly nightshade) contains hallucinogenic agents, as do henbane and mandrake which were also used in medieval love magic. Sometimes the consecrated host and the consecrated wine from Mass were defiled by being used in love spells. So too were holy water, holy oil and consecrated candles. 'During 1499 Bernadina Stadera was accused to have desecrated three hosts writing magical words on them, probably with blood.'[8]

The ingredients of a potion were traditionally boiled together in a pot or cauldron, possibly on a specific day that was considered well-omened. One recipe specifies that its love potion should be brewed on a Friday, while the moon is waxing. During the brewing of the potion a spell may also have been uttered. One short example runs as follows:

GODDESS OF LOVE
HEAR MY PLEA
LET [lover's name] DESIRE ME!

Surviving love incantations from late medieval and early modern Italy invoke the stars, the prophet Daniel and St Martha.[9]

One particularly revolting love spell reportedly condemned by the Church in the tenth and eleventh centuries required the woman seeking love to insert a live fish in her vagina, and retain it there until it was dead. She must then cook it and serve it to her desired lover.[10] During the cooking the addition of other ingredients regarded as aphrodisiac was strongly recommended. For the wealthy sorceress, wine, saffron and cardamom were considered suitable additions. For those who preferred a cheaper spell, more readily available herbs such as parsley, sage, rosemary and thyme were thought to be equally efficacious. As the traditional song *Scarborough Fair* still dimly reflects, parsley, sage, rosemary and thyme were generally considered effective components of love potions.[11]

✠ ✠ ✠

We shall return to the specific accusation of witchcraft against English royal women shortly. First, however, there is another point to consider. In addition to fifteenth- and sixteenth-century accusations of witchcraft against royal ladies, several further clandestine and love marriages occurred in the royal family at the end of the fourteenth century and in the first half of the fifteenth century. All but one of these involved junior royalty, and none of them was bigamous. The first case, however, caused something of a scandal. It centred on Elizabeth of Lancaster, the younger daughter of John of Gaunt by his first wife, Blanche of Lancaster.

Elizabeth, who was brought up by her father's future mistress and ultimate third wife, Catherine de Roët, has been described as headstrong. Certainly she seems to have been governed by her passions, and to have been somewhat free of moral restraint. In June 1380 Elizabeth was betrothed to John Hastings, third Earl of Pembroke. At the time of the betrothal Elizabeth was 17 years old while her future husband was only 8. Perhaps not surprisingly under the circumstances, Elizabeth seems to have been less than enthralled by the proposed marriage, and in the course of the next five or six years she began to seek elsewhere the sexual fulfilment which her boy bridegroom was too young to provide. She was seduced by her relative, Sir John Holland – the elder half-brother of Richard II (being a son of Joan of Kent by her earlier marriage).

Elizabeth's relationship with John Holland was clearly sexual, because by the beginning of 1386 she found herself pregnant. Fortunately her father showed understanding of her predicament. The marriage (still unconsummated) with the Earl of Pembroke was annulled, and on 24 June 1386, Elizabeth of Lancaster and Sir John Holland were married at Plymouth. Holland was subsequently created first Duke of Exeter, and the couple went on to have five children.

In 1400, following the usurpation of Elizabeth's brother, Henry IV, her husband became implicated in the 'Epiphany Rising' against the new king. He was arrested and later executed. But Elizabeth of Lancaster was not the sort of woman to retire into a cloister or spend her time in quiet widowhood. A few months later she married again. Her new husband was Sir John Cornwall, first Baron Fanhope and Milbroke. He and Elizabeth appear to have enjoyed a happy marriage, and in due course two further children were born.

✠ ✠ ✠

The marriage of Elizabeth's brother, Henry IV, with Joanna of Navarre was certainly no secret, but reputedly it was based on love rather than politics. Joanna was born in about 1370, the daughter of King Charles II of Navarre. Her first marriage had been with the Duke of Brittany, to whom she had borne several children prior to his decease in 1399.

In England, 1399 was also the year that marked the deposition of King Richard II by his cousin Henry of Lancaster (the eldest son of John of Gaunt by his first wife, Blanche). Henry's claim to succeed Richard was not undisputed – either at the time or subsequently.[12] Nevertheless, Parliament was persuaded to enthrone the Lancastrian prince with the title Henry IV. At the time of his accession the new king was a widower, with several living sons. In spite of this, he decided to remarry, choosing as his queen consort the widowed Duchess of Brittany. Although this wedding might have the appearance of an arranged, political union, actually the marriage was probably a love match. Henry had met the widowed Joanna during his exile from Richard II's England, and had apparently fallen in love with her. He and Joanna were married five days after the Feast of Candlemas, on 7 February 1403, and for the next ten years Joanna of Navarre was Queen Consort of England. The marriage, however, remained childless.

Ostensibly Joanna was on good terms with her stepchildren, Henry IV's sons by his first wife. In particular she was thought to enjoy a cordial relationship with the future Henry V, because in his frequent arguments with his father Joanna tended to support 'Prince Hal'. It therefore caused some astonishment when, in 1419, six years after Henry V's accession, the queen dowager (as Joanna then was) was accused of having used witchcraft in an attempt to poison him. This accusation against Joanna was brought by one of her own confessors. The evidence was insubstantial, and Joanna was probably innocent. Nevertheless, she was tried for the offence. Subsequently she was imprisoned for several years at Pevensey Castle. When Henry V was dying, however, he set her free.

On her release Joanna retired to Nottingham Castle, where she then lived very quietly. She subsequently had a good relationship with her stepgrandson, Henry VI, and when she finally died, in 1437, she received a royal burial at Canterbury Cathedral, where her body lies beside that of Henry IV, adjacent to the former site of the shrine of St Thomas Becket. However, Joanna never quite escaped the taint of what had happened. She was remembered by history as 'the Witch Queen'.

❖ ❖ ❖

Henry V's brother, Humphrey, Duke of Gloucester (1390–1447), engaged in two surreptitious unions. His first clandestine union was with Jacqueline of Hainaut. However, possibly more important was his second secret marriage, with Eleanor Cobham. This second secret wife was also to become the second Lancastrian royal lady to be accused of witchcraft.

In some ways Humphrey's story recalls that of his grandfather, John of Gaunt. Perhaps the latter may have been Humphrey's model. In 1425 (at a time when he still believed himself married to Jacqueline of Hainaut) the beautiful and clever Eleanor Cobham became Humphrey's mistress, and in 1428, after his marriage to

Jacqueline had been declared null and void, Humphrey married Eleanor.[13] Like his grandfather's third marriage to Catherine de Roët, Humphrey's marriage to Eleanor was regarded as something of a *mésalliance*. Nevertheless, the marriage itself was initially a happy one, though it seems to have been childless.[14]

However, in 1441 Eleanor fell foul of the authorities, and found herself condemned for witchcraft including treasonable necromancy. Eleanor's great mistake had probably been to seek to explore the horoscope of the young King Henry VI in the hope of discovering his likely date of death. Of course, if the young king had died without children then Eleanor's husband would have succeeded to the throne and Eleanor herself would have become Queen of England.

Her confessor or chaplain, John Hum (Hume/Home), was one of those involved, and it was Hum who accused the duchess. He was a canon of Hereford and St Asaph and served as chaplain and secretary to both Eleanor and her husband. Others of Eleanor's associates who were arrested were:

> master Thomas Southwell a canon of St Stephen's chapel at Westminster … and master Roger Bolyngbroke a man expert in necromancy,[15] and a woman called Margery Jourdemayne surnamed the witch of Eye beside Winchester [*sic* for Westminster]: to whose charge it was laid that these four persons should, at the request of the said duchess, devise an image of wax like unto the King, the which image they dealt so with, that by their devilish incantations and sorcery they intended to bring out of life, little and little, the King's person, as they little and little consumed that image.[16]

Although Eleanor denied most of the charges brought against her, she did admit to involvement with Margery Jourdemayne, 'the Witch of Eye next Westminster', from whom she had obtained certain potions.[17]

Margery Jourdemayne (born before 1415, executed 27 October 1441) had an unusual name. It would be tempting to think that this may have been a feature of fifteenth-century women reputed to have magical or supernatural powers, because a roughly contemporary *sortilega* (fortune teller) in fifteenth-century Colchester likewise had the rather strange name of Jeweyn Blakecote.[18] Did women of this profession tend to be foreign? Is it possible that Margery Jourdemayne's name is our first recorded example of a professional or 'stage' name; that her French surname was *jour demain* and meant 'Tomorrow' and was perhaps meant to imply that Margery had the power to foretell the future?[19] These seem tempting speculations. But in fact *Jourdemayne* was Margery's married name. Her birth surname is unknown. Her husband was William Jourdemayne, who came from a family of yeomen established in Middlesex since at least the end of the previous century. The surname is undoubtedly old French in origin, but *jour de main* may simply have been an appellation for a workman employed on a daily basis.[20]

Unfortunately for Eleanor Cobham, Margery had something of a reputation – and also a record. 'From the early 1430's Margery seems to have kept the company of a number of respected and learned clerics and courtiers'.[21] She is reported to have foretold that Edmund Beaufort, first (or according to some calculations, second) Duke of Somerset, would die 'at a castle'. When Edmund was killed in 1455, at the first battle of St Albans, he discovered, as he lay dying, that he was at the Castle Inn! We shall have more to say about Edmund Beaufort later. But as for Margery, she may also have been previously involved in reputed plots against the life of Henry VI.

Eleanor admitted that she had known Margery Jourdemayne for some ten years, and that she had made use of her services. However, her statement at her trial was that the potions she obtained from Margery were merely intended to help her conceive a child by her husband. Despite her denials of the other charges, Eleanor was found guilty. The case against her was pursued strongly – probably partly for political reasons, in order to bring down her husband or at least reduce his power and influence.

After being forced to do penance in various parts of London on Monday 13 November, Wednesday 15 November and Friday 17 November 1441, escorted by the mayor and other officials, the unfortunate ex-duchess was imprisoned for life. A letter from King Henry VI to his chancellor survives, which gives orders for her transportation to Cheshire, and Henry commanded that those who escorted her 'lette not, for sekenesse or ony dissimulacion of hir, to carie hir thedir as we have appointed'.[22] She died in prison in 1452. Margery Jourdemayne and others of Eleanor's co-accused were less fortunate, however. Margery was burned at the stake, while the other confederates were hanged, drawn and quartered.

✤ ✤ ✤

Henry V's other brother, John of Lancaster, Duke of Bedford (1389–1435), married first Anne of Burgundy and second Jacquette de St Pol, a member of the house of Luxembourg who, as a result of her marriage became an English royal duchess. In the end John's marriages both proved childless. He left only one surviving child; his bastard daughter, Mary.

But in 1436, after Bedford's death, his widowed duchess, Jacquette, remarried in secret. Her second husband, Richard Woodville, was the son of John of Lancaster's chamberlain. Jacquette's initially secret union with this Sir Richard Woodville ultimately produced a large family. This family included a daughter, Elizabeth Woodville, who, in her turn, was to contract a secret royal marriage, as a result of which she also involved both herself and her mother in accusations of witchcraft. We shall explore Elizabeth's story in the next chapter. First, however, we should examine the last and arguably most important of the alleged secret marriages of the royal house of Lancaster – a case which touched the throne itself.

✤ ✤ ✤

The death of King Henry V at Vincennes on 31 August 1422 had left his consort, Catherine of France, a young widow. At the time of his death she was just approaching her twenty-first birthday. In the wake of Henry's corpse, Catherine returned to England, where her infant son, Henry VI (still less than one year old) was residing. Thereafter she lived a quiet life, although she appeared in public on important ceremonial occasions.

Catherine's mother, the French queen, Isabeau of Bavaria, had enjoyed the reputation of being something of a nymphomaniac. It is possible that Catherine inherited Isabeau's strong sexuality, for one chronicler reported that, after the death of Henry V, Catherine found herself 'unable fully to curb her carnal passions'.[23] Within two years of her husband's death she had apparently begun to form an amorous attachment to the late king's young cousin, Edmund Beaufort, later Count of Mortain (1427), Earl of Dorset (1438) and Duke of Somerset (1444) – a descendant of John of Gaunt's third marriage and a member of his legitimised Beaufort bastard line of descendants. Edmund (whom we encountered earlier as one of the clients of the 'Witch of Eye', Margery Jourdemayne) was about 19 years old, and still unmarried and untitled, when he attracted the attention of the youthful queen mother.

The Parliament held at Leicester in 1426 seems to have been aware of Queen Catherine's new attachment, because the House of Commons petitioned the chancellor – Edmund's uncle, Henry Beaufort, Bishop of Winchester – to allow widowed queens to remarry at their own behest, upon payment of a fine. Perhaps the Commons had been induced to do this by Edmund himself – or indeed, by his uncle, the chancellor. Unfortunately, as Colin Richmond has remarked, regarding the liaison between Queen Catherine and Edmund Beaufort 'almost everything is obscure'.[24] But at all events, the government was unsympathetic and hostile. The late king's surviving brothers, John, Duke of Bedford, and Humphrey, Duke of Gloucester, were completely opposed to any union between Queen Catherine and Edmund Beaufort. Perhaps Edmund was already perceived as a man with strong political ambitions and a taste for power. Certainly he was to emerge as such later.

In the face of official opposition the proposed bill was dropped. In its place, a rather different new bill was presented to Parliament by the government in 1427, and duly passed into law. This ruled that widowed queens of England could only remarry with the consent of an adult king. Given that Henry VI was still only a child at the time, the purpose of this new legislation was clearly aimed at curbing Queen Catherine's amorous activities. The text of the bill is not now to be found in the Rolls of Parliament for 1427, but two copies survive elsewhere, and a translation of the first copy is quoted in Appendix 3 (below).[25] The second copy is accompanied by contemporary annotations to the effect that the Lords Spiritual were worried lest the bill might prevent a marriage between a couple who had already had sexual intercourse. Did the bishops and abbots know – or suspect – that Edmund Beaufort was already Queen Catherine's lover?

Like so many points in this story, how far Catherine actually went in express-
ing her love for Edmund Beaufort is unclear. But some authors have canvassed
the notion that her second son, known to history as Edmund Tudor, but whose
first name was clearly derived from that of Edmund Beaufort, was also fathered
by the latter.[26] Edmund Tudor's date of birth is not precisely known, but he must
have been born by 1430 at the latest, to allow time for the birth of his younger
brother or half-brother (see below).

Edmund Tudor's *ostensible* father was Owen Tudor, who was reportedly a
member of Queen Catherine's household, but who may actually have had a connection with the household of Edmund Beaufort.[27] In 1430 or 1431 Catherine is
alleged to have married Owen Tudor, an attractive, if comparatively lowly, young
man whom she had reportedly met either at a dance or while he was swimming.
Rather curiously, a marriage between Catherine and Owen Tudor has been generally assumed, although, interestingly, there is no more *documentary* evidence of
such a marriage than there is in the later case of Edward IV and Eleanor Talbot
(see below). Moreover – also as in the case of Edward IV and Eleanor – there
was no strictly contemporary talk about Queen Catherine's alleged second marriage. Her reported *mésalliance* remained a secret from the general public until
after Catherine's death on 3 January 1437. Nevertheless, secret marriages were
very easily contracted in the fifteenth century. Moreover, in the case of Queen
Catherine and Owen Tudor, despite the complete lack of documentary evidence
we do have the undoubted fact that the widowed queen gave birth to three or
possibly four children of whom Owen was later reputed to be the father.[28]

Actually, as we have seen, the paternity of Queen Catherine's second son,
Edmund Tudor, has been questioned. Unfortunately the available chronological
evidence is not precise enough to give us much help in determining this matter.
Conversely, Catherine's third son, Jasper Tudor, born in about 1431, has generally
been accepted as having been the son of Owen Tudor. There is no *written* evidence
available in the case of either Edmund or Jasper to help us resolve the question of
paternity. Nevertheless, there is clear evidence of a different kind, though its significance has been hitherto overlooked. This evidence takes the form of heraldry.

Coats of arms belong to individuals, not to families. Nevertheless the sons of an
armigerous father are allowed to use versions of the father's coat of arms, marked
by some point of difference, called a mark of cadency. During the Plantagenet
period marks of cadency sometimes took the form of a 'bordure' (coloured
surround or border) added to the father's arms. Thus, for example, Thomas
of Woodstock, Duke of Gloucester, the youngest son of Edward III and Philippa
of Hainaut, bore his father's arms with the addition of a silver (or white) bordure.
Similarly, after his legitimisation, John Beaufort, the eldest son of John of Gaunt,
bore the English royal arms, surrounded by a blue and silver (or white) bordure
as a mark of cadency. This coat of arms was later inherited by Edmund Beaufort
(*see Plate 6*). Sons of Edmund Beaufort would have been entitled to use the same
arms, but with some change in the colour or design of the bordure.

Owen Tudor also bore a coat of arms. However, it was nothing like the royal arms, and there was no reason why it should have been. Owen's shield was red in colour, and bore a chevron coloured ermine, surrounded by three helms in white or silver (*see Plate 5*). If Edmund and Jasper Tudor were Owen Tudor's sons they should have borne a version of the same coat of arms as their father, with some mark of difference – either a coloured bordure or a label.

But, astonishingly, neither Edmund nor Jasper Tudor used arms remotely resembling those of Owen Tudor. Instead both brothers bore the royal arms with a blue bordure, marked in Edmund's case with alternate golden martlets (heraldic birds) and fleurs de lis, and in Jasper's case, with gold martlets only (*see Plates 7 and 8*). These coats of arms, which owed nothing whatever to the arms of Owen Tudor, were clearly derived from the arms of Edmund Beaufort. The blue and gold bordures of Edmund and Jasper Tudor were simply versions of the blue and white bordure of Edmund Beaufort, modified for cadency. Apart from this modification the three coats of arms were identical. The arms of Edmund and Jasper Tudor, which were entirely appropriate for putative sons of Edmund Beaufort (who would, via that paternity, have inherited some English royal blood), were wholly inappropriate for sons of Owen Tudor (who would have had no single drop of English royal blood in their veins). The whole purpose of medieval heraldry was to show to the world who one was. And the coats of arms of Edmund and Jasper Tudor proclaimed, as clearly as they could, that these two 'Tudor' sons of the queen mother were of English royal blood, while their bordures suggest descent from Edmund Beaufort. The only possible explanation seems to be that Beaufort was their real father.

Subsequently Catherine also bore a daughter, and there are unconfirmed rumours of yet another son, although many authorities consider that story questionable. In the absence of any heraldic evidence relating to these children nothing can be said about their paternity.

Queen Catherine died on 3 January 1437, while her 'Tudor' children were still very young. Shortly after her death, Edmund Beaufort married Lady Eleanor Beauchamp, by whom he subsequently fathered a number of children. Curiously, Eleanor Beauchamp was the aunt, and probably also the godmother,[29] of Lady Eleanor Talbot, whose reputed secret marriage to Edward IV will be explored in our next chapter. Eleanor Beauchamp's marriage to Edmund Beaufort was initially secret and unlicensed, which only goes to prove that Edmund Beaufort was as capable as anyone of marital mischief. The marriage between Edmund and Eleanor was only pardoned and granted recognition by the Crown on 7 March 1438.[30]

We should note that Edmund Beaufort probably did not marry Eleanor Beauchamp until after Queen Catherine's death.[31] It was also not until after her death that Catherine's alleged marriage with Owen Tudor become a matter of public discussion. Owen himself lived on until 1461, when he was captured after the battle of Mortimer's Cross, and subsequently beheaded at Hereford.[32] His last words are reported to have been 'that hede shalle ly on the stocke that was wonte to ly on

Quene Katheryns lappe'.[33] Owen's body was buried at the Franciscan (Greyfriars')
priory church in Hereford, and there is a curious sequel to the story of Catherine
and Owen's alleged marriage, associated with the ultimate fate of Owen's burial.

In the 1530s, at the time of the dissolution of England's religious houses,
Henry VIII did very little to rescue any royal burials from the doomed churches.
The body of his illegitimate son, the Duke of Richmond, was rescued from
Thetford Priory – but by the Howard family (dukes of Norfolk). As for Henry
himself, he had just two bodies rescued – those of his sister, Mary Tudor, Queen
of France (from Bury St Edmund's Abbey) and of his grandfather, Edmund Tudor,
from the Greyfriars' Church in Carmarthen. Curiously, however, the body of
Henry VIII's supposed great-grandfather, Owen Tudor, was not rescued from the
Hereford Greyfriars' Church. Could it have been that Henry VIII knew more
about his true paternal ancestry than later historians? If his grandfather, Edmund
Tudor, had been the son not of Owen Tudor, but of Edmund Beaufort, then
Henry VII would have had no real family connection with Owen. However, he
would arguably have had a rather better Lancastrian claim to the throne than was
previously suspected, being descended from John of Gaunt and the Beauforts on
both his father's and his mother's side (*see Family Tree 4*).

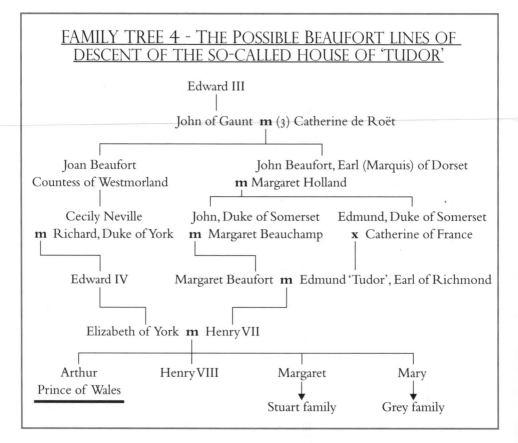

FAMILY TREE 4 - THE POSSIBLE BEAUFORT LINES OF DESCENT OF THE SO-CALLED HOUSE OF 'TUDOR'

Edward III

John of Gaunt **m** (3) Catherine de Roët

Joan Beaufort
Countess of Westmorland

John Beaufort, Earl (Marquis) of Dorset
m Margaret Holland

Cecily Neville
m Richard, Duke of York

John, Duke of Somerset
m Margaret Beauchamp

Edmund, Duke of Somerset
x Catherine of France

Edward IV

Margaret Beaufort **m** Edmund 'Tudor', Earl of Richmond

Elizabeth of York **m** Henry VII

Arthur
Prince of Wales

Henry VIII

Margaret

Mary

Stuart family

Grey family

In this case there would be no justification for applying the surname 'Tudor' to the English sixteenth-century royal family. As Richmond has remarked, 'the idea of renaming sixteenth-century England is an appealing one'.[34] Interestingly, Dr Cliff Davies has recently presented powerful evidence that the so-called Tudor royal family itself scarcely ever used the surname Tudor. 'Until the final years of Elizabeth's reign, the term was very rarely used to refer to the governments of the kings and queens we now know as 'Tudors'.[35] Davies has his own very cogent reasons to explain this point, but perhaps an additional one might have been the fact that the so-called 'Tudors' knew very well that their progenitor was not Owen Tudor but Edmund Beaufort.

Interestingly, there has long been other evidence of Edmund Beaufort's ambitious nature, which may have had the Crown as a target, if not for himself then at least for one of his sons. Henry VI's marriage to Margaret of Anjou remained childless for some years, and Henry VI has been reported to have been averse to sexual contact. However, in 1453, when Henry was mentally ill, Margaret of Anjou became pregnant and subsequently gave birth to a son, known as Edward of Westminster. He became Prince of Wales, and, in the normal course of events, would have succeeded to the throne in due course – if his Yorkist cousin, Edward IV, had not pre-empted the Lancastrian succession. However, it has long been questioned whether Edward of Westminster was truly fathered by Henry VI, and the leading contender for his paternity is none other than Edmund Beaufort, Duke of Somerset!

In fact, Richard, Duke of York's overtly expressed claim to the throne seems to have arisen not so much out of his objection to the rule of the Lancastrian dynasty as such, as from the great personal hostility which seems to have existed between York and his cousin Somerset – alias Edmund Beaufort.

Indeed the traditional account of the outbreak of the Wars of the Roses – while almost certainly a later fantasy – pictures York and Somerset plucking their rival roses and shouting at one another in the Temple Gardens.[36] It may well have been that York knew very well that the next potential 'Lancastrian' king, Edward of Westminster, was not a true Lancastrian but a descendant of the originally bastard Beaufort line. York and his family may also have suspected more than they could prove about the paternity of Edmund and Jasper 'Tudor'. At all events York's son, Richard III, would later (in 1484–85) make a point of proclaiming the bastard descent of his rival, Henry Tudor (later Henry VII). If Richard was speaking of Henry's maternal Beaufort descent then his use of the word bastard was not strictly accurate, since the Beauforts had been legitimised. However, if Richard III's words were a veiled allusion to the belief that Henry VII's father was the illegitimate son of Catherine of France by Edmund Beaufort, then his allegation of bastard descent, albeit unproven (and in those days unprovable), was possibily accurate. In the final analysis, only future DNA research might be able to establish clearly whether the so-called Tudor dynasty was perhaps not Tudor at all, but Beaufort, and therefore bearing the Plantagenet Y-chromosome in the veins of its male lineage.

✠ ✠ ✠

In the sixteenth century the pattern of secret second marriages for royal ladies
which the Duchess of Bedford and Queen Catherine fostered and promoted
during the Lancastrian epoch was to be perpetuated among Catherine's 'Tudor'
descendants. In the first half of the sixteenth century Mary Tudor, Queen of
France, entered into a secret second marriage with Charles Brandon, Duke of
Suffolk, while her elder sister, Margaret, Queen of Scotland did likewise with
Archibald Douglas, Earl of Angus and subsequently with Henry Stewart, Lord
Methven. Perhaps the environment which permitted those domestic second and
third marriages of his sisters – coupled with the domestic marriage policy adopted
by his grandfather, Edward IV, together with the possibly ambitious sexual politics of his putative great-grandfather, Edmund Beaufort, Duke of Somerset – all
exercised some influence upon Henry VIII. The various Tudor royal marital she-
nanigans will be considered shortly. Before that, however, we have now arrived at
the first disputed English royal marriage which raises doubts about the identity
of a king's consort. It is time to explore the little-known but fascinating story of
how the Yorkist king Edward IV interpreted royal marriage policy.

9

TALBOT'S DAUGHTER
AND THE GREY MARE

L'histoire est une suite de mensonges sur lesquels on est d'accord
History is a set of lies agreed upon

Emperor Napoleon I of France

King Edward was, and stoode, marryed, and trouth-plyght, to oone Dame
Elianore Butteler [*Talbot*] (doughter of the old Earl of Shrewesbury) with
whom the saide King Edward had made a precontracte of matrimonie longe
tyme bifore he made the said pretensed mariage with the said Elizabeth Grey
[*Woodville*] in manner and fourme aforesaide.

Act of Parliament of 1484

Our first clear example of a disputed kingly marriage is the case of
Edward IV (reigned 1460–83). Edward was the first monarch of the
new, Yorkist dynasty, which held the throne from 1460 until 1485, and
he seems to have gained an impressive (though perhaps exaggerated) reputation
for the strength of his libido.[1]

In the context of matrimony, Edward IV's name has been linked with four
women. Chronologically the first of the four was the noble and royally descended
Eleanor Talbot (Butler), with whom Edward had a relationship from about 1460
until maybe 1462 or 1463. The *fact* of this relationship is generally accepted. The
only question mark is in respect of its *nature*. Was it a marriage, as Parliament
declared in 1484, or an illicit relationship? Edward's second partner was Elizabeth
Wayte (Lucy), the daughter of a gentry family from Hampshire. She became the
king's mistress in about 1461–62 and bore him probably two children. We could
ignore her, were it not for the fact that 'Tudor' historians later invented (solely in
order to be able to deny) an alleged marriage connection between her and the

king (see below). Edward IV's third partner was Elizabeth Woodville (Grey), the eldest daughter of Jacquette, Duchess of Bedford (whom we met in the previous chapter), by her second husband, Richard Woodville.[2] The last of the four was Bona of Savoy, a kind of foreign princess[3] whom Edward never actually married, but with whom a marriage was negotiated on his behalf by the king's powerful cousin, the Earl of Warwick.

Edward IV is generally accepted to have contracted a clandestine marriage with Elizabeth Woodville in 1464. Although this marriage was initially a secret, the young king did subsequently acknowledge Elizabeth as his queen, and the children she gave him as his heirs. However, his marital situation is complicated by his alleged earlier marriage to Eleanor Talbot, in 1460 or thereabouts.[4]

The story of the Talbot marriage was only made public after Edward IV's death in April 1483, in circumstances we shall first review very briefly, and then examine in more detail. On Edward IV's death, his eldest son by Elizabeth Woodville was initially accepted as King Edward V. However, the new king was a minor, and needed someone to act as his regent or 'Protector'. This position belonged by right to the senior prince of the blood – in this case the boy's paternal uncle, Richard, Duke of Gloucester. However, the boy's mother, Elizabeth Woodville, tried to seize power for herself and her family. The Woodvilles were unpopular with the English aristocracy, most of whom backed the Duke of Gloucester for the role of Protector. As Gloucester made his way south to London to take office, the queen mother fled into sanctuary at Westminster Abbey.

Soon after Gloucester was officially recognised as Edward V's Protector, Bishop Stillington of Bath and Wells, former Chancellor to Edward V's father,[5] precipitated a constitutional crisis by revealing to a royal council meeting that Edward IV had married Eleanor Talbot, daughter of the Earl of Shrewsbury, several years before his marriage with Elizabeth Woodville. Since Eleanor had still been alive at the time of Edward's secret marriage to Elizabeth, this allegation, if true, meant that the king's second marriage was bigamous.[6] Consequently all the children of that Woodville marriage – including Edward V – were bastards.

After considering the case, the royal council – which on this occasion was actually a large body comprising *all* those peers who were then in or near London – accepted the evidence, set aside Edward V, and offered the throne to Gloucester, who thus became King Richard III. The decision was later ratified by a full Parliament. What subsequently became of Edward V is unknown, but he is popularly believed to have been murdered, and has gone down in history as the elder of the two so-called Princes in the Tower.[7]

During the reign of Richard III Elizabeth Woodville was demoted from queenship, while Edward IV's marriage to Eleanor Talbot was publicly proclaimed. Later, however, Richard's opponent, Henry VII – who, as we shall see, had his own axe to grind – restored Elizabeth Woodville's queenship and did his best to write Eleanor out of history completely. These later manoeuvrings make it difficult, now, to get at the truth.

✠ ✠ ✠

Edward IV had not been born close to the throne. He seized the Crown from his distant cousin, Henry VI, in 1461. It had been Edward's father, Richard Duke of York, who had first formally advanced the Yorkist claim to the English throne in 1460.[8] York was the descendant of Edward III's third son, Lionel, Duke of Clarence. He therefore argued that he was of a more senior royal line of descent than the Lancastrian kings, because the latter were only descended from Edward III's *fourth* son. York arguably had a valid case,[9] and one possible motive why he chose to advance his claim to the throne *at this stage* was considered in the previous chapter. However, the Duke of York never personally attained the Crown, because he was killed by his Lancastrian opponents in December 1460. It was early in the following year that the Yorkist claim was finally made good – by the duke's eldest son, Edward Earl of March (Edward IV).

At the time of his accession Edward IV was 19 years of age and not yet married. The young king was 6ft 2in in height, and had brown hair.[10] At this young age he was still of athletic build, though later he would run to fat. He seems to have been drawn to women a little older than himself, and both Eleanor Talbot and Elizabeth Woodville fit into this category. The pattern of royal upbringing, which we have already documented, makes it unlikely that Edward was still a virgin in 1460. But in spite of his later reputation, we know the names of very few of his sexual partners. Moreover, unlike Charles II (see below), Edward seems to have engendered very few royal bastards – with the exception of the numerous progeny he had by Elizabeth Woodville, who were later technically ruled to be illegitimate.[11] Since his relationship with Elizabeth Woodville proves that the king was fertile it is curious that, if he had numerous illicit relationships, these resulted in so few illegitimate children. Contemporary English evidence (as opposed to foreign or later propaganda) seems to suggest that, while not faithful to his consort(s), the king was probably more of a serial monogamist in the matter of mistresses, than the keeper of a large harem.

Since Edward is reputed to have had a strong sex drive, it is probable that, if he were attracted to a woman, he would not readily have accepted her refusal of his advances. Thus, if the woman did not immediately succumb to his love-making, he might have said the first words that came into his head in order to achieve his objective. Some have suggested that this is precisely what happened in the case of both Eleanor Talbot and Elizabeth Woodville. But while it might be easy to imagine Edward thoughtlessly uttering those dangerous words 'I'll marry you' in two – or even more – cases, such conduct cannot completely explain his relationships with Eleanor Talbot and Elizabeth Woodville, for reasons which we shall see presently.

Actually, nothing is known about any girlfriends of Edward IV prior to his accession, and his first known attachment was with Eleanor Talbot. She was the daughter of John Talbot, Earl of Shrewsbury, the granddaughter of Richard Beauchamp, Earl of Warwick, and the niece of Richard Neville, Earl of Warwick ('the Kingmaker'), and of Eleanor Beauchamp (Beaufort), Duchess of Somerset. Eleanor, who was descended several times over from King Edward I (see, for example, Family Tree 3) has been much maligned by generations of historians, who have spent some five centuries casting aspersions on her birth, her ancestry and her morals. However, it has now been proved beyond any possible doubt that Eleanor's family was precisely as stated.[12] Eleanor's morality is also now established beyond any reasonable doubt.

In fact, as we shall see, there are good and serious reasons for doubting the commonly held explanation that Eleanor was merely Edward IV's mistress. Nevertheless, most previous writers have discounted Eleanor's claim to be married to Edward IV. The general tendency has been to assume that Eleanor simply became the king's mistress, and that is how she is usually described by historians. This conclusion is chiefly based on two assumptions. The first assumption is that Richard III's subsequent use of Eleanor's story was a wicked lie, published purely for his own selfish political advantage. The second assumption is that the later actions of Henry VII in respect of Eleanor were completely pure and disinterested. This seems rather naïve and simplistic. The notion that Richard III was simply making use of Eleanor's name might or might not be true. But to simply *assume* that to have been the case is to consciously or unconsciously adopt a partisan position, because actually we have no surviving clear evidence in the matter. Indeed the famous nineteenth-century historian, James Gairdner, openly stated it as his opinion that there was no justification for making such an assumption.[13]

Likewise to assume that the subsequent actions of Henry VII were disinterested is also partisan – and very naïve in the light of Henry VII's other known actions. To quote his very own words on the subject, Henry had the strongest possible interest in making sure that Eleanor's claim to be Edward IV's wife 'maie be for ever out of remembraunce and allso forgot',[14] because of course, if Eleanor Talbot was Edward IV's *own* true wife, then Henry VII's *own* wife, Elizabeth of York – the eldest daughter of Edward IV and Elizabeth Woodville, and the supposed Yorkist heiress, mother of the 'Tudor' dynasty and ancestress of all future English sovereigns – was nothing more than a bastard with no claim to the throne.

In our attempt to understand the complex issue of Edward IV's marital conundrum, it is vital to remember what we already know about the nature of marriage at this period. We have learned that in the fifteenth century there were no marriage certificates, so that documentary proof of *any* marriage at this time would be very hard to come by. We also need to remember that, while they were not recommended by the Church, secret marriages were very common practice, and were universally accepted as valid. Finally we need to remember that such secret marriages required nothing more than an exchange of promises to marry on the part of the contracting couple, followed by sexual intercourse. No witnesses – even no priestly celebrants – were necessary. Inevitably, such secret marriages can be exceedingly hard to authenticate. Even at the time (as the medieval Church court records show very clearly) many matrimonial disputes resulted from this complicated situation.[15]

Unfortunately some modern historians seem to have found it very difficult to understand fifteenth-century marriage practice, and have therefore made serious mistakes in their explanations of the alleged relationship between Edward IV and Eleanor. Many have written of something which they call a 'precontract' – thereby implying that this royal relationship was something which fell short of being a true marriage. This is nonsense. Although the word 'precontract' was used in Richard III's Act of Parliament, its reference there was retrospective, and indeed 'precontract' is a word which *can* only be used retrospectively. One could not *make* a thing called a 'precontract' in the fifteenth century – or at any other time. One could only make a *marriage* – either openly or in secret. Later, if one of the contracting parties committed bigamy, then, *in relation to the second and bigamous marriage*, the term '*pre*-contract' could be used retrospectively, to refer to the *first* – and valid – marriage. Historians have frequently failed to understand this basic point, and have used the term 'precontract' inappropriately and incorrectly.

✠ ✠ ✠

Eleanor Talbot was of royal descent on both her father's and her mother's side. Indeed, two of her first cousins, Isabel and Anne Neville, subsequently married the two younger brothers of Edward IV, and one of them – Anne Neville – ultimately became Queen of England. Thus Eleanor can certainly be considered to have been of potentially queenly birth. Her dual descent from the royal family and her aristocratic status also both militate against the notion that Eleanor would have embraced with delight the dubious honour of becoming the king's mistress. No lady of such a high social status as Eleanor had accepted the post of royal mistress in England for well over a century. Even the less well-born Elizabeth Woodville, a few years later, firmly rejected that position, and insisted upon marriage.

As for Eleanor's character, like her sister the Duchess of Norfolk, and others among her closest relatives, she clearly had strong religious beliefs. This is demonstrated by her endowments at Corpus Christi College, Cambridge (then basically a religious foundation) and by her subsequent retirement into the quasi-religious life of a tertiary of the Carmelite Order. The Carmelite religious devices which figured on her later signets fully confirm her religious devotion.[16] Moreover, Eleanor's friend and protégé, Dr Thomas Cosyn, the Master of Corpus Christi College, Cambridge, later explicitly described her as *Deo devota* ('vowed to God').[17] A lady of such strong religious convictions is an unlikely candidate to have accepted the immoral role of a royal mistress.

Moreover, there would have been absolutely no reason for Eleanor to make such a compromise. She was a widow, while the king was unmarried. Thus, if Edward loved and wanted her, no impediment stood in the way of the honourable solution of marriage. Upper class widows at this period – particularly young and attractive widows – regularly contracted second marriages.[18] There was clearly no legal impediment to prevent a King of England from marrying a widow, for, as we have already seen, at the start of the fifteenth century Henry IV had married the widowed Joanna of Navarre, while in the fourteenth century the Black Prince had married the widowed Joan of Kent.

Eleanor was probably five or six years older than Edward IV, for she seems to have been born about the end of February 1436. Her father, John Talbot, first Earl of Shrewsbury, had been a hero of the Hundred Years' War between England and France, and in the second half of the fifteenth century his name was familiar to everyone in England. Thus, when the later Act of Parliament, which formally declared that Eleanor had been married to Edward IV, referred to her as the 'doughter of the old Earl of Shrewesbury', it was saying something very important, and using a name which was a national byword at the time. As for Eleanor's mother, she was of even higher birth than her husband. She was John Talbot's second wife, Lady Margaret Beauchamp, the eldest daughter of Thomas Beauchamp, Earl of Warwick, and elder sister of Eleanor, Duchess of Somerset.

No contemporary portraits of Eleanor now survive, but in 1468 her sister (who by that time had become the Duchess of Norfolk) was described as 'very beautiful'.[19] It is therefore likely that Eleanor was also a beauty. Although her mother, Margaret Beauchamp, may have had fair hair, some of Eleanor's closest relatives – including her sister and at least one of her nieces – seem to have inherited the dark colouring of her father, Lord Shrewsbury.[20] Eleanor, too, may therefore have had dark brown or black hair, and brown eyes. Both she and her sister also seem to have had aquiline noses (a feature found in both their parents). A skeleton in Norwich Castle Museum which may well be Eleanor's is that of a healthy young woman who had been about 5ft 6in in height.[21] The modern reconstructed picture of Eleanor published here is based upon the skull of that skeleton, and its colouring is inspired by surviving portraits of Eleanor's sister and niece.

Eleanor had been married at a young age to Thomas Butler, the son of one of her father's associates, Ralph Butler, Lord Sudeley. The child-bride almost certainly finished her upbringing at Sudeley Castle, in the home of her parents-in-law. In 1452, when she reached the age of 16 (the age at which a marriage with a child-bride could be consummated), Lord Sudley gave a small group of manors to his son and daughter-in-law, and thereafter Eleanor and Thomas probably lived mainly at Burton Dassett in Warwickshire. However, in 1459, after only seven years of real marriage, Eleanor was left a young and childless widow.

Her relationship with her father-in-law, Lord Sudeley, seems to have remained cordial, for Lord Sudeley reached an agreement with the young widow whereby, while one of her husband's manors was returned to him, another was ceded to

Eleanor outright.[22] Moreover, there is some evidence that a little later Eleanor used her influence with Edward IV to protect Lord Sudeley and his interests (see below). Nevertheless, after losing her husband, Eleanor seems to have left Warwickshire for good, and moved to East Anglia, where she joined the household of her younger sister, Elizabeth Talbot, Countess Warenne, wife of the son and heir of John Mowbray, third Duke of Norfolk.

Recently discovered evidence shows that the future Edward IV, then Earl of March, was in the eastern counties during the summer of 1460, visiting a cousin of the Duke of Norfolk.[23] Eleanor may also have travelled to the eastern counties at about that time, in order to visit her sister. If so, and given that the Duke of Norfolk was the father-in-law of Eleanor's sister, Edward might easily have met Eleanor during his visit. Several of her relatives and connections were closely linked to Edward, and could have presented Eleanor to him.[24] Their second possible meeting could well have taken place in the late spring or early summer of 1461, when Edward was returning south to London after the bloody battle of Towton. The new king's route was via Coventry, Warwick and Daventry. On about 8 June, travelling between Warwick and Daventry, he would have passed very close by Eleanor's manors of Fenny Compton and Burton Dassett, the first of which her former father-in-law had granted to her absolutely, and the second of which she held as part of her jointure. By this time the widowed Eleanor would have completed her period of mourning for her dead husband. Therefore, if there was a secret marriage between Edward and Eleanor it could well have taken place in early June 1461, and the most likely venue for this event would have been one of Eleanor's Warwickshire manors.

We have seen already that it would be easy to imagine a situation in which Edward IV, overcome by the strength of his own passion, and in love with a religious and aristocratic lady who would not consent to be his mistress, might have uttered a casual promise which was never seriously meant. In fact a number of historical novelists have made use of precisely this scenario to explain the story of Edward and Eleanor. But unfortunately, however enticing the picture may be, in reality it does not provide an adequate explanation of what happened in this case.

The problem is that such a scenario could only have been enacted completely in private. It would then have remained a secret. In the present instance, however, a key feature of the accounts which survive is the fact that there was reportedly at least one witness to the marriage. Moreover, the named witness was of significant status: an ecclesiastic who was an expert in canon law, and who was able to evaluate very precisely the significance both of the event and the words uttered. He was Canon (later Bishop) Stillington. This witness is a very important figure in Edward IV's marital history, and we shall have more to say about him and his role shortly.

One other fact which undermines the notion that Edward IV thoughtlessly uttered words which he did not mean simply in order to achieve his sexual objective is that, while such an explanation would certainly have entitled Eleanor to claim Edward as her lawful husband, *in fact she never did so*. As we shall see, Eleanor's conduct was tactful and discreet – more closely resembling that of Maria Smythe (the undoubted secret wife of George IV) than that of Lucy Walter (probable mistress of Charles II).

Even so, evidence survives which suggests that Eleanor had certain claims upon the king. There is some evidence that he gave her property, and that he treated her and her feelings with a degree of respect. Also, as we have just seen, there is evidence that an expert witness to the marriage existed; a witness who later stated very publicly – and at considerable cost to himself – that Edward was married to Eleanor. All of this necessarily presupposes that the alleged secret marriage between Edward and Eleanor was no mere casual uttering of unmeant promises on the part of a king eager merely for sexual fulfillment. If the marriage took place it must have been a serious, if private, exchange of marriage vows – similar to the ceremony later alleged to have been secretly conducted between Edward and Elizabeth Woodville.

In fact one near-contemporary source does actually report that Edward played out with Eleanor a scene that was remarkably similar to the one he was subsequently believed to have enacted with Elizabeth Woodville. According to the slightly later account of Philippe de Commynes, the young king 'promised to marry her, provided that he could sleep with her first, and she consented'. Edward 'had made this promise in the Bishop [of Bath]'s presence. And having done so, he slept with her'.[25] Stillington's reported presence is chronologically interesting, because it suggests that the marriage must have taken place soon after Edward's accession, probably in 1461.[26] There are also other reasons for believing this. The Act of Parliament passed in 1484 formally ruled that Eleanor had married Edward *before* 1464, legislating that this had been the king's only true and valid marriage. This act also said that Edward and Eleanor were married for a 'long tyme after' 1464. Since Eleanor died in 1468, a 'long tyme after' must have meant about four years. At the same time the act stated that they were married a 'long tyme bifore' 1464. If that expression also referred to a period of about four years then the couple must have married in about 1460/61.

Elsewhere, Commynes presents the case for the marriage even more strongly, stating explicitly that Stillington 'had married them'.[27] This seems credible, because as we have just seen, a secret marriage between Edward IV and Eleanor cannot have been 'off the cuff', and can only have been entered into after some planning. In addition to Commynes' evidence, both Domenico Mancini and Polydore Vergil (while not mentioning Eleanor by name) refer to Edward IV's involvement with a member of the Earl of Warwick's family,[28] and Mancini also specifically states that Edward made a promise of marriage.[29]

It is not clear why secrecy might initially have been seen as an essential element of Edward's alleged contract with Eleanor. Nevertheless, there are possible explanations. For example, Edward may have feared the reactions of his family – and particularly those of his mother, Cecily Neville, the dowager Duchess of York.

Cecily certainly seems to have been strongly opposed to Edward's later relationship with Elizabeth Woodville. Based on less certain evidence she is also reported to have disapproved of his relationship with Elizabeth Wayte (Lucy).[30]

The second possibility is that a deliberately secret marriage was merely Edward's dishonourable way of tricking and deceiving Eleanor. In theory, the fifteenth-century chivalric code placed a high importance on keeping one's word.[31] However, Edward IV was certainly capable of telling lies, and there are known instances when he did so. Apparently he was able to reconcile this behaviour with his sense of honour. For example in 1471, on his return from exile, it was said that 'the lies that he told were mere "noysynge", necessary to fulfil his true intention, which was in itself validated … by his true claim to the throne'.[32]

The third possibility is that Edward was following an ancient tradition by coupling first and awaiting results. If Eleanor had become pregnant perhaps he would then have acknowledged their marriage. This may also have been how he handled things in connection with his subsequent secret marriage with Elizabeth Woodville.

What positive evidence now survives of a relationship between Edward and Eleanor? At the time of Eleanor's death she owned certain landed property in addition to the manors she had acquired from the Sudeley family as a result of her first marriage, and her later accommodation with her father-in-law. At some stage she had acquired further estates in Wiltshire and perhaps elsewhere. Where the property in question can be identified, it can be traced neither to Eleanor's birth family, nor to the Sudeley family. It therefore seems probable that she received it as a gift from the king. There are two reasons for suggesting the lands were a royal gift. First, we have the fact that at least one of the estates – the manor of Oare-under-Savernake – seems to have comprised royal land.[33] Second, we have the curious circumstance whereby on Eleanor's death Edward IV's government seems to have taken deliberate steps to avoid any investigation of Eleanor's tenure of this property.[34]

Further possible evidence of Eleanor's relationship with Edward IV emerges from the king's treatment of her father-in-law, Ralph Butler, Lord Sudeley. Like other peers, Ralph was summoned to – and attended – Edward IV's first Parliament. Ralph was then in his late sixties. The old man had recently suffered family bereavements and was probably in poor health. On 26 February 1462 Edward IV generously granted him exemption for life from personal attendance in council or Parliament, and from all royal appointments such as local commissions.[35] Could it have been Eleanor who obtained this exemption for her former father-in-law? Was she also responsible for the royal grant to him, three months later, of 'four bucks in summer and six does in winter within the king's park of Woodstock'?[36]

The suggestion that Eleanor could have been responsible for Edward's grants to Lord Sudeley is strengthened by the fact that later, when Eleanor was no longer intimate with the king, the latter treated Lord Sudeley's exemption as a dead letter, with the result that Lord Sudeley was once again regularly appointed to commissions from the end of 1462.[37] Previous writers had difficulty in understanding Edward IV's actions in respect of Lord Sudeley – perhaps because they overlooked the significant fact that the king's kindness dated from precisely the period when his alleged partner was Ralph's friend and former daughter-in-law. It must also be significant that subsequently Edward IV's treatment of Lord Sudeley changed dramatically. In February 1469 the king was to break the old man completely and confiscate all his property. However, that was eight months after Eleanor's death.

We have seen that in the case of Henry V's widow, Queen Catherine, silence had prevailed during her lifetime in respect of her relationship with the man who fathered her later children. Similarly during the 1460s, nothing was said publicly about the precise nature of Edward IV's relationship with Eleanor. Allegations to the effect that this had taken the form of a secret marriage seem to have surfaced for the first time during the 1470s. The story of Edward's marriage to Eleanor was then a particularly live issue during the period 1483–85. Subsequently, discussion of the matter was very firmly suppressed in England in the autumn of 1485, following the accession of the 'Tudor' dynasty. However, on the European mainland the topic continued to be a live issue from roughly 1483 to 1534.[38] There the claim continued to be advanced that Edward and Eleanor had been secretly married in the presence of at least one witness.

Edward IV's relationship with Eleanor Talbot was of relatively short duration. In 1461–62 the king seems to have become involved in an affair with Elizabeth Wayte (Lucy), who bore him an illegitimate child.[39] Much later, during the 'Tudor' period, there were rumours that it might have been Elizabeth Wayte, rather than Eleanor Talbot, whom the king had secretly married. These rumours may have stemmed in part from faulty memories. However, they may also have been politically motivated. Either way, they appear to indicate that Edward's relationship with Elizabeth Wayte must also be dated to the early period of his reign, and certainly prior to 1464.[40]

Meanwhile, in the absence of any public statement about a wedding with Eleanor, negotiations had been started by Edward IV's cousin (and Eleanor's uncle), Richard Neville, Earl of Warwick, for a royal diplomatic alliance with Bona of Savoy. These negotiations were in process from 1463 to 1464. The Earl of Warwick had been one of the strongest supporters of his cousin, the king, and he had thought to use his power to influence the king in the important choice of a suitable consort. The earl may well have been aware that his niece, Eleanor, had attracted the king's attention soon after the latter's accession. However, it is obvious that in 1463–64 he had absolutely no idea that the king might have contracted a marriage with her. While some might see this point as significant, actually it proves nothing, since Warwick was obviously equally ignorant in respect of Edward's undoubted (but secret) involvement with Elizabeth Woodville. As far as the earl was aware, in 1464 the king was still free to marry, and he had accordingly been urging Edward to accept Bona of Savoy. At the same time he had been strongly promoting and advocating Edward's suit at the French court.

In mid-September 1464, at a council in Reading, Warwick urged the king to agree finally to the dynastic alliance with Bona.[41] To everyone's astonishment – and to Warwick's embarrassment and fury – the king responded by announcing that he was already married. Perhaps even more astonishing to those few people (such as Canon Stillington and perhaps the Duchess of Norfolk) who may have known of the king's attachment to Eleanor, might have been the fact that the person Edward now named as his wife was not Eleanor Talbot, but Elizabeth Woodville.

✠ ✠ ✠

It had probably been late in 1463, or possibly very early in 1464, according to modern year dating[42] – when Edward IV first met Elizabeth Woodville, the dowager Lady Grey (later known to those who disliked her as 'the Grey Mare'). Elizabeth was the eldest child of the large family born to Jacquette of Luxemburg, dowager Duchess of Bedford, and her second husband, Richard Woodville (Lord Rivers). Like Eleanor Talbot, Elizabeth Woodville was a little older than the king. Her precise date of birth is not recorded but she is thought to have been born in 1437, soon after her parents' marriage. Indeed it is possible that Jacquette had already been pregnant at the time of her second marriage. Elizabeth's place of birth is also uncertain, but her parents spent a lot of time in France during the early years of their marriage.

Very little is known about Elizabeth's life before she met Edward.[43] However, it is certain that in about 1456 the 20- or 21-year-old Elizabeth married Sir John Grey (c.1432–61), the eldest son and heir of Lord Ferrers of Groby. During the four or five years of their marriage the fertile Elizabeth bore Sir John two sons.[44] Elizabeth has been described as a beauty, with very fair hair. It is true that some manuscript illustrations show her with golden hair. However the portrait of her at Queens' College, Cambridge, shows dark auburn hair, so the details of her appearance remain doubtful.

Elizabeth's reason for an interview with the king is often stated to be that she came to petition him for the return of land he had confiscated following the death in battle of her Lancastrian first husband. This is inaccurate. Despite the fact that Sir John had been a Lancastrian supporter, his land had not been confiscated by Edward IV. The truth was that Elizabeth Woodville's mother-in-law was contesting Elizabeth's right to her jointure. The case between the two women was being hotly contested in Chancery, and it was in order to improve her chances of winning that Elizabeth sought the help of a distant relative, Lord Hastings, who, in return for a promise of some share of the proceeds, agreed to present Elizabeth to the king.[45]

Once again, there are no surviving contemporary accounts of what took place when Edward and Elizabeth first met. We owe their story as it has come down to us principally to Sir Thomas More (Henry VIII's chancellor, and subsequent opponent in religious matters). Unfortunately Thomas More is far from being a consistently reliable source for Yorkist history! However, according to More's account Edward was rapidly captivated by the beautiful Elizabeth, and asked her to go to bed with him in return for his promise to grant her suit in respect of her jointure. Elizabeth refused, and the king therefore decided to contract a secret marriage with her in order to get his way. This all sounds remarkably similar to the account of Edward's earlier relationship with Eleanor.

The Woodville secret marriage was reportedly celebrated at the manor house which was the home of Elizabeth's parents, at Grafton Regis, Northamptonshire. The date of the wedding is traditionally given as Tuesday 1 May 1464 – four weeks and two days after Easter.[46] This date is plausible. During the Middle Ages marriage was not permitted to take place during the penitential season of Lent (i.e. from Ash Wednesday until Easter) and sexual intercourse during this period was also subject to the rule of abstinence.[47] In point of fact, however, 'the details cannot be confirmed and may be fictional. 1 May, or May Day, was already associated with romantic love'.[48]

According to popular accounts, the marriage is generally reputed to have been celebrated in the presence of the bride's mother, Jacquette, Duchess of Bedford. However, other versions of the story state that the ceremony took place 'in the presence only of the priest, two gentlemen, and a young man to sing the responses', the celebrant having been 'the Dominican Master Thomas Eborall'.[49] In reality we have no better proof of the people who attended Edward IV's Woodville marriage than we have of those who attended his alleged Talbot wedding.[50] In almost every respect, what we know of Edward's Woodville marriage sounds very similar to what we know of his relationship with Eleanor Talbot. Indeed, there would probably have been little prospect of the story of the Woodville marriage being believed by later historians if (like the story of the Talbot marriage) it had remained a secret throughout Edward's lifetime, and if the fertile Elizabeth had not gone on to give the king a large family of children!

Of course, if Edward had already contracted a secret marriage with Eleanor, then his Woodville marriage was bigamous. Subsequently, the king's apparent besottedness with Elizabeth Woodville was ascribed to witchcraft on the part of the bride and her mother, and the latter was prosecuted on these grounds in 1469–70. 'The sorcery suit ... apparently presumed that necromancy had been necessary to secure such a marriage!'[51] Whatever the real motivation underlying the king's decision, the rapidity with which Edward had succumbed to Elizabeth's charms apparently lent itself readily to supernatural explanations.

Like the alleged earlier Talbot marriage, the Woodville marriage was not made public at the time. As we have seen, it was only publicly announced four months later – to general amazement – and to the fury of Eleanor Talbot's powerful uncle, the Earl of Warwick, whose marriage negotiations with Bona of Savoy were then just approaching a successful conclusion.

Although she was an unpopular choice with most of the English aristocracy, Elizabeth Woodville was subsequently crowned queen with some splendour. Edward's Woodville union went on to produce a horde of children, including the so-called Princes in the Tower and Elizabeth of York, future mother of the house of 'Tudor'. As for Elizabeth's conduct in the role of queen, that has received various judgements. Trained, perhaps, by her aristocratic mother, royal style seems to have come naturally to Elizabeth, and many who saw her were impressed. On the other hand she alienated much of the old nobility by her nepotism. Her political involvement, while often unclear and even disputed, seems also to have attracted adverse comment. Her interventions in the case of Sir Thomas Cook and in the executions of the Earl of Desmond and the Duke of Clarence are cases in point.[52]

As for Eleanor Talbot, she had borne the king no children.[53] After the public announcement of Edward's Woodville marriage, she seems to have continued (or resumed) living quietly at her sister's dower house, East Hall, at Kenninghall in Norfolk. She continued her association with Corpus Christi College, Cambridge. It is also often stated that she became a nun. This is incorrect, but she did progressively retire into a quasi-religious life as a laywoman attached to the Carmelite order – a course which Edward IV may privately have welcomed. She remained completely silent regarding her relationship with the king. Nor did she ever make any attempt to contest Edward's Woodville marriage in the Church courts.

Precisely why Edward should initially have kept his Woodville marriage a secret and then decided to publicly reveal and acknowledge it is yet another of the many mysteries in this complex case. Speculations regarding his motivation have included witchcraft, or that Edward was eager to avert the proposed marriage with Bona of Savoy (but surely he could just have said 'no'), or that Elizabeth Woodville may have been pregnant in September 1464 (but in that case she must subsequently have miscarried, since her first recorded child by the king was not born until February 1466). The mystery cannot finally be resolved. However, it does very strongly reinforce the fact that Edward IV's marital conduct was consistent only in its unpredictability, owing nothing, apparently, to any normal considerations of royal policy or diplomacy. Given Edward IV's strange conduct with Elizabeth Woodville, the possibility of an earlier secret marriage with Eleanor, followed by bigamy, certainly cannot be ruled out purely on grounds of logic.

✠ ✠ ✠

The king's announcement at Reading may chiefly have surprised his then Keeper of the Privy Seal, Canon Robert Stillington, because as we have seen, slightly later sources identify Canon (later Bishop) Stillington as having been present at the king's marriage to Eleanor Talbot, either as a witness or as the priestly celebrant.[54] If in September 1464 Canon Stillington enquired further about the king's Woodville wedding then, as an expert in canon law, he must have been worried by what he found out. Since the marriage to Elizabeth Woodville had reportedly been solemnised several months previously, on 1 May 1464, this meant that it post-dated by about three years the king's alleged contract with Eleanor. Such chronology would have made the Woodville marriage potentially bigamous, and under canon law it could have been considered invalid by the Church courts, making any children born of it automatically illegitimate.[55] The fact that the king had publicly acknowledged the Woodville wedding made no difference to any of this.

Some historians have expressed surprise that Canon Stillington took no action in respect of Edward IV's marital situation in the autumn of 1464. Once again this is to misunderstand the situation. Stillington was not in a position to take any action. Only Eleanor – the supposedly wronged party – could have cited Edward IV before the Church courts. However, she did nothing. While many medieval English women in a similar marital situation did successfully seek legal remedy in the Church courts to substantiate their married status, for Eleanor such a course of action was probably never a realistic possibility.[56]

If Stillington had indeed married Edward IV to Eleanor – or even witnessed their marriage vows – he possessed potentially dangerous knowledge. Once the Woodville marriage had been made public, a marriage contract with Eleanor could never be acknowledged. The whole topic had to be kept secret, and reportedly the king 'held them not his friends nor good subjects which mentioned it'.[57] It would therefore not have been surprising if the king sought to buy off Stillington. Significantly, immediately after the public announcement of his Woodville wedding, the king decided to grant Robert Stillington an annual income. He also decided to appoint the canon to the next vacant English bishopric.[58] Apparently these moves worked. Through the remainder of the 1460s Stillington held his peace.

The death of Eleanor Talbot in June 1468 made things easier, and the king must have breathed a sigh of relief. With Eleanor safely buried in the choir of the Norwich Carmel, Edward probably thought he was safe. But another factor now emerged. In 1464, when Edward IV's Woodville marriage was made public, the heir to the throne had been Edward IV's 14-year-old brother, George, Duke of Clarence (coincidentally a neighbour of Stillington's in the south-west of England, and a friend of the Duke and Duchess of Norfolk). Naturally, when Elizabeth Woodville started producing children by the king – especially when she gave birth to the couple's three sons, in 1470, 1473 and 1477 – Clarence's position changed dramatically.

During the 1470s someone seems to have decided to enlighten Clarence. Previously there had been no sign that the duke had any knowledge of the king's alleged Talbot marriage. However, by about 1476–77 he certainly seems to have heard about it. Never the most thoughtful of men, Clarence unwisely revealed his secret knowledge, causing a panic in the mind of Elizabeth Woodville. Incidentally, for her too, this may well have been the first intimation of the nature of her husband's former relationship with Eleanor. Mancini tells us that she now began to fear that her own marriage was invalid, and that her son would never succeed to the throne unless Clarence was silenced.[59] As a result, Elizabeth incited Edward IV first to arrest, and then later to execute his brother.

Significantly, the Duke of Clarence's execution on Wednesday 18 February 1478 was closely linked in time with the arrest and imprisonment of Bishop Stillington. The bishop's imprisonment is thought to date from about 15 February, just prior to Clarence's execution.[60] Apparently either the king or the queen had drawn the obvious (though possibly erroneous) conclusion that Stillington must have been the source of Clarence's information.[61] Stillington remained in the Tower until about the end of the second week of April.[62] Commynes tells us that he was released only on payment of a fine.[63] Stillington was not formally granted a pardon until Saturday 20 June 1478. However, that pardon wiped his slate clean with a 'declaration that Robert, Bishop of Bath and Wells, has been faithful to the king and done nothing contrary to his oath of fealty, as he has shown before the king and certain lords'.[64]

⌖ ⌖ ⌖

Given the fact that neither Eleanor nor Edward IV ever made any public statement about a marriage between them during their respective lifetimes, one problem which confronts us in trying to assess fairly whether or not this marriage was a reality is the fact that none of our surviving written sources for their relationship is precisely contemporary. The situation in relation to Edward's Woodville marriage was rather different. Although that wedding was also secret, and no contemporary documentary evidence exists to prove what took place, the king himself acknowledged the Woodville union later in that same year in which it had allegedly been contracted.

By contrast, talk of the Talbot marriage first seems to have surfaced only nine years after Eleanor's death when, as we have seen, the matter was apparently brought to the attention of Edward IV's younger brother, George, Duke of Clarence. Even then, the subsequent Act of Attainder against Clarence did not refer to Eleanor or mention her alleged marriage with the king. For Elizabeth Woodville any such reference in an Act of Parliament – even if accompanied by an official denial of the Talbot marriage – would have been the equivalent of shooting herself in the foot! Nevertheless, the act did condemn the duke for speaking against the king, 'and agaynst the persones of the blessed princesse oure alther soveraigne and liege lady the Quene, of my lorde the Prince theire son and heire, and of all the other of thaire moost noble issue'.[65] An account of the case against Clarence written five years later also records that:

> the queen then remembered the insults to her family and the calumnies with which she was reproached, namely that according to established usage she was not the legitimate wife of the king. Thus she concluded that her offspring by the king would never come to the throne unless the duke of Clarence were removed.[66]

The earliest surviving explicit written reference to the marriage between Edward IV and Eleanor dates from six years later, when both Eleanor and the king were dead. This was Richard III's Act of Parliament – quoted in part at the opening of this chapter – which recognised Eleanor as Edward's true wife on the basis of the evidence then presented to Parliament – evidence which does not now survive. It was penned in 1483–84, in a political context which is regarded as highly significant by those historians who oppose any idea of a marriage between Edward IV and Eleanor. Of course the question of Eleanor's marriage was of great importance in 1483, since it constituted the chief basis upon which Edward IV's son, Edward V, was set aside, and the throne passed to Richard III – younger brother of Edward IV and of the executed Duke of Clarence.

As we shall see in due course, when we explore the alleged marriage between Charles II and Lucy Walter, such later evidence does indeed sometimes need to be treated with caution, because it can be biased. However, in the case of the alleged marriage between Edward IV and Eleanor Talbot we can – and should – balance the later evidence from the two opposing camps of Richard III and Henry VII. Thus we can confront the bias alleged against Richard III in 1483–84 with the later 'Tudor' bias. It must be misleading – and unhistorical – to consider the possible bias of the *first* side only, while ignoring that of the second. An examination of the different ways in which the two opposing camps handled the question of Eleanor's alleged marriage with Edward IV is revealing, and it may be legitimate to draw certain conclusions from their conduct.

So what actually happened in 1483–84? When Edward IV died unexpectedly, in April 1483, his elder son by Elizabeth Woodville was proclaimed king as Edward V. The queen mother then sought to claim the role of regent for her under-aged son. According to the continental European political scene familiar to her mother, Jacquette, this would have been an entirely normal procedure. According to English precedent, however, the regent's powers belonged not to the widowed queen but to the closest living male paternal relative of the new sovereign – in this case Edward IV's only surviving brother, Richard, Duke of Gloucester. A contest ensued between the queen mother and her supporters on one side, and the Duke of Gloucester and the majority of the English nobility on the other. It was in this context that, on Monday 9 June 1483, Robert Stillington,

Bishop of Bath and Wells, finally went public in respect of the Talbot marriage. Reportedly the Bishop made a vital and earth-shattering statement to a meeting of the royal council – in effect an incipient but still unofficial Parliament – which was held on 9 June between 10 am and 2 pm at the Palace of Westminster.[67]

Stillington declared that Edward IV's marriage with Elizabeth Woodville had been bigamous because at the time of the Woodville marriage the king was already married to Eleanor Talbot, who was still living in 1464. We are told that the bishop himself claimed to have been present at Edward's marriage to Eleanor, in consequence of which he now pronounced that all the children born of the Woodville marriage, including Edward V, were illegitimate (and therefore debarred from inheriting the throne). Stillington's revelation is the key element of the events of the summer of 1483, and it was chiefly upon the basis of his statement that Edward V was set aside.[68] The throne passed to Richard Duke of Gloucester as the next male heir, and he was proclaimed king as Richard III.[69]

The decision to change the order of succession was made by those members of the House of Lords who were then in London.[70] It was ratified by a full Parliament the following year in the form of the celebrated Act of *titulus regius* of 1484 (see Appendix 3). This act makes it clear that evidence had been presented (though it does not itemise what that evidence was). It then sets out in detail the reasons for Richard III's enthronement. Amongst those reasons, it states in completely unequivocal terms that Edward IV was married to Eleanor Talbot,[71] and that his subsequent 'pretensed marriage' to Elizabeth Woodville was invalid.[72] There can be very few (if any) other medieval royal relationships which have been accorded such impressive legal confirmation as to be authenticated by an Act of Parliament!

At the time, not one single member of the royal family raised a voice in protest at this turn of events. The dowager Duchess of York, mother of both Edward IV and Richard III, together with their sister, the Duchess of Suffolk and her family, closed ranks in support of the new king. In the Low Countries the other sister of Edward and Richard, 'Madame la Grande', dowager Duchess of Burgundy – who, as the sequel would show when Henry VII took the throne, was very well able to give practical expression to any disapproval she might feel at the course of events in England – likewise said and did nothing. Even the demoted queen, Elizabeth Woodville, found not a word to say. She was an intelligent woman and (as Mancini makes clear) had for some years been only too well aware of the consequences which must inevitably follow for her children if the validity of her own marriage to the king was called into question.[73]

As for Eleanor's family, her sister, Elizabeth Talbot, Duchess of Norfolk, attended Richard's coronation, was well treated by the new king, and seems to have enjoyed a good relationship with him.[74] Other members of Eleanor's extended family also served Richard, apparently without any qualms. Indeed, her Catesby connections openly supported him until his defeat by Henry 'Tudor' at the battle of Bosworth in August 1485.[75]

However, once Richard was gone, the new monarch showed, by his actions, that he had some interesting priorities. Amongst his first orders as king were the execution of Catesby and the reimprisonment of Bishop Stillington.[76] Early in his first Parliament, Henry VII enacted his own laconic act of *titulus regius*, which said, in effect, that he was king because he was king. He also arranged for a bizarre and unique procedure: the repeal, unquoted, of the *titulus regius* of 1484. When Acts of Parliament were annulled it was usual at least to précis the original text in the Act of Repeal.[77] Henry, however, neatly avoided this by quoting only the first, innocuous, thirteen words of Richard's Act. He also made unique provision for all copies of the 1484 act to be destroyed 'upon Peine of ymprisonment ... so that all thinges said and remembered in the said Bill and Acte maie be for ever out of remembraunce and also forgott'.[78]

Historians working in England for Henry VII subsequently assisted the process of induced national amnesia by allowing reference to Richard III's claim of a previous marriage of Edward IV to stand, while at the same time substituting for the name of the Earl of Shrewsbury's daughter, that of the king's mistress, Elizabeth Wayte (Lucy). They pretended that Richard III's case had been that Edward IV had contracted a prior marriage with Elizabeth Wayte, but that she had categorically denied this. It was probably a deliberate, but rather clever lie.

The complete destruction of Richard's act (and the case against the Woodville marriage which it encapsulated) was of vital importance to Henry, because under its terms, his intended bride, Elizabeth of York (whom Henry now sought to pass off as the heiress of the house of York) had been declared a bastard. Of course the most logical procedure for Henry VII would have been to disprove the allegation of bigamy in Parliament, by bringing evidence to show that the whole story of the Talbot marriage was a complete fabrication. The fact that instead of doing so, Henry chose to suppress the act entirely – forbidding any copy of it to be kept, and prohibiting any discussion – strongly suggests that the case set out in Richard's *titulus regius* was, in fact, unassailable. From Henry VII's actions alone one could legitimately deduce that Edward IV probably had contracted a secret marriage with Eleanor Talbot, thereby making a complete mess of his matrimonial policy.

✠ ✠ ✠

Eleanor's story and that of Elizabeth Woodville have many clear similarities. Both were widows, from Lancastrian backgrounds, both were attractive, both were a few years older than the king. And in both cases, apparently, Edward's solution was the same. He went through a clandestine form of marriage and kept the affair quiet. Of course, the final outcome was very different in the two cases. One key distinction between Eleanor Talbot, (who failed to get the king to honour his contract with her) and Elizabeth Woodville (who succeeded), was the latter's proven fecundity, which Edward is said to have considered a great point in her favour.[79] Another key difference was Elizabeth Woodville's great determination and strength of character. It is plausible that a third difference may lie in the possibility that Eleanor herself decided, in the end, that marriage with Edward was not really what she wanted out of life.

Curiously, Eleanor's death, which the king must have greeted with some relief, and which she herself seems almost to have been prepared for,[80] appears in many other ways to have been unexpected. Her sister and executrix, the Duchess of Norfolk, was out of the country at the time, as were all Eleanor's closest living relatives.[81] As a result, the necessary legal processes following Eleanor's death were not, in fact, started until two weeks later, when Elizabeth Talbot returned to England.

Probably the Duchess of Norfolk could not have refused Edward IV's command to accompany Margaret of York to Flanders. However, she stayed away for several weeks. She sailed from Margate with the king's sister on Thursday 23 June, was present at the exchange of vows between Margaret and Charles the Bold on Monday 27 June, and attended all the wedding festivities. On 30 June, while her sister Eleanor was dying in England, the Duchess of Norfolk was still in the Low Countries. She only set off to return to England on Wednesday 13 July.[82]

Eleanor probably died at East Hall, the old manor house at Kenninghall, which her sister held in dower. Writing in the sixteenth century, John Leland recalled a local tradition which probably relates to Eleanor's demise:

> There apperith at Keninghaule not far from the Duke of Northfolkes new place a grete mote, withyn the cumpace whereof there was sumtyme a fair place, and there the saying is that there lay a Quene or sum grete lady, and there dyed.[83]

The Duchess of Norfolk buried her sister in the choir of the Whitefriars' Church in Norwich. This church stood just across the River Wensum from Norwich Cathedral. The site now comprises premises owned by the firm of Jarrolds. Almost nothing is left of the Friary today, but one surviving medieval archway bears a modern plaque, commemorating Eleanor's burial. Eleanor's tomb could still be seen in the priory ruins in the seventeenth century, but all trace of it has long since vanished. However, bones which may be Eleanor's were excavated from the priory site in 1958. They are now preserved in a nice, clean cardboard box in the storerooms of Norwich Castle Museum.[84]

As for Elizabeth Woodville, eclipsed and demoted from the rank of queen during the reign of Richard III in favour of Eleanor Talbot, she subsequently found herself restored to her former rank by Henry VII. For very good reasons of his own the new king wished to marry Elizabeth of York, the eldest daughter of Edward IV, and her mother's namesake. It was Henry's aim to present his consort to the country as the heiress of the house of York, and for this it was essential that her mother should have been Edward IV's true wife. Hence Elizabeth Woodville was publicly re-enthroned. At the same time, and for the same reason,

Eleanor Talbot was carefully written out of history. And just in case anyone remembered the complicated story of Edward IV's bigamous secret marriages, Henry's historians invented the lie that Edward IV had been alleged to have married Elizabeth Wayte (Lucy), but that this story had been disproved.

For about two years Elizabeth Woodville's luck seemed to be in. She found herself back at court as the mother of the new queen consort, and the prospective grandmother of the new ruling dynasty. Sadly, her luck did not last. In 1487, when Henry VII was facing a threat to his throne from someone who may have been (or have claimed to be) one of Elizabeth Woodville's sons by Edward IV,[85] Henry urgently needed to get her out of the way. He could not risk her seeing – and perhaps identifying – the pretender. She was therefore disgraced and deprived of her dower lands. Left with only a small pension, she retired to Bermondsey Abbey. Thus, ironically, Elizabeth Woodville came closer to being a nun than Eleanor Talbot had ever been!

Despite a brief fantasy that she might become Queen of Scotland, Elizabeth spent the remaining five years of her life at the abbey, dying there in more or less complete poverty in April 1492. She had nothing to leave her children but her blessings. At her own request her body was buried at Windsor, on the north side of the altar of St George's Chapel, in the same tomb as Edward IV. Thus, in one sense, Elizabeth Woodville was buried as a queen. Yet her wooden coffin was so cheap that it fell to pieces completely in the damp Windsor soil, leaving virtually nothing to be found, four hundred years later, by the late eighteenth-century antiquarians who explored the tomb. Moreover, the accounts of Elizabeth's funeral make very sad reading. The entire event was such a pitiful exercise in penny-pinching on the part of her son-in-law, Henry VII, that even second-hand candles were used.[86]

10

THE INFANTA AND THE NYGHT CROWE[1]

Debating with myself the contents of your letters, I have put myself in great distress, not knowing how to interpret them; … praying you with all my heart that you will expressly certify me of your whole mind concerning the love between us two. For of necessity I must ensure me of this answer, having been now above one whole year struck with the dart of love.

Henry VIII to Anne Boleyn, 1527

[She] asked the king … to consider carefully that she was a gentlewoman born of good and honourable parents and with an unsullied reputation. She had no greater treasure than her honour which she would rather die a thousand times than tarnish.

Letters and Papers, Foreign and Domestic; Henry VIII, vol. X, p. 245[2]

The concubine's little bastard, Elizabeth, will be excluded from the succession.

E. Chapuys (Imperial Ambassador to England), 1536

Henry VIII, the grandson of Edward IV and Elizabeth Woodville, is famous for having had six wives. Sad to say, however, in sober fact this claim to fame is nonsense. Two of Henry's 'marriages' – to Catherine of Aragon and Anne Boleyn – overlapped, and since it was no more permissible in the sixteenth century than it is today to have two wives at the same time, it is instantly apparent that at best only one of these two marriages can have been valid.

Books and television series that focus on 'the six wives' can be chronologically very misleading. To allot equal chapters or episodes to each of the six women with whom Henry celebrated weddings would seem to imply that his relationships with them were all of equal duration. In fact, however, the 'marriage' to Catherine of Aragon – which, in modern terms, nearly made it to a silver wedding anniversary – by itself lasted ten years longer than all the other five 'marriages' put together. Or to look at things in a slightly different way, Henry knew Catherine of Aragon for a total of thirty-five years. He knew Anne Boleyn for at least ten years (though his marriage to her lasted only three years). On the other hand he knew both Jane Seymour and Catherine Howard for perhaps two years at the most. His second longest marital relationship was with Catherine Parr. That lasted for about four years. The 'marriage' to Anne of Cleves lasted merely a matter of months. In terms of their time duration, Henry's most important royal relationships were undoubtedly those with Catherine of Aragon and Anne Boleyn, and these two relationships were also of overwhelming importance in other ways.

However, like other members of the 'Tudor' dynasty, Henry VIII had a great talent for rewriting history to suit himself. In point of fact, after various vicissitudes, the king's own ultimate judgement (for what that is worth) was that his marriage to Catherine of Aragon and his marriage to Anne Boleyn were *both* invalid. Certainly both marriages were annulled in England,[3] and the annulment of a marriage means, not that it is terminated, but rather that it is declared never to have existed at all. If the annulments of Henry's marriage to Catherine of Aragon and Anne Boleyn were legal, that would reduce the number of Henry VIII's wives to a maximum of four.

If we pursue this course, we can reduce the number of Henry's wives even further. His marriage to Anne of Cleves, never consummated, was also annulled. Moreover, one must take account of the fact that Henry's love-match with Catherine Howard was likewise finally annulled, so that Catherine, like her cousin Anne Boleyn, went to the block not as Queen of England, but as a private lady.[4] Thus we can see that Henry VIII may only have had two legal wives. Indeed, this was actually the king's own view of the matter. At the end of his reign Henry himself stated quite clearly that he had only made two valid marriages – with Jane Seymour and with Catherine Parr – since all his other 'marriages' had by that time been ruled to be null and void.

In this chapter, however, we shall not be considering the king's last four marital experiments in any detail. This is because we are exploring secret and bigamous royal marriages. It was only Henry's involvement with Anne Boleyn which resulted in a secret and potentially bigamous marriage. None of his subsequent putative marriages was secret, or raised issues of royal bigamy.[5] Because there is a question of bigamy in respect of Anne Boleyn, we must also consider the question of the king's relationship with Catherine of Aragon. Of course, Henry's connection with Catherine of Aragon was neither secret nor bigamous – though it may have been open to question in another respect.

✠ ✠ ✠

Like his grandfather, Edward IV, Henry VIII does not really seem to have had huge numbers of documented extra-marital relationships. His childhood and youth were strictly controlled, and after he became king, although there certainly were mistresses, these never circulated in large numbers simultaneously. Henry VIII is also like his grandfather Edward IV in another respect. For it is a curious fact that, like Edward, Henry too produced very few royal bastards – at least, if one excludes his children by Catherine of Aragon and Anne Boleyn, all of whom were later officially designated as bastards! Later reports that Anne Boleyn herself was Henry's bastard daughter can certainly be discounted. In fact, apart from his children by Catherine of Aragon and Anne Boleyn, the only officially recognised bastard of Henry VIII was Henry Fitzroy, Duke of Richmond, the king's son by Elizabeth Blount.

On the surface, the importance which Henry himself gave to Richmond appears to make it unlikely that other bastard children of the king would have been left completely unacknowledged. Mary Boleyn (Anne Boleyn's elder sister) was undoubtedly the king's mistress for a time, and Henry's paternity of Mary's two Carey children has sometimes been alleged. However, the fact that the king himself did not give any official recognition to either of these two children makes his blood relationship with them questionable.

On the other hand, Mary Boleyn's children were born under somewhat different circumstances than Elizabeth Blount's son. Elizabeth had been unmarried when she bore the Duke of Richmond, so that her son was not the product of a double adultery and his mother had no husband to assume the role of the child's legal father.[6] Mary Boleyn's marital situation was not the same. In 1520 – probably before she became the king's mistress – she married Sir William Carey.[7] Her daughter, Catherine Carey, was not born until 1524, and her son Henry Carey, in 1526. Thus both of Mary's children had a ready-made legal father on hand to assume responsibility for them. It is possible that Catherine Carey was, in fact, the king's child. However, unlike Richmond she was merely a daughter. That fact, coupled with the probable double adultery which might have led to her conception, may account for her lack of recognition.

The paternity of Catherine's younger brother, Henry Carey, is even more doubtful. But even if he really was the king's son, the fact that Henry VIII had by the time of Henry Carey's birth commenced his relationship with the boy's aunt, Anne Boleyn, may have been enough to deter royal recognition, since Henry VIII was certainly aware that his relationship with Mary Boleyn jeopardised his chances of contracting a legal marriage with Mary's younger sister Anne (see below).

✠ ✠ ✠

The overall reputation of Henry VIII is an interesting historical phenomenon which needs careful perusal. Henry was a revolting man who treated women selfishly and sometimes cruelly. He was a major vandal who destroyed many works of art and much of England's cultural heritage for selfish motives, including his own financial gain. He was a well-educated man who, however, used his education cynically for his own ends. In short, as a person there is really nothing much to recommend him. Yet despite all this he has somehow managed to acquire the somewhat cuddly image of 'Bluff King Hal'. Given the very extensive evidence against him, probably only a tyrannical dictator who wrote his own version of history could have achieved this, and indeed, the 'Tudor' propaganda machine was a powerful government tool in the sixteenth century.

It is not, perhaps, surprising that part of the self-image which Henry VIII sought to disseminate was that of a macho man for whom women fell easily. Of course, a number of women did fall in with his wishes, but this could well have been merely because of the political power which he exerted. No doubt some of his women – mistresses and 'wives' – were at times afraid of him, and they may have given in to his wishes for this reason. Others would have been interested in what they could get out of a relationship with the King of England, and may have been happy to risk succumbing to Henry's advances for this reason, rather than because they found his conversation delightful, his personality charming, his physique handsome or his sexual attraction irresistible.

In fact, the evidence regarding Henry VIII as a sexual being is somewhat equivocal. He failed to father a large number of children. Moreover, the male children he did engender were all defective and died young – in some cases very young indeed. Thus all of Catherine of Aragon's sons died in infancy, while Edward VI never made it to full adulthood, and even the Duke of Richmond died before managing to father any children of his own.

On whom should we blame Henry's failure to engender living sons by Catherine of Aragon? It can hardly have been the queen's fault, since as we shall see, during the first ten years of her 'marriage' with Henry, Catherine of Aragon was pregnant on at least six occasions. Obviously the queen was fertile. Equally obviously the king was also fertile and was fulfilling his conjugal duties. Since Catherine even carried most of her foetuses to term, and more than once successfully gave birth to a live child, it may have been merely a mixture of bad luck and lack of hygiene that brought about the couple's failure to produce more living heirs.

However, in the last ten years of his life Henry VIII fathered no children at all. His marriage with Anne of Cleves was never consummated. The king himself gave evidence to this effect as part of the proceedings for the annulment of the marriage. It is also unclear whether Henry ever really had a sexual relationship with either Catherine Howard or Catherine Parr. In fact, Henry's last provable act of sexual intercourse took place in 1537. Interestingly, this was only a short time after the death of Anne Boleyn, who may have encountered difficulties of her own in her sexual relationship with Henry, since she is reported to have stated that he was impotent.[8] Yet during their relatively short marriage, Anne, like Catherine before her, seems to have had fairly regular pregnancies – perhaps three of them in three years. So initially, from a sexual point of view, her 'marriage' to Henry must have been successful. As we shall shortly see, however, an important event which took place in 1536 may have changed things dramatically for Henry towards the end of his relationship with Anne Boleyn.

Overall, the evidence now available makes Henry VIII's sexual activity in later life somewhat questionable. Indeed, after the age of about 45 the king's sex-life seems to have become nearly non-existent. Some writers have sought to explain this by suggesting that Henry had contracted some sexually transmitted disease, possibly syphilis. However, there is no record of syphilis symptoms in Henry's medical record, nor is there any record from his doctors that they prescribed the standard sixteenth-century syphilis treatment of mercury. In reality, therefore, the evidence for Henry having syphilis is nil.[9] It is, perhaps, more likely that the king suffered from some form of erectile dysfunction in later life. This could have been psychologically based, or the result of ageing, or caused by the general ill-health which the king suffered during the last ten or eleven years of his life as a result of an accident (see below). Recent research has suggested that Henry may also have suffered from late onset diabetes during this period.

Much is known about Henry VIII's medical history. His father and brother both died of tuberculosis, but Henry VIII escaped this disease. In 1514 he had an attack of smallpox, but he was a healthy young man at that time, and he survived with no apparent lasting ill effects. An attack of malaria in 1521 was more debilitating, because of course, an initial dose of malaria results in a recurring cycle of attacks of fever every few years for the rest of the patient's life. Later, a serious jousting accident in 1524, when the king forgot to close his visor, nearly cost him an eye. He was lucky. Nevertheless, the lance blow to his head left the king suffering subsequently from serious migraines. Later still there was a tennis injury to his leg and foot in 1527, following which the king began to suffer from a varicose ulcer.

The key fact, however, is that in January 1536 Henry was unhorsed in a tournament and was very seriously injured. He seems to have been unconscious for two hours after the accident, and his life was thought to be in danger for a time. Although Anne Boleyn had conceived three times by the king, and was actually pregnant at the time of his accident, the shock of the news caused her to miscarry, and she had no subsequent pregnancies. The jousting accident, which, among other things, seriously exacerbated the effects of the king's leg ulcer, is thought by modern medical researchers to have been the cause of Henry's obesity, his later general ill-health and his mood-swings.[10] It is, perhaps, significant that, following this accident, the king is reported to have accused Anne Boleyn of using witchcraft against him, while she began to cast aspersions on his sexual potency.

Another part of Henry VIII's reputation is his supposed attractive physique. It is curious, therefore, that actually none of his surviving portraits shows any sign of this. The excuse has sometimes been offered that portraits of the king mostly depict him later in life, and even a recent television documentary which explored the causes of Henry VIII's later obesity continued to affirm that when he was young Henry was very attractive.[11] Nevertheless, the fact is that we do possess portraits of the young Henry, and the youth depicted is not strikingly handsome or prepossessing in facial terms. One theory which has been voiced is that what was chiefly admired by contemporaries was actually not the king's facial features but his shapely legs!

One portrait of Henry as a beardless youth seems to show quite a strong resemblance between the king and his great uncle, Richard III. Henry is depicted as a rather lanky youth with brown hair, and a thin and slightly anxious-looking face. Another portrait shows a rather fat and unhealthy-looking, but still beardless, young Henry who would hardly stand out in a crowd. This particular painting casts some doubt on the young king's reputation for exercise and sport! Depictions of the king in 1520, at the 'Field of the Cloth of Gold', show a short-haired, bearded Henry VIII, with an already extensive waistline. This is the Henry familiar to us from paintings by or after Holbein. Thus it is clear that by the time he became involved with Anne Boleyn, Henry VIII looked pretty much as we are accustomed to imagining him. Possibly there was some sexual attraction there, which Holbein and his school somehow failed to capture or convey to us, but the Henry who became involved with Anne Boleyn could hardly be described as classically handsome.

So were the contemporary written reports of Henry's charming physical appearance perhaps just another product of the royal propaganda machine? Indeed, would anyone actually have dared to write that the king was physically unattractive? Of course, when Thomas More and other courtiers penned such descriptions they could be fairly confident that the majority of their readers, whether they lived in the English countryside, or abroad – or were as yet unborn – would have very little opportunity to check up on this matter. Many of the readers would never actually have set eyes on the king. Nevertheless, it is a fact that foreign diplomats – who might have risked being unflattering without too much fear of the consequences – do seem to have admired the appearance of the youthful Henry.

In the final analysis it is difficult to reach an objective conclusion on this point. We may simply note that, while previous writers have tended to accept at face value the contemporary *written* descriptions which describe the young Henry VIII as a handsome man, actually the surviving pictorial evidence does not seem to back up this view. This is yet another respect in which Henry VIII appears to resemble his maternal grandfather, Edward IV. For Edward, too, was generally described as a handsome young man. But in Edward's case also, the king seems to have put on a great deal of weight later in his life. Moreover the surviving portraits of Edward IV also fail to show to us the handsome young king we have been asked to believe in. Only some miniatures in contemporary illuminated books seem to depict the tall, good-looking

Edward IV that has been described to us. Interestingly, another point which Edward IV and Henry VIII seem to have had in common is brown hair. The once popular myth that Edward IV had fair hair has been exploded.[12] All his portraits show brown hair, and surviving locks of his hair confirm this. Likewise, despite frequent stories about the red hair of the Tudor dynasty, Henry VIII seems usually to be depicted in his portraits with hair which is basically brown – with perhaps just a hint of auburn.[13]

✠ ✠ ✠

Since we are concerned with secret and bigamous royal marriages, it is only Henry's contract with Anne Boleyn, and the preceding one with Catherine of Aragon, which we shall explore in detail here. It is true that the question of bigamy was later raised also in the case of Catherine Howard. Indeed the latter might perhaps have saved her life if she had been willing to declare that her marriage to the king was invalid because of a previous marriage contract with Francis Dereham.[14] Nevertheless, Catherine Howard firmly denied that she had been married to any man before the king, and in consequence of this she went to the block. Of course, even if Henry's marriage to Catherine Howard had been bigamous, the bigamy would have been hers, not his, so that *royal* bigamy would not really have been involved.

As for Henry's weddings, as we have seen, only one of the six was secret. This was his putative marriage to Anne Boleyn, which took place at an unknown date towards the end of January 1533. At that time Henry was still officially married to Catherine of Aragon, so the contract with Anne was arguably not only secret but also bigamous. Even if Henry's earlier marriage to Catherine had indeed been invalid, as the king himself argued, it is by no means certain whether this would have made the marriage to Anne legal. At the time of his wedding with Anne, Henry VIII was still a Catholic, and England as a whole remained in full communion with Rome. It is within this context, therefore, that the wedding with Anne Boleyn must be judged, and modern Catholic canon law states very clearly that when 'in doubt, the validity of a marriage must be upheld until the contrary is proven'. Moreover, 'even though the previous marriage is invalid … it is not thereby lawful to contract another marriage before the nullity or the dissolution of the previous one has been established lawfully and with certainty'.[15]

Let us first examine the marital history of Catherine of Aragon, since this has an inevitable bearing on what followed, up to and including Henry's subsequent contract with Anne Boleyn. An Infanta of Spain, descended on both her father's and her mother's side from the ancient royal house of Trastámara, Catalina de Castilia y Aragón was born on 16 December 1485. She was the youngest daughter of Isabel the Catholic, Queen of Castile, and her husband and cousin, King Ferdinand V of Aragon. The royal couple were known to their contemporaries, and are remembered in history, as 'the Catholic Monarchs'.[16]

✗ PRINCESS ROYAL

Negotiations for an English royal marriage with a Trastámara infanta had briefly been explored by Richard III (following the death in 1485 of his wife, Anne of Warwick), but in the event, lack of time and the course of events put an end to such a scheme. However, the new king Henry VII embraced the idea with enthusiasm, on behalf of his progeny. It has been argued that he did so because of the antiquity of the Trastámara dynasty, and the prestige which such a marriage might lend to his own much newer and more dubious royalty.[17] These may have been considerations, but so too may have been the fact that the Trastámara family had a Lancastrian claim to the English throne which was far superior to that of Henry VII himself.[18] The Infanta Catalina was a direct and legitimate descendant of Edward III's son, John of Gaunt.

The marriage negotiations between the English and Spanish courts were long and not always amicable. Although a successful conclusion was reached by March 1501, Catherine (as she is known in England) was apparently not expected when she landed at Plymouth on Saturday 2 October 1501, and no preparations had been made to receive her. According to local tradition (unsupported, however, by any documentary evidence) she and her attendants were accommodated for one night at the Abbot of Forde's guesthouse at Charmouth in Dorset,[19] while Henry VII made rapid preparations for Catherine's formal reception at Exeter. From Exeter the princess then began a formal and ceremonious journey to London. On Monday 4 October the king and Prince Arthur met her at Dogmersfield, Bishop Stillington's former manor house in Hampshire. Catherine reached London on Friday 12 November and was received there with pageants laid on by the civic authorities in her honour.

The young princess was considered attractive; 'she was very short, and had fair skin, which may have come from her English heritage. She had long auburn hair, and she often wore it loose. She was slightly plump, which was considered both attractive and a sign of fertility'.[20] Her marriage to Henry VII's eldest son, Arthur, Prince of Wales, was celebrated at St Paul's Cathedral on Sunday 14 November 1501 (being the feast of St Erkenwald). The marriage ceremony was followed by a week of celebrations, including banqueting and jousting.

Following their marriage, King Henry VII dispatched the young couple to Ludlow Castle, where they cohabited for a few months. According to the testimony of Catherine herself, however, the marriage with Prince Arthur was never consummated.[21] Many years later, when her second marriage was in dispute, Catherine made a formal statement to the effect that she and Arthur had shared a bed for a total of no more than seven nights, and that when Arthur died she had still been *virgo intacta*. Significantly, her statement, which was made solemnly under the seal of the confessional, had actually been backed up by Henry VIII himself, many years earlier. For after his own subsequent marriage to Catherine in 1509, Henry had declared openly at his court that his bride had been a virgin on their wedding night.[22]

✗ COHABIT = TO LIVE TOGETHER WITHOUT BEING MARRIED. SO, THAT WORD IS WRONG HERE.

Catherine's first marriage was short-lived. In the spring of 1502 Prince Arthur fell ill, and he died on 2 April.[23] This raised the question of what should be done with his young widow. At an early stage the possibility was mooted of marrying Catherine to the new heir to the English throne, Arthur's younger brother, Henry (then Duke of York). Both Ferdinand and Isabel in Spain, and Henry VII in England, appeared to favour this proposal. There was much renewed negotiation. By September 1502, however, a draft agreement had been reached, and this was made into a formal treaty in June 1503.

The treaty specified that within two months (i.e. by August 1503) *matrimonium per verba de praesenti* should take place. This has sometimes been described as a betrothal, but it was in fact a marriage (*matrimonium*) since it was in the form of present-tense vows ('I marry you').[24] However, in a sense the marriage would remain incomplete because it would not immediately be consummated owing to Henry's age at the time (he was 12 years old).[25] This *matrimonium* would be a simple and private exchange of promises. It was to be followed by a formal church wedding ceremony once a papal dispensation permitting the marriage had been issued; after the second instalment of Catherine's dowry was paid, and after Henry reached the age of 15 (which would be on 28 June 1506). In actual fact the *matrimonium per verba de praesenti* took place immediately after the treaty was ratified, on Sunday 25 June 1503. CATHERINE WAS A YOUNG WIDOW CONSEQUENTLY FREE TO MARRY AGAIN

There were, of course, some difficulties about a marriage between Catherine and Henry, given that Catherine had already been married to Henry's brother, Arthur. Whether or not it had been consummated, Catherine's marriage to Arthur created a brother–sister relationship between Catherine and Arthur's younger brother, which according to the Church's laws constituted an impediment to their marriage. However, it was an impediment which the Church laws allowed to be removed by the granting of a papal dispensation. * NOT TRUE

Interestingly, Catherine's parents at first assumed that their daughter's marriage with Prince Arthur *had* been consummated. Indeed, they had been so advised by Puebla, their ambassador in London, who cited Catherine's confessor, Alessandro Geraldini, on this point. However, in a letter which she sent to the Catholic Monarchs, Catherine's duenna, Doña Elvira Manuel, strongly denied that the marriage had been consummated. Ferdinand and Isabel then sent for Geraldini so that they could discuss the matter with him face to face. Subsequently, after some reflection, the Spanish and English sovereigns agreed that the safest course would be to cover every possible eventuality.

The granting of the papal dispensation was itself delayed, first by the death of Pope Alexander VI, on 18 August 1503, and then by the subsequent election of the very short-lived Pope Pius III (who died on 18 October of the same year). It was not until late in 1504 that a third pope, Julius II, finally got round to sending a document – in the form of a papal brief (or letter) – about Catherine's marriage to the girl's mother, Queen Isabel, who received it just before she died (26 November 1504).

Curiously, Julius II's papal brief was dated 26 December 1503, and the reasons for his delay in dispatching it are not clear. They might possibly have been connected with the fact that the new pope had initially been reported as saying that he was not sure whether he had the authority to grant a dispensation in this case. However, it is highly probable that this remark, together with the papal reluctance and delay, were all based not on genuine religious scruples but on political issues. In fact, Pope Julius wanted to use the granting of a dispensation as a lever to encourage Catherine's father to be more accommodating in respect of Naples!

The initial papal brief was subsequently followed by the issue of a formal papal bull, which was also dated 26 December 1503. However, a copy of the bull was not received in England until March 1505. The brief sent to Spain and the bull sent to England have different wording. The brief states baldly that Arthur *had* consummated his marriage with Catherine. The bull – probably reflecting the Spanish court's later checking of this matter, and the resulting doubt about what exactly had taken place – is more vaguely worded. It gave permission for Catherine's marriage to Henry even if (*'forsan'*) her marriage to Arthur had been consummated.

The death of Catherine's mother, Queen Isabel, weakened Spain, which had come into existence as one single country only through the marriage of Catherine's parents, the Queen of Castile and the King of Aragon. Queen Isabel's heir in Castile was Catherine's elder sister, Juana, who was married to the Habsburg Archduke Philip of Austria. From Henry VII's point of view the widowed King Ferdinand was a less attractive ally now than previously, and on 27 June 1505, shortly before he celebrated his fourteenth birthday, Prince Henry (obviously acting on his father's orders) rejected his marriage to Catherine on the grounds that he had not properly consented to it. However, this was not intended to be an absolute repudiation of the marriage. It was merely yet another negotiating ploy on the part of the English court. *In the 15th century, nobility's children did not consent, to a marriage imposed to them, they did obey*

In 1506 the position in Spain changed again, following the death of the Archduke Philip of Austria, and the mental instability of his widow. As a result King Ferdinand's position once again became more secure. However, Henry VII was still playing politics over the question of his son's marriage, and in London some kind of marriage alliance with the Austrian Habsburgs was now under consideration – though various options were being talked of, one of which involved a Habsburg betrothal for Henry VII's daughter, Mary.

The situation did not change fundamentally until 21 April 1509, when King Henry VII died. It is possible that, on his deathbed, Henry VII expressed the wish that the marriage between his son and the infanta should now go ahead. Certainly Henry VIII stated this to the Spanish ambassador. However, it is equally possible that the new king was now, for the first time, free to express his own wishes in the matter, and was doing so. Catherine was familiar to him. She was a foreign princess but she now spoke good English. Henry had known her for most of his life, and for this reason she had an obvious advantage over an unknown and unseen foreign bride. As a potential marriage partner she was also readily available, reportedly attractive, and 'fertile-looking'. On 8 May 1509 Henry VIII told the Spanish ambassador that he now wanted the marriage settled quickly and without any further difficulties.

As for Henry VIII himself, he seems to have had a very sheltered upbringing, and it is thought unlikely that he had any opportunity for sexual experimentation prior to his father's death. In the first five or six years of their marriage he appears to have had very great respect for Catherine, whose influence over him at this period was considerable. Henry was in every way very attentive to his new queen. As we have already seen, he himself stated to his court that when he married Catherine she was a virgin. However, the new king must have been quick to consummate his marriage and by the late summer of 1509 Catherine was already pregnant for the first time. Sadly, on 31 January 1510, she had a miscarriage. The dead baby was a girl.

Within a few months Catherine was pregnant again, and this time she appears to have carried the baby to term. She successfully gave birth to a son on 1 January 1511. He was baptised Henry, and created Prince of Wales. Almost at once the king and queen set off for the shrine of Our Lady of Walsingham in Norfolk to give thanks for the birth, and it may have been on this occasion that the king reportedly walked barefoot for a distance of about the last two miles from the manor house at East Barsham to the shrine — twice the distance covered barefoot by most pilgrims, who traditionally only took off their shoes at the Slipper Chapel at Houghton-in-the-Dale.[26] Tragically, however, the little prince only lived about two months, dying on 22 February.

In 1512 no pregnancies were reported, but Catherine was said to be pregnant again in 1513, reportedly giving birth to a live child soon after the battle of Flodden (September 1513). During several months prior to the birth she had been acting as regent of the kingdom while Henry VIII was in France, and she seems to have carried out the duties very conscientiously and effectively. The sex of the child she bore in 1513 is not mentioned but probably it was a girl, because had it been a son the fact would have been more likely to be recorded. In any case, the child must have died soon after its birth.

There was another pregnancy in 1514, and this resulted in the stillborn birth of a son in either November or December of that year. In the second half of 1515, the queen was again pregnant, and this time she successfully gave birth to a live and healthy daughter (Mary) on 18 February 1516. Shortly before this, in January, Catherine's father, King Ferdinand of Aragon, died. He was succeeded by his grandson (Catherine's nephew), Charles – the future Emperor Charles V.[27] Of course, Catherine had known her father well, and maintained close links with him. However, she did not know her nephew in the same close family way. Thus her ability to act as a diplomatic link was decreased by her father's death.

No pregnancy was recorded for the queen in 1517 (the year in which Elizabeth Blount became Henry VIII's mistress), but on 9–10 November 1518 Catherine of Aragon gave birth to her last child, a stillborn daughter. Meanwhile the king's extra-marital relationship with Elizabeth Blount was ongoing, and in 1519 Elizabeth gave birth to an illegitimate son by the king – Henry Fitzroy (later Duke of Richmond). Meanwhile, however, despite her increasing age and his own involvement with Elizabeth Blount, Henry VIII continued to sleep with his wife, at least at times. According to the king, the last sexual act between himself and Catherine took place some time in 1524. By that time Henry's relationship with Elizabeth Blount was over,[28] but it was in about 1523 that he probably found himself a new mistress in the person of his own very distant cousin, Mary Boleyn (Carey).[29] Mary Boleyn is important in the story of Henry VIII's early marital manoeuvrings, because she was Anne Boleyn's elder sister.[30] Thus her sexual relationship with the king created problems very similar to those raised by Catherine of Aragon's marriage to Prince Arthur. _PRINCESS_

Mary Boleyn was probably born about 1499. She was therefore eight years younger than the king (whereas Queen Catherine was six years older than Henry). In 1514, when Henry VIII's sister, Mary, married King Louis XII of France, the teenaged Mary Boleyn had been sent abroad with the princess as one of her attendants. She served for some time as a lady in waiting at the French court, where she seems to have gained both sexual experience and something of a reputation. _MARY + ANNE BOLEYN SERVED AT THE COURT OF FRANCE_

Following her return to England, in 1520 Mary Boleyn married Sir William Carey, a friend of the king and a member of the Privy Council. Nevertheless, for a Boleyn girl, descended from the earls of Ormonde, the dukes of Norfolk and ultimately from the royal house of Plantagenet, this marriage could be seen as a less than glittering match. Various reasons have been suggested as to why Mary married Carey, but the most likely explanation seems to be that her father was aware that Mary was flighty and he wanted to get her settled quickly before her French reputation caught up with her. Mary's first child, Catherine Carey, was probably born in 1524 and, as we have seen, it is possible that Catherine was Henry VIII's daughter. The fact that she was only a girl, coupled with her birth having been the possible product of a double adultery, are probably more than sufficient to explain why, if she was his daughter, Henry did nothing to recognise the little girl, who, after all, did have a legal father already in the person of her mother's husband.

Henry's relationship with Mary Boleyn seems to have ended in about 1525,[31] and it was in the course of the next twelve months that the king began to show an interest in Mary's younger sister, Anne. At the Shrove Tuesday joust on 20 February 1526 Henry VIII appeared in the guise of a tortured lover, with the motto 'declare I dare not'. This probably marked the approximate start of his courtship of Anne. _RETURNED FROM FRANCE AND START SERVING AS ONE OF THE MAIDS OF QUEEN CATHERINE COURT._

Like her elder sister, Anne had completed her education abroad, at the courts of the Archduchess Margaret of Austria in the Low Countries, and subsequently at the French court. When she returned to her homeland it was said that no one would take her for an English woman. She seemed more like a French girl, having acquired a Continental 'finish' which made her stand out.

Anne's first recorded appearance at the English court had been on Tuesday 4 March 1522, when she performed the part of 'Perseverance' in the court pageant for Shrove Tuesday – the last celebration before the start of the penitential season of Lent. Anne, then about 21 or 22 years of age, was not classically beautiful.[32] No contemporary portrait of Anne survives, but she seems to have had a rather long face and neck and she was dark, with a sallow complexion, brown eyes and black or very dark brown hair. Later reports of a mark or mole on her neck and a slight deformity to one hand are impossible to verify.[33] In 1522 she seems not to have made any immediate impression or impact on the king, who was then just beginning his relationship with her elder sister. It was not until four years later that we find evidence of the first signs of his interest in her.

Of course, Henry had no thoughts of marriage with Anne at this stage. His sexual relationship with Catherine of Aragon may have ended in the previous year. Nevertheless, at this time neither his marriage to Catherine nor the legitimacy of Mary, his daughter by the queen, seem to have been questioned by anyone. His intention as far as Anne Boleyn was concerned was simply that she should succeed her sister (and Elizabeth Blount) as his mistress.

Meanwhile, in June 1525 Henry Fitzroy, the king's illegitimate son by Elizabeth Blount, had been promoted by being created Duke of Richmond and Somerset and appointed lieutenant of the North. In the same year the Princess Mary was appointed to head the council of the Welsh Marches, and a household was established for her at Ludlow Castle, where Edward V and Prince Arthur had both lived as Princes of Wales. In Mary's case, although she was recognised as the heiress to the throne, she was not formally proclaimed Princess of Wales, since, as a girl, she was necessarily heiress *presumptive* rather than heiress *apparent*. AS A SPANIARD MOTHER QUEN CATHERINE AND PRINCESS MARY WHERE VERY LOVING TO EACH OTHER, TO SEPARATE AND HURT THEM, HEARRY ADVISED by ANNE, SEND MARY TO LIVE AWAY ALONE It was not until 1527 that Henry VIII began to voice doubts about the validity of his marriage to Catherine. The basis of his questioning was biblical. In the Old Testament (Leviticus 18, 1–19) a sexual relationship with the wife of a brother was forbidden. At the same time the book of Deuteronomy (21, 5) exhorted a man whose brother died childless to beget offspring for him by his widow. This apparent contradiction is probably explained by the different concepts of 'wife' and 'widow'. Of course one should not seduce the wife of one's brother while he was alive, but begetting children by her if he had died was another matter. Nevertheless, the Catholic Church regarded the widow of a brother as falling within the prohibited degrees. This meant that a brother's widow *could* be married, but only with a papal dispensation like the one which had been granted by Pope Julius II in 1503–05 – allowing the marriage of Catherine and Henry irrespective of whether Catherine's marriage to Arthur had ever been consummated. NOT TRUE, THE CATHOLIC CHURCH, AND RELIGION IS NOT THAT CRUEL TO FORBID A WIDOW OR WIDOWER TO MARRY AGAIN.

In the spring of 1527, based on the fact that the children of his marriage to Catherine of Aragon had mostly died (and all the sons had died), Henry began to question whether his marriage was accursed. Did the pope actually have the requisite authority to set aside the rules in Leviticus?

At first the king put this question to Cardinal Wolsey, Archbishop of York and Papal Legate, and to Archbishop Warham of Canterbury (5–6 April 1527). These churchmen were probably not surprised by this development. They well understood that the king's failure to produce a living son and heir by Catherine of Aragon constituted a problem for England. Wolsey seems to have assumed that in due course, when suitable grounds had been found for setting aside the marriage with Catherine, Henry would choose a French princess to replace her as England's queen and the mother of the future heir to the throne. The important thing, however, was to find a valid reason for quietly ending the marriage with Catherine. To this end, in May the consideration of the king's case was adjourned *sine die* pending the seeking of expert opinions on the matter.

Meanwhile in June, perhaps unwisely, Henry himself discussed the matter directly with Catherine. The queen's reaction was predictably furious. She told the king that she had been a virgin when she married him, and that he himself knew this perfectly well. On this basis, Catherine argued – both then and consistently thereafter – that their marriage was unquestionably valid. However, she completely failed to address – or even grasp – the issue which was preoccupying Henry and also the Papal court: namely the question of whether or not Pope Julius II had possessed the authority to grant a dispensation for a marriage between Henry VIII and his brother's widow. Throughout the protracted matrimonial dispute which followed, Catherine seems to have consistently failed to understand that this question of papal authority to grant a dispensation was the key issue, for she never commented upon it, maintaining throughout her consistent claim that she had married Henry as a virgin bride.

After her interview with Henry, Catherine also wrote at once to her nephew, the Emperor Charles V, seeking his help. Since the Emperor's troops were holding Rome and had the pope virtually imprisoned, Charles was, in one way, well placed to help his aunt and cause problems for the king. This was because at this stage Henry had no thought in his head of trying to circumvent papal authority. Indeed, in the summer of 1527 the king sent a request to Rome for a new papal bull which would permit him to marry a person to whom he was related in the first degree by either a legal or an illicit tie, provided that this person was not his brother's widow. Clearly the king had Anne Boleyn in mind, and his request was a roundabout allusion to the fact that Mary Boleyn had previously been his mistress. Henry considered that he needed papal authorisation for a valid marriage to Anne because of his prior relationship with Mary Boleyn. He was also firmly of the belief, at this stage, that only papal authority could properly end his marriage with Catherine. It was only later that Henry was forced, by the lack of papal assistance, to take matters into his own hands.

ADULTERY, IN A MARRIAGE IS A CAUSE OF DIVORCE WITH PAPAL DISPENSATION.
GIVEN CATHERINE KNOW BETTER THAN ANYONE ELSE, THAT HENRY AND HIS
COURT NONSENSICAL ARGUMENTS WHERE TO BULLY HER INTO AGREEING →

He probably did so reluctantly, and with nagging doubts about the validity of such a solution.

Meanwhile Anne Boleyn had been refusing to follow her sister into the royal bed as the king's mistress. The strength of the king's feelings for her is demonstrated by the seventeen surviving letters which he wrote to Anne in 1527 and 1528 (see chapter heading). It was Anne's refusal to be his mistress, coupled with his own perception that he needed a new wife, who could produce a male heir to the throne, which finally encouraged Henry to see these two matters as having a single solution. Anne's refusal and Henry's offer of marriage superficially reflect the relationships of his grandfather, Edward IV, with Eleanor Talbot and Elizabeth Woodville. However, Henry intended, at first, to seek a different solution. Whereas Edward IV had opted for secret marriages, Henry wanted to act openly. At some stage in 1527 he therefore offered Anne marriage, and, following her acceptance of this proposal, the king formally applied for a papal dispensation which would set aside the diriment impediment which stood in the way of his marriage to Anne. However, matters progressed with frustrating slowness.

At first both Henry and Anne were happy to trust Cardinal Wolsey, Archbishop of York and Chancellor of England. By 1529, however, Anne had decided that Wolsey was either not serious, or he was incapable of achieving the desired solution. She therefore helped to bring about the cardinal's fall from power, and she began to suggest to Henry that authority over the Church in England belonged to him as king – a notion canvassed the previous year by William Tyndale in his book *Obedience of a Christian Man*. In the summer of 1531, Henry finally sent Catherine of Aragon – officially reduced to the rank of 'Princess dowager of Wales' – away from his court. The following year Anne, now convinced that Henry VIII did really intend to marry her, finally began to sleep with him. In September 1532 she was created Marchioness of Pembroke in her own right, with the remainder to her offspring, and this probably approximately marks the date at which the couple began their sexual relationship. ANNE NEVER LOVED HENRY, SHE AND HER FOLLOWERS USED HIM.

By December 1532, Anne Boleyn was pregnant. Of course, Henry VIII's marriage to Catherine of Aragon had still not been annulled, either by the pope or by the English Church. However, urgent action was now essential. Although the king had sought to avoid – and had intended to avoid – a secret marriage with Anne, on a date in January 1533 which is not precisely known, secretly and privately, the couple married.[34] Since the issue of Henry's marriage to Catherine remained unresolved, the marriage to Anne was, of course, bigamous.

Although the marriage had been secret and private, Anne Boleyn was formally recognised as Queen of England on Holy Saturday 1533 (12 April). On 28 May 1533, four months *after* Henry's marriage to Anne, the newly appointed Archbishop Cranmer, who had just succeeded Warham as archbishop of Canterbury,[35] finally formally annulled the king's marriage to Catherine of Aragon and declared the secret marriage of Henry and Anne to be valid. (Almost a year later, on 23 March 1534,

TO A FORCED DIVORCE, SHE WAS A GOOD QUEEN, A DEVOTED AND LOVING WIFE AND MOTHER OF A LEGITIMATE HEIR TO THE TRONE AND SHE NEVER COMMITED ADULTERY. OF COURSE, SHE HAD MANY REASONS TO SAY NO the Papal court in Rome finally gave the opposite decision, and recognised Catherine of Aragon's marriage to Henry VIII as valid.) On Sunday 1 June Anne was crowned queen in Westminster Abbey. Fourteen weeks later, on Sunday 7 September, she gave birth to a daughter (the future Queen Elizabeth I).

It has often been said that Anne's failure to give Henry VIII a son immediately was a disaster for her and for their marriage, but in fact this seems not to have been so. In a very short time Anne was pregnant again. However, her miscarriage, in August 1534, *was* seen as a disaster. Moreover from this time onwards Henry seems to have begun to experience difficulties in his sexual relationship with Anne – possibly because he felt under such tremendous pressure to father an heir. At all events it was not until late in 1535 that Anne became pregnant for the third time.

Nevertheless, the popular notion that, having got Anne, Henry VIII then quickly lost interest in her seems to be unjustified. It is true that there were tensions in the relationship and it was sometimes stormy, but even as late as April 1536 the king was still making [ASKING] every effort to secure recognition for Anne as Queen of England from Catherine of Aragon's nephew, Charles V [EMPEROR]. By this time there was no longer any case to fight on Catherine's [QUEEN] behalf, for she had died on the early afternoon of Friday 7 January 1536, at Kimbolton – possibly from cancer, though her doctor and other contemporary opinion believed that she had been slowly poisoned.[36] Henry's treatment of Catherine of Aragon [QUEEN] had been unpopular, particularly with his female subjects. Moreover it was generally considered that whether or not his marriage to Catherine had been valid, their daughter, Mary [PRINCESS], had been conceived in good faith [LEGITIMATE] and should not have been declared illegitimate. As a result, public opinion both in England and abroad tended to be against Anne Boleyn, who was scathingly castigated as a whore.

Anne Boleyn had a genuine and active interest in religion, and she was a Catholic (it would be quite wrong to think of her as a Protestant). Nevertheless, she was a reforming Catholic, with evangelical tendencies, and she encouraged / the king to move in this direction. The final break with papal authority in Rome cannot be ascribed to Anne Boleyn. This came about rather as a result of Thomas Cromwell's policies and was encapsulated in the first Act of Supremacy (1534). In fact Anne disapproved of Cromwell's aim to close the English religious houses and confiscate their property for the royal treasury. She would have preferred reform of the religious houses, with an emphasis on education. Anne incited her almoner, John Skip, to preach against Cromwell's policies in the Chapel Royal on Passion Sunday 1536. This was an embarrassment to Cromwell. The king's attempt to persuade Charles V to recognise the Boleyn marriage in 1536 was another embarrassment to Cromwell, who had hoped that the king's meeting with the imperial ambassador, Chapuys, would be used rather to switch English foreign policy from an alliance with France to an alliance with the emperor. As a result of these two incidents it was ultimately Cromwell (not Henry VIII) who decided that Anne Boleyn must go. THE CATHOLIC RELIGION TEACHES, THAT YOU NEVER COMMIT ADULTERY WITH A MARRIED MAN OR WOMAN IF SHE WANTED TO REFORM THE TEACHING OF THE 10 COMMANDMENTS TO HER OWN NEEDS, THEN SHE WAS NOT RELIGIOUS AT ALL,

The minister made use of the rather free and easy court Anne Boleyn had created to manufacture evidence against her. On 30 April 1536 he arrested and interrogated Mark Smeaton, one of the court musicians. Probably by the use of torture, Cromwell extracted damning confessions from Smeaton, stating that Anne had been guilty of adultery with Smeaton himself and with others. With this confession Cromwell then confronted the king. Henry, ill-tempered since his recent jousting accident, reacted with predictable fury. Anne, her brother George and several others with whom she was accused of committing adultery were arrested and sent to the Tower of London. Rather cleverly, Archbishop Cranmer, who was an ally and supporter of Anne, was banned from the royal presence while the case against the queen was pursued, in order to ensure that the archbishop could do nothing to defend her. *Cromwell followed orders of Henry, not the other way round.*

Of course, the case against Anne Boleyn was a complete fabrication. Moreover, the argument that adultery by the queen was a treasonable offence was also a lie. Only later in Henry's reign was legislation enacted to this effect. Nevertheless, the members of the grand jury which was to hear the indictments against Anne were carefully selected by Cromwell to ensure that the outcome would be the one he wanted. First her supposed lovers were tried and found guilty. Only then was the case against Anne herself heard. By this clever strategy it was possible to use the evidence of the earlier convictions to condemn Anne.

She maintained her innocence throughout, and on the last night of her life she swore twice on the Blessed Sacrament that she was not guilty of the charges. On 17 May – the day when her alleged lovers were all executed – Anne's marriage to Henry VIII was annulled by Archbishop Cranmer. This was a strange and illogical action in one way, since, if she had never been validly married to the king, it is difficult to understand how Anne could possibly have committed adultery. Moreover the grounds for the annulment were the king's prior relationship with Mary Boleyn, which everyone had known about all the time. However, the real issue here was neither truth nor credibility. The intention was merely to ensure that Anne Boleyn was finished completely and for ever.

Thus it was not as a queen but as a private person that Anne was executed on Tower Green on the morning of Friday 19 May, by an imported French executioner wielding a sword rather than an axe. The marriage which Henry VIII had gone to such pains to contract had been written off in seconds, and the woman whose love he had so much desired had been cast aside without a word raised in her defence. Everything was done in a hurry. No one had even thought to provide a coffin, so Anne's body was hastily tucked into a chest for arrows, and in this undignified container it was interred in a shallow, unmarked grave in the adjacent chapel royal of St Peter ad Vincula. Anne's execution left Henry VIII completely free to marry whom he willed.

✠ ✠ ✠

The legal points at issue in the case of Henry VIII's relationships with Catherine of Aragon and Anne Boleyn are complex. First, we should note in passing that Catherine of Aragon was at no time defending papal authority; in fact she was sidelining it. *Her* claim was that she had needed no dispensation to marry Henry VIII: that she had never really been married to his brother, Arthur, because that first 'marriage' had remained unconsummated. Obviously she felt strongly in the matter, and the case she presented was heartfelt, but she completely missed the key point. Catholic teaching on the point of canon law at issue here means that she *did* require a papal dispensation to marry Henry VIII, whether or not her marriage with Arthur had been consummated. Moreover, it is abundantly clear from their actions at the time that Catherine's parents, Henry VII, Henry VIII and Pope Julius II all understood this and acted accordingly. Thus Catherine's emotional protestations that she had been a virgin when she married Henry were sincere but completely irrelevant. IN THIS days, OF COURSE, but NOT THEM WHEN THE bride and groom HAd TO SHOW THE bloodstain bridl SHEETS OF THE defLOWERING ACTIVITY.

Now let us consider the case put by Henry VIII. This was far from consistent. He argued that Catherine's marriage to his elder brother (whether consummated or not) created a diriment impediment to his own marriage to Catherine. The question then was: did Pope Julius II have the authority to set aside this impediment? Henry VII, Catherine's family and the papacy in Rome all believed that the pope *did* have this authority – and Henry VIII had himself accepted this viewpoint for more than twenty years. Only from 1527 or thereabouts did he begin to question it.

However, Henry VIII was by no means clear in his attitude to the papacy since, while requesting an annulment of his marriage to Catherine by the current pope, Clement VII, on the grounds that Pope Julius II had exceeded his authority, Henry was also asking Pope Clement to grant a dispensation to permit him to [BULLING] marry Anne Boleyn (whose sister had previously been Henry's mistress – thereby causing an identical diriment impediment to the one which had stood in the way of Henry's marriage to Catherine of Aragon). Henry's position was therefore completely nonsensical. Either the pope *did* have the authority to grant dispensations in such circumstances or he did not!

In the final analysis, of course, Henry simply cut through the Gordian knot by discarding Catherine and marrying Anne. Even then, however, his conduct of affairs was exceedingly inept. He failed to have his marriage to Catherine annulled in England until *after* he had married Anne. Thus, by any standard his marriage to Anne must have been bigamous and hence invalid. Moreover, his reason for discarding Catherine was that he and she were related within the prohibited degrees at the first and highest level, and that *no power on earth could set this impediment aside*. It should therefore have been obvious, even to Henry, that, since an identical impediment existed in his relationship with Anne Boleyn, no legal marriage between Anne and himself would ever be possible. By his own argument no power existed on earth which could set the impediment aside! Logically, whatever held good in the case of his marriage with Catherine also applied to his marriage with Anne. In the end, Henry himself did accept this logic, and declare that he had not been legally married either to Catherine or to Anne – but this was only after both ladies were dead.

Finally, there is an alternative point of view to consider: namely that the pope *did* *(does)* have authority to set aside the diriment impediment. Since Julius II did precisely this in the case of Catherine of Aragon, arguably that made her marriage to Henry legal. On the other hand, no one set aside the impediment in the case of Anne. Based on this point of view, Henry's marriage to Catherine was valid but his marriage to Anne was not. BECAUSE THERE WAS NO RELEVANT CASE FOR ANNE

To sum up, there are two possible ways in which to assess the legal position as it stood at the time.[37] One (Henry VIII's own final viewpoint) is that he was not legally married either to Catherine of Aragon or to Anne Boleyn. The other is that he was legally married to Catherine but not to Anne. There is no way in which it can be argued, on the basis of the law as it stood at the time, either that Henry VIII was legally married to *both* Catherine and Anne, or that he was legally married to Anne, but not to Catherine. IF THE MEDIEVAL MARRIAGE LAW APPLIED TO HENRY VIII AND QUEN CATHERINE, AND POPE JULIUS II SET ASIDE THE SAY IMPEDIMENT, THEN THEIR MARRIAGE WAS TOTALLY LEGAL

OTHER CATHOLIC CHURCH IMPEDIMENT TO MARRIAGE IS CONSANGUINITY MEANING WITH YOUR blood RELATIVES, FAMILY THEY WERE NOT RELATED IN THAT WAY

11

REVIEW OF SECRET
AND BIGAMOUS MEDIEVAL
ROYAL MARRIAGES

Despite the fact that the so-called Tudor period is usually classified by historians as 'early modern', the Henry VIII case has been included here in our medieval section, because the medieval marriage laws, which pertained in the earlier cases we have considered, still applied to Henry VIII, Catherine of Aragon and Anne Boleyn. Not until 1538, two years after Anne Boleyn's execution, did State registration of marriages become a legal requirement in England. All the alleged secret royal marriages which we have so far examined took place under a common legal framework. Throughout the period we have been looking at there were no marriage certificates. Marriages were not contracts in civil law. Instead, they were subject to the religious (canon) law of the Catholic Church (since the period we explored in this section was before the English Church broke away from the authority of the pope in Rome, and began to evolve its own rules).

In addition to their common underlying legal framework, the four key cases we have examined also have certain other features in common. These key cases are the marriage of the Black Prince, the alleged second marriage of Queen Catherine, the alleged marriages of Edward IV, and the alleged marriages of Henry VIII. We shall try to highlight these interesting key features as we review the four cases, and assess their potential significance.

Our first case of a secret royal marriage was that of the heir to the throne, the Black Prince, eldest son of Edward III. In 1360 it is alleged that the Black Prince secretly married Joan of Kent. Of course there is no documentary evidence of such a secret marriage, but the allegation is credible because in the following year (1361) the prince and his bride contracted an official union, approved by the

why? He was called the black prince

king and the pope. It is interesting to note that the alleged secret marriage was followed by a public royal ceremony which conferred official royal status on the partnership, because in various different forms this is a feature which we can trace in all four of the cases under review.

The couple subsequently went on to live together publicly for a number of years (until the Black Prince died), and to produce children. The birth of children (creation of a family) is another significant feature of the partnership. The circumstantial evidence for the marriage is therefore so strong as to warrant no doubt about the matter. The marriage of the Black Prince was also important because it set a precedent for a key member of the royal family to contract a domestic marriage with a subject on the basis of affection and personal inclination, rather than contracting an arranged marriage with a foreign bride, selected for reasons of policy.

Several other secret marriages in the royal family in the next century reinforced this precedent. In the cases of John of Gaunt and Catherine de Roët, Humphrey, Duke of Gloucester and Eleanor Cobham, and Jacquette, Duchess of Bedford and Richard Woodville there was again no official marriage document, because such documentation did not exist at this period. However, in two cases out of the three we have the evidence of recognised children, and in all three cases there is evidence of the couple openly living together as husband and wife for a number of years.

Our first case of a crowned royal personage and an alleged secret marriage is that of Queen Catherine, widow of Henry V. This case is very interesting. Again, of course, there is no documentary evidence of a marriage. We would not expect any. There *is* evidence of children, although the precise number of children is very much open to question. Two children (Edmund and Jasper Tudor) seem certain, but various authorities have stated that there were three, four, or even five children born to the couple. Conversely, other authorities have raised questions about the paternity of at least one of the children. Indeed, in this present study I have extended the question mark about Queen Catherine's offspring by arguing that the armorial evidence shows that at least two of her children were fathered not by Owen Tudor, but by Edmund Beaufort.

We may have evidence of an association of some kind between Catherine and Owen Tudor lasting several years. However, there was no contemporary general opinion that they were married. The situation is complicated by Catherine's acknowledged predilection for Edmund Beaufort. All in all, the picture in this case is far from clear, and there are really no grounds for stating as a fact that Catherine was married to Owen Tudor. Nevertheless, curiously, the current articles in the *Oxford Dictionary of National Biography* on Catherine and on Owen *do* both state their marriage as a fact![1] This is an excellent example of how history tends to impose a definitive interpretation on the events of the past, sometimes in defiance of logic, and in spite of what the contemporary evidence actually shows.

However, the existence of children (a family) once again proves the existence of a partnership of some kind for Queen Catherine – either with Edmund Beaufort or with Owen Tudor – or possibly with both of them. Moreover, as in the case of the Black Prince, an alleged secret marriage was followed by a public feature which conferred official royal status. In this case, however, it was not a public ceremony of any kind, but rather the public and open granting of titles, together with a version of the royal arms, to the two eldest sons of Queen Catherine's new partnership. The grant of royal arms was an extraordinary feature, with no possible intrinsic justification if the father of the children was indeed Owen Tudor. Nevertheless, at one level this feature can be interpreted as conferring some kind of official status of Queen Catherine's partnership, whoever her partner was, and whether or not she was ever married to him.

Next we have the case of Edward IV. Here again, writers of history have sought to impose an interpretation, and in this case the general view hitherto has been that Edward IV was *not* married to Eleanor Talbot, but that the allegation of the marriage was merely fabricated later, to serve the interests of Richard III in his aspiration to be king.

Again, in the case of Edward and Eleanor, we have no marriage certificate, but we now know better than to expect one. In this case we also have no children, and there is no evidence of the couple living together for an extended period. On the other hand there certainly *is* evidence of a relationship between Edward and Eleanor – including new evidence, recently uncovered by the present writer. This indicates that the relationship between the couple was a fact. That fact must then be coupled with other evidence, showing that Eleanor would have been unlikely for several reasons to have accepted an illicit relationship. There is also evidence that Elizabeth Woodville was later worried about the validity of her own marriage to Edward IV, and took rather desperate measures to defend herself and her children.

Finally, we have the fact that ultimately, and on the basis of further evidence which was subsequently destroyed, the marriage of Edward and Eleanor was formally recognised in an Act of Parliament. This act was later repealed and deliberately suppressed by Henry VII, who had good reasons for wanting to defend the notion that Edward IV was married to Elizabeth Woodville. Overall, I would argue therefore that the alleged marriage between Edward and Eleanor deserves to be taken more seriously than the alleged marriage between Queen Catherine and Owen Tudor, and that only a rather blinkered and partisan attitude on the part of many historians could explain why these two alleged marriages have been treated so differently in the past.

As for the marriage of Edward with Elizabeth Woodville, probably it was bigamous. Like the marriage of the Black Prince and the alleged second marriage of Catherine of France it was also secret initially, but subsequently it was given official royal status – this time by a public coronation of Elizabeth Woodville as queen. This partnership also had something else which the partnership with

Eleanor Talbot lacked, namely the creation of a family. Indeed, the Woodville marriage raises an important point which we shall confront again later, namely the fact that even if a marriage was not strictly speaking legal, it may nevertheless need to be accepted as a kind of fact.

Finally we considered the case of Henry VIII, Catherine of Aragon and Anne Boleyn This case is in some ways very similar to that of Edward IV, in that Henry's alleged second marriage (to Anne Boleyn) was secret and arguably bigamous, like that of Edward IV with Elizabeth Woodville. However Anne's secret and private marriage was followed by a public royal ceremony identical to that which occurred in the case of Elizabeth Woodville – a coronation. In the case of Anne Boleyn this was certainly a deliberate attempt to confer official status and recognition on a dubious marriage – which raises the interesting question of whether a similar significance should be seen as underlying Elizabeth Woodville's grand coronation. And like Elizabeth Woodville's marriage, that of Anne Boleyn – while it may have been strictly speaking illegal according to the code of the day – may nevertheless have to be accepted on some level as a fact. *Why?*

Henry VIII's unions with Catherine of Aragon and Anne Boleyn both produced children, and in this respect they differed from the case of Edward IV, who had no children by Eleanor Talbot. However, Henry's children by both partners were subsequently bastardised and excluded from the throne – like the children of Edward IV and Elizabeth Woodville. Moreover, the cases of both Edward and Henry were subject to subsequent parliamentary rulings: namely the section of the *titulus regius* of 1484 which declared the marriage of Edward IV and Eleanor Talbot valid, and set aside the marriage of Edward and Elizabeth Woodville, and the Act of Succession of 1536 (together, of course, with its predecessor in 1534 and its successor at the end of Henry's reign, not to mention the subsequent succession legislation of Edward VI) which attempted to establish which of Henry VIII's children could succeed to the throne, and in what order, together with their legitimate or illegitimate status.

Another feature in which the cases of Edward IV and Henry VIII seem to be similar is in the ultimate fate of the alleged royal brides. Eleanor Talbot retired into private and semi-religious seclusion and died in slightly mysterious circumstances. *Queen* Catherine of Aragon was forced into retirement, concentrated her attention largely on her religion, and her death was thought by contemporaries to have been suspicious. Neither Eleanor nor Catherine was buried as a queen.

As for Elizabeth Woodville, she was demoted from royal rank. Although her queenship was later briefly reasserted by her son-in-law, in the end she lost everything she owned, and her funeral was a curious mixture between a royal burial and that of a poor person. Anne Boleyn was likewise deprived of her queenly status. She was executed of course, having lost everything she owned, and she was buried as a criminal. Not even her daughter (when she finally ascended the throne) ever made any attempt to reinstate Anne's reputation or give her a royal reburial. *Even she where buried without the honor as a queen of England, you cannot demote queen Catherine because she was a royal princess, daughter of the powerfull Catholic sovereings, promoters of the discovering of the new world.*

Three

Reformation, Registration, Cohabitation

12

THE VIRGIN QUEEN

Master Tyrwhit and others have told me that there goeth rumours abroad which be greatly against my honour and honesty (which above all other things I esteem), which be these; that I am in the Tower; and with child by my Lord Admiral [Thomas Seymour]. My lord, these are shameful slanders.

Elizabeth [I] to the Duke of Somerset (Lord Protector), 1549

The Queen is in love with Robert [Dudley].

Philip II of Spain

Ther was a privie staires where the Quene and my Lord of Leicestre did mete, and if they had not used sorcery there should have bene young traitors ere now begotten.

The Earl of Southampton, 1572

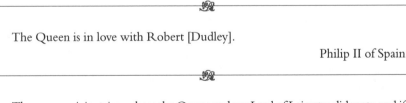

The introduction of the registration of marriages by Thomas Cromwell in 1538 began to change the situation in respect of marriages in England. However, direct government involvement was still at one remove, since registration was by the Church rather than directly by the State. From this date onwards, records were kept of all marriages in churches and diocese – at least in theory. In addition, while marriage remained principally a religious matter, the Elizabethan *39 Articles of Religion* (1562) did not recognise marriage as a sacrament, so its official status in England was changed somewhat from what it had been prior to the Reformation. However, it was not until 1837 that *State* registration of marriage at a national level came into force in Britain, bringing in its wake the formal and automatic issue of marriage certificates and allowing the civil law to take full command in the matter of marriage.

In theory, after 1538 a written record of each and every marriage was meant to be preserved. In fact, however, historical and genealogical research shows that this is not invariably the case. This is firstly because not all early sixteenth-century church records of marriages have survived. Secondly, ongoing disputes regarding the choice of religion meant that some marriages took place other than in the newly Anglicanised parish churches. Moreover, the age-old tradition of the secret marriage was by no means quick to go away. As a result we can certainly find some instances in both the sixteenth and the seventeenth century of alleged secret royal marriage of which no written record exists.

As we shall see in the next chapter, at least one such royal marriage – that of James [II] with Anne Hyde – is generally credited, despite the lack of documentation to authenticate it. The widespread belief in that particular royal marriage is founded largely upon the subsequent history of the couple (who, despite James' infidelity, lived together until Anne's death, producing a number of children, two of whom survived to adulthood) and upon the public recognition which was accorded to the partnership. In the case of the other alleged secret royal marriages of Elizabeth I and the Stuart dynasty the allegations have been generally (if not universally) disbelieved. Nevertheless, despite Cromwell's legislation of 1538, the lack of a written record in these cases seems far from being the key issue in deciding whether or not the allegations should be believed.

✤ ✤ ✤

The first case we shall examine concerns Henry VIII's daughter, Elizabeth, the so-called 'Virgin Queen'. The questions surrounding Elizabeth's dubious personal legitimacy and the doubts about the validity of her succession to the throne – doubts which were widespread in Europe at the time – depend upon the complex and difficult issue of the legality of her mother's marriage to her father (see above), and upon the subsequent succession legislation enacted by Henry VIII and Edward VI. Her father declared Elizabeth a bastard in 1536, and he never subsequently changed her status, although he did eventually restore her to the line of succession *as though she were legitimate*. Later her half-brother, Edward VI, once again removed Elizabeth's rights to claim the Crown. Thus, in the end, it was only thanks to the *coup* of her half-sister, Mary (followed by the latter's childless death) that Elizabeth actually came to the throne. The succession would otherwise have passed to her cousin, Jane Grey. (For the relevant documentary evidence, see Appendix 3.)

Despite her extremely dubious legitimacy as a princess and as a queen, Elizabeth had many suitors.[1] These included foreign princes – notably Philip II of Spain (widowed husband of her dead half-sister, Queen Mary) and *Monsieur* (Hercule-François of France, Duke of Anjou and Alençon, the youngest son of Henri II of France and Catherine de Medici). Philip II sent an official proposal of marriage to Elizabeth after her accession. Of course, she knew him, for he

QUEEN

had been in England as the husband of her half-sister, Mary I. Indeed Philip had sought to help Elizabeth when Mary suspected her of disloyalty. From Elizabeth's point of view, however Philip's previous relationship with Mary was against him, as, of course, was the fact that he was a Catholic.[2]

As for *Monsieur*,[3] the queen's last foreign suitor, he courted her in person and despite the difference in their ages, he seems to have established a genuinely affectionate relationship with Queen Elizabeth. When the Duke finally left her to return to the European mainland, the queen is said to have penned the following poem to voice her regret at his departure:

On Monsieur's Departure [4]
I grieve and dare not show my discontent,
I love and yet am forced to seem to hate,
I do, yet dare not say I ever meant,
I seem stark mute but inwardly do prate.
I am and not, I freeze and yet am burned,
Since from myself another self I turned.
My care is like my shadow in the sun,
Follows me flying, flies when I pursue it,
Stands and lies by me, doth what I have done.
His too familiar care doth make me rue it.
No means I find to rid him from my breast,
Till by the end of things it be supprest.
Some gentler passion slide into my mind,
For I am soft and made of melting snow;
Or be more cruel, love, and so be kind.
Let me or float or sink, be high or low.
Or let me live with some more sweet content,
Or die and so forget what love ere meant.

Elizabeth only officially ended her engagement to Anjou in 1583, after the fiasco of his attempt to take the city of Antwerp.[5] However, the match had been opposed by notable members of the queen's council, including the Earl of Leicester, who warned the queen of the dangers of childbearing at her age. Only William Cecil (Lord Burghley) and the Earl of Sussex had given this proposed marriage their full and consistent support.

At various periods of her life Elizabeth also had suitors in her own kingdom, and it has been suggested that she may have contracted a secret marriage with one of them. The idea of such a secret marriage is by no means impossible. There were several secret marriages in the sixteenth-century royal family! Both her father's sisters – Margaret, Queen of Scotland and Mary, Queen of France – contracted secret marriages, as did Elizabeth I's royal cousin, Lady Catherine Grey (younger sister of Jane, the 'Nine Days' Queen').

Elizabeth's first domestic suitor (during her youth, before she became queen) was Admiral Sir Thomas Seymour. Later, another serious contender was Robert Dudley, later Earl of Leicester. Seymour would probably have liked to marry the young Elizabeth, for several reasons. In the end, however, he settled instead for a secret marriage with her widowed stepmother, Queen Catherine Parr. The secret marriage of Thomas with the queen dowager brings him firmly into the context of our present study, irrespective of his aspirations to marry the future Queen Elizabeth I.

Thomas Seymour was undoubtedly ambitious and he seems to have had his eyes fixed on some kind of royal bride. He had previously made an offer for the hand of Anne of Cleves, whose marriage with his brother-in-law, Henry VIII, had been annulled on 9 July 1540. When this proposal was rejected, Thomas decided to try Catherine Parr instead:

> He courted Katharine in secret and married her with indecent haste in May 1547 – just four months after Henry had died. Their marriage was without permission from his brother [the Lord Protector] or the Privy Council – it would not have been granted as theoretically Katharine could have been pregnant by King Henry.[6]

By the end of 1547 Catherine Parr *was* pregnant – by Thomas Seymour – and reportedly very happy at the prospect of having a child. Meanwhile, however, her husband was romping about in a very inappropriate manner with their stepdaughter, Elizabeth. He is said to have visited the young girl in bed, and on one occasion, to have ripped her gown. Thomas's behaviour became the subject of gossip and scandal and in 1548 Elizabeth was forced to leave her stepmother's household. Based on the evidence of subsequent correspondence, the personal relationship between the two women seems to have remained good, but apparently neither of them was happy with the behaviour of the admiral, and Catherine Parr may have felt some concern for her stepdaughter, whom she wished to protect. On 30 August the queen dowager gave birth to a daughter, who was christened Mary. But as a result of the birth, Catherine contracted puerperal fever, and she died five days later.

Subsequently Seymour's conduct was investigated by the government, and both he and Elizabeth were arrested. She stoutly maintained that her honour had never been compromised and that she was still a virgin, and nothing to the contrary was ever proved against her. But as for Thomas Seymour, he was executed by his brother, for high treason, on 10 March 1549. If Elizabeth had not already been given sufficient cause to fear marriage by the conduct of her father in respect of her mother and her mother's cousin, Catherine Howard, then the fate of Thomas Seymour may well have been enough to convince her that marriage could be an extremely dangerous adventure. Meanwhile, however serious Thomas Seymour's interest in the young Elizabeth may have been, it is difficult to take him seriously as a prospective husband, since he was married to Elizabeth's stepmother for the entire period of his close relationship with the young girl.

As for Elizabeth's relationship with Robert Dudley, this was particularly serious and long-lasting, and there is ample contemporary evidence of a genuine mutual attachment between them. Indeed, the interesting marital history of Robert Dudley contains three secret marriage allegations – one of his alleged partners being the queen. Dudley has also been suspected of murdering his first wife in order to free himself to marry the queen. However, once again chronology seems to rule out the possibility of a royal secret marriage for Dudley.

Elizabeth's relationship with Dudley is linked to a complex modern theory connected with the authorship of the literary works traditionally attributed to William Shakespeare. This theory is variously known as the 'Tudor Rose' or 'Prince Tudor' hypothesis, and we shall henceforth refer to it here as 'TR/PT'. Various versions of this theory have advanced claims that Elizabeth was married to Dudley and/or had a child or children by him. They have also produced competing interpretations of the queen's relationships with Thomas Seymour and with Edward, Earl of Oxford. The 'TR/PT' is a most complicated story. However, unfortunately we cannot entirely ignore it, since it impinges directly upon the question of a possible secret marriage of Elizabeth I. We must therefore examine briefly the evidence (such as it is) for the complex 'TR/PT'. At the same time we shall try to review the contemporary sixteenth-century evidence of Elizabeth I's relationships with Dudley and others.

The complex modern 'TR/PT' theories concerning Elizabeth I's supposed relationship with the author of the 'Shakespeare' corpus of literature have many variations. What all the versions seem to have in common, however, is the premise that Elizabeth I was the mother of the man (whoever he was – and he has been variously identified) who really wrote the plays and poems attributed to William Shakespeare.

The first version of 'TR/PT' suggested that Elizabeth I was secretly married to Robert Dudley, Earl of Leicester, by whom she had two sons: Francis Bacon and Robert Devereux, second Earl of Essex. This theory was launched in the 1890s by a writer called Orville Ward Owen, and subsequently developed by Alfred Dodd, who presented his version in 1910. As we have seen, the belief that Elizabeth I was in love with Leicester is an old one, dating back to the lifetime of the couple. Indeed, this belief is almost certainly well founded. The proposition that the queen and the Earl of Leicester were married is also far from new, although this aspect of the story has less evidence to support it.

During the 1930s, Percy Allen advanced a different 'TR/PT' theory: namely that Elizabeth I had been amorously involved with (but not married to) Edward de Vere, Earl of Oxford, by whom she had an illegitimate son called William Hughes, who was the real author of the 'Shakespeare' literature. This version of events has since evolved further variant forms. First, subsequent writers modified the original theory to identify Henry Wriothesley, Earl of Southampton (rather than William Hughes) as the illegitimate child of the queen by Oxford – and also the true 'Shakespeare'. Then, in the 1970s an updated version of the story was used in a novel by Margaret Barsi-Greene. She reverted to the notion of a relationship between the queen and Robert Dudley, Earl of Leicester. However, in her version of the theory this couple never married. Barsi-Greene changed the name of the child yet again, making one William Hastings the illegitimate child of Elizabeth by Robert Dudley. According to her account, Hastings was the real 'Shakespeare'.

By 2001 'TR/PT' had progressed to the point where Elizabeth was attributed no less than four illegitimate children by Leicester, including Robert Cecil, first Earl of Salisbury, Robert Devereux, second Earl of Essex, Mary Sidney and Elizabeth Leighton. In addition the 'Virgin Queen' was said to have had another son much earlier, by Thomas Seymour. This son was the Earl of Oxford, who later incestuously fathered yet another illegitimate son by his own mother, the queen; this final 'Tudor' royal bastard being Henry Wriothesley.

It was an American actor called Paul Streitz who published this latest, highly complex version of 'TR/PT'. Not surprisingly, perhaps, his account has been seriously questioned by historians, and grave flaws have been found in the evidence he presented. Moreover, Streitz has been accused of selectivity, since he 'covers only the evidence that suits his purpose while he omits anything that might conflict'.[7]

So what does the contemporary, sixteenth-century factual evidence show us? As we have seen, Elizabeth was born in 1533, seven to eight months after her father's bigamous marriage with her mother, Anne Boleyn, who was certainly pregnant at the time of the marriage. Although Elizabeth's birth may have come as something of a disappointment to her father, there is no possible doubt that she was initially recognised as heir to the throne, and the Act of Succession of 1533–34 (see below, Appendix 3. Item 5) was intended to consolidate her position in this respect. Later, however, following her mother's disgrace, the annulment of her parents' marriage and the execution of Anne Boleyn, Elizabeth was declared illegitimate and was removed from the succession. Her childhood and youth were varied and strange. She passed through the hands of an assortment of carers, and eventually, following her father's death, she settled in the household of her stepmother, Queen Catherine Parr.

Here she found herself in close proximity to Sir Thomas Seymour, the younger of the two maternal uncles of her half-brother, King Edward VI. Some writers – including, as we have seen, some advocates of the 'TR/PT' hypothesis – assert that an illicit relationship then developed between the young Elizabeth and Sir Thomas. It is a fact that there were contemporary rumours that Elizabeth and Thomas Seymour had an illicit sexual relationship, and these rumours may even have contained an element of truth.

The latest version of the 'TR/PT' strongly advocates belief in such a relationship, and Streiz, for example, tries to use letters from Elizabeth to Seymour's elder brother, the Duke of Somerset (Lord Protector of England during the minority of his nephew, Edward VI) to prove that Elizabeth fell pregnant by Thomas Seymour, and that she subsequently bore a son who became Edward 'de Vere', seventeenth Earl of Oxford. However, the evidence for these assertions is highly questionable.

Thus, Streitz asserts that Thomas Seymour proposed marriage to the young Elizabeth, and he bases this assertion upon a quotation from a published letter alleged to have been written by Elizabeth. Unfortunately, the letter in question is now dismissed as a forgery, fabricated, apparently, by an earlier would-be historian.[8] Streitz then goes on to give an account of Elizabeth's alleged pregnancy by Seymour based on the evidence of an authentic letter written by the young Elizabeth, which however Streitz misinterprets. In point of fact the passage which Streitz takes to refer to a forthcoming child actually refers to Elizabeth's female custodian of the time! AT 17 OF COURSE YOU CAN HAVE A CHILD.

Next, in support of his premise that Edward de Vere was the queen's son by Thomas Seymour, Streitz attempts to argue that de Vere was born some two years earlier than his traditionally accepted birth date of 12 April 1550. But even if de Vere was born earlier, it seems impossible that Elizabeth could have been his mother. There are surviving accounts written by those who saw her during the summer of 1548, which offer no evidence that the future queen then appeared to be pregnant. Streitz also seeks to make much of a Latin phrase in a source from 28 June 1563, which described Edward de Vere as *minorem quatordecem annorum*. But here again, Streitz misinterprets his source. The Latin phrase actually means that Edward was 'less than 14 years of age'. When accurately translated, it appears to be entirely compatible with Edward de Vere's standard and generally accepted birth date of 12 April 1550.[9]

We are left, then, with a situation in which all the evidence presented by 'TR/PT' advocates in an attempt to prove that Elizabeth had a child by Sir Thomas Seymour appears to be flawed. There may in fact have been an amorous (and possibly sexual) relationship between Elizabeth and Seymour, but there is no evidence that such a relationship (if it existed) ever produced any offspring. Moreover, this alleged relationship is of no direct interest to us in our present context, since not even the 'TR/PT' advocates have sought to claim that Elizabeth and Sir Thomas Seymour were ever *married*.

Genuine and more intriguing evidence that the 'Virgin Queen' may have had offspring is contained in Elizabeth I's 1571 Act of Treason. This was very strangely worded, so that it appears explicitly to allow for the succession to the throne of bastard offspring of the queen. The phrase used in the text of the act refers to 'the natural yssus of her Ma'j body'.[10] What precisely is meant by this wording is open to interpretation, but the word 'natural' was often used to mean 'illegitimate'. If it does indeed refer to illegitimate children of the queen, as contemporaries

ISSUE OF HER LOINS ?

seem to have understood, then the act certainly warrants serious consideration. However, there is nothing in it – or in contemporary comments upon it – to justify the assumption made by recent advocates of the 'TR/PT' that the act was intended to refer to the Earl of Oxford. In fact, as William Camden wrote later, 'I my selfe being then a young man have heard them oftentimes say that the word [naturall] was inserted into the Act of Purpose by *Leicester*, that he might one day obtrude uppon the English some bastard sonne of *his*, for the Queenes naturall issue'.[11] This takes us back to the chief focus of the present chapter – namely the rumours, current in the seventeenth century and subsequently, of a possible marriage between Elizabeth I and Robert Dudley, Earl of Leicester. As we have noted already, in addition to sixteenth-century rumours of such a relationship, some modern versions of the 'TR/PT' argue in support of such a marriage. They suggest that the queen's union with Leicester led to the birth of a son – variously identified – who was the real author of the works of 'Shakespeare'. It is time, then, to consider the history of the Earl of Leicester.

✤ ✤ ✤

Robert Dudley, later Earl of Leicester, was born on 24 June 1532 or 1533. Condemned to death in 1553, in the wake of his father's attempt to alter the succession in England by enthroning Lady Jane Grey, Dudley was saved from the block by the intervention of Philip II of Spain, husband of Queen Mary and King-Consort of England. When Elizabeth I succeeded to the throne in 1558, Dudley was made her Master of the Horse. In 1562 he became a privy councillor, and in 1564 he was created Earl of Leicester. Finally, in the year prior to his death he became Lord Steward of the Royal Household. He died on 4 September 1588.

Allegations of secret marriages constitute a significant part of Dudley's life story. Not only has it been alleged that Dudley secretly married the queen, he is also said to have secretly married two of her cousins, Lettice Knollys, Countess of Essex, and Lady Douglas Sheffield (nee Howard).[12] However, Dudley's *first* marriage was far from secret. On 4 June 1550, at the Royal Palace of Sheen, and in the presence of King Edward VI, the young Dudley married Amy Robsart, the only daughter of a Norfolk gentleman. Amy was approximately of the same age as Dudley himself. However, their marriage remained childless. Moreover, following the accession of Elizabeth I in 1558, Dudley saw very little of his wife, who never accompanied him to court. Indeed, Dudley was rather unkindly commanded by the queen 'to say that he did nothing with her [Amy], when he came to her, which he seldom did'.[13]

If Amy Robsart was not present at the court in person, she was nevertheless well known and much talked about there, being the subject of avid speculation. In fact in the course of 1559, when news reached the court that Amy was unwell, the view was openly expressed that her life was the only thing that stood in the way of her husband's marriage to the queen. Thus there was speculation on the part of the Spanish ambassador, de Quadra, and others, that Dudley was sending Amy poison. Naturally, when Amy finally died in mysterious circumstances, on 8 September 1560, this caused a major scandal. The truth about Amy Robsart's death has never been established beyond question but, despite widespread contemporary suspicions, it seems unlikely that her husband had her murdered. As things turned out, in the long run Amy's suspicious death caused Robert Dudley many more problems than it solved!

After the death of Amy Robsart, Robert Dudley had a relationship with Douglass Howard (Lady Douglass Sheffield), who in 1574 bore him a probably bastard son, also called Robert Dudley. The Earl of Leicester himself always treated this younger Robert Dudley as illegitimate. However, claims were made after the earl's death that he and Douglass (who had been a widow at the time of their relationship) had been secretly married. Robert Dudley junior lost his early seventeenth-century legal battle to establish his legitimacy, despite the fact that his mother wrote a document claiming that she had indeed been married to Lord Leicester. The case was raised again in the nineteenth century in an attempt to revive the earldom of Leicester, but on that occasion too, the claim was dismissed.

However there seems to be no doubt that in 1575 Leicester did engage in a secret marriage, this time with the queen's cousin, Lettice Knollys, dowager Countess of Essex. The marriage took place at Leicester's house in Wanstead, with only a handful of friends and relations in attendance. The reason for the secrecy was that Leicester did not want the queen to know what he had done, and for nine months the secret was indeed kept. This is interesting proof that clandestine marriages could remain concealed if the contracting parties so wished.

Dudley's chronology shows that from 1550 until 1560 he was unquestionably married to Amy Robsart – a marriage which the queen may have resented but could not undo. In the early 1570s he was entangled with (though probably not married to) Douglass Howard. Then from 1575 until his death in 1588 Dudley was married to the queen's cousin, Lettice Knollys. Again, the queen was jealous and resentful, but the fact of Dudley's marriage to Lettice seems certain.

It follows that only between 1560 and 1575 could Dudley have seriously contemplated a marriage with the queen. Yet during this period the queen was entertaining the prospect of marriage with three successive French princes, with her cousin Lord Darnley (who eventually married Mary, Queen of Scots), and with an Austrian archduke.

If the queen and Robert Dudley did ever go through a form of marriage, this would almost certainly have involved Dudley in bigamy. But the fact that in 1575 Dudley secretly married Lettice Knolly presumably shows that he was still free to marry at that time. All the evidence suggests that, whatever the true nature of the affectionate relationship between Elizabeth I and Dudley, it was never formalised as a marriage.

13

OLD ROWLEY
AND MRS BARLOW

The Duke of Monmouth is in so great splendour at Court and so dandled by the King, that some doubt, if the King should have no child by the Queene (which there is yet no appearance of), whether he would not be acknowledged for a lawful son.

Samuel Pepys, 31 December 1662

I never gave nor made any contract of marriage, nor was married to any woman whatsoever, but to my present wife Queene Caterine.

Charles II, 1679

… we should immediately insist upon our title to the crowns of England, Scotland, France and Ireland, and the dominions and territories thereunto belonging, as son and heir apparent to Charles the Second, king of England, our royal father lately deceased.

The Duke of Monmouth's proclamation as King, 21 June 1685[1]

Elizabeth I's childless death in 1603 finally brought the so-called 'Tudor' dynasty to an end. She was succeeded on the English throne by the house of Stuart, in the person of her young cousin James VI of Scotland (I of England), son of Mary Queen of Scots by her second husband, Lord Darnley. By blood and descent, James I and VI was the next rightful heir to the English throne, but his succession had been contested during Elizabeth's reign because he was a 'foreigner'. Nevertheless, ultimately he did succeed. Despite his somewhat equivocal sexuality, James had a flourishing family, and all subsequent British monarchs have been his descendants.

1 The marriage of Henry III and Eleanor of Provence, redrawn after Matthew Paris (ms Royal 14C.Vii, f. 124v). *Copyright Muhammad Hanif*

2 Medieval witches brewing a potion, redrawn from a fifteenth-century woodcut. *Copyright Muhammad Hanif*

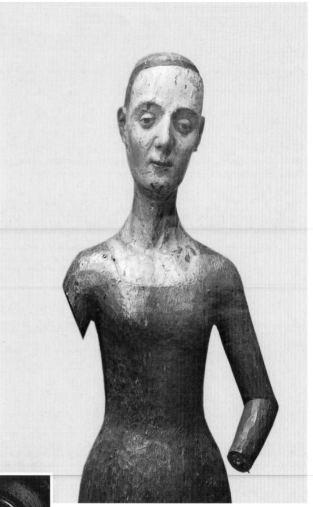

3 Funeral effigy of Catherine of France. *Copyright Dean and Chapter of Westminster*

4 Edmund Beaufort, Duke of Somerset, Beauchamp Chapel, St Mary's, Warwick.

5 The arms of Owen Tudor. *Copyright Odejea/ Wikimedia Commons*

6 The arms of Edmund Beaufort, Duke of Somerset. *Copyright Ipankonin/Wikimedia Commons*

7 The arms of Edmund 'Tudor'. *Copyright Ipankonin/Wikimedia Commons*

8 The arms of Jasper 'Tudor'. *Copyright Ipankonin/ Wikimedia Commons*

9 Edward IV, after a miniature in Caxton's *Chronicles of England* of 1480.

10 Eleanor Talbot, reconstructed image, based on a skull from the Whitefriars site in Norwich, and on portraits of Eleanor's sister and niece. *Copyright Mark Satchwill*

11   Elizabeth Woodville, after the portrait at Queens' College Cambridge.

12 Henry VIII, after Holbein.

13 Catherine of Aragon.

14 Anne Boleyn.

15 Elizabeth I, after the portrait by Zucchero at Hatfield House.

16 Robert Dudley, Earl of Leicester, after the portrait of 1587–88 at Kenilworth Castle.

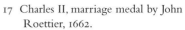
17 Charles II, marriage medal by John Roettier, 1662.

18 Lucy Walter, engraving by E. Scriven, 1810.

19 James II.

20 'Charles III', eighteenth-century engraving after Anker Smith.

21 Clementina Walkinshaw, Countess of Albestroff, from an anonymous English School portrait, around 1760.

22 The young King George III.

23 George IV as Prince of Wales, engraving by William Satchwell Leney, 1794.

24 Maria Smythe (Fitzherbert), engraving by Conde, 1792, after a portrait by Richard Cosway.

25 Caroline of Brunswick as Princess of Wales, engraving by Schiavonetti from *The Lady's Monthly Museum*, 1800.

26 Monument to Maria Smythe (Fitzherbert), St John the Baptist Catholic Church, Brighton. Although the tomb inscription records Maria's surname as that of her second husband, Thomas Fitzherbert, her effigy is depicted wearing *three* wedding rings.

27 Queen Victoria alias 'Mrs Brown'.

28 'Brown Study' – a contemporary cartoon of John Brown with his tame lion.

29 Albert Victor, Duke of Clarence.

30 George V as a young prince.

31 Admiral Sir Michael Culme-Seymour.

32 Grave of Laura Culme-Seymour, Ta' Braxia Cemetery, Malta. *Copyright Robert Galea-Naudi*

In due course James was succeeded by his second son, Charles I, whose heir, the subject of this chapter, and the future King Charles II, was born at St James's Palace on 29 May 1630. He was the second son of Charles I and Henrietta Maria of France. Actually, an elder brother had been born about a year earlier, but he had died almost immediately, so that from the moment of his birth, Prince Charles was heir to the thrones of England, Scotland and Ireland.[2]

Charles [II] grew up to be tall (6ft 2in in height as an adult), and dark. While not conventionally handsome, he had a striking and attractive appearance. In the 1650s, at the time when we are chiefly concerned with him, Mme de Motteville described the young prince as 'well made with a swarthy complexion agreeing well with his fine black eyes, a large ugly mouth, a graceful and dignified carriage and a fine figure'.[3]

Prince Charles's youth had been overshadowed by the outbreak of the English Civil War, which began in 1642. At the age of 12, Charles had accompanied his father, King Charles I, at the battle of Edgehill, and he subsequently participated in the campaigns of 1645, when he was the titular commander of his father's forces in the West Country. But early in 1646, when it became evident that the king was losing the war, Charles [II] left England, going first to the Scilly Isles and then to Jersey. Finally he sailed to France, where his mother, Queen Henrietta Maria, had sought refuge two years earlier, following the birth of her last child, Princess Henrietta, in Exeter.

After the execution of his father in 1649, Charles II spent eleven difficult years as an exiled and impoverished titular monarch, and it was during this period that his relationship with a girl called Lucy Walter developed. As we shall see, there are allegations that Charles married Lucy, who bore him a son, James, later created Duke of Monmouth.

In 1660 Charles II (later affectionately known as 'Old Rowley') was restored to his thrones, and two years later he married Catherine of Bragança, the Infanta of Portugal. Sadly, that royal marriage remained childless. However, Charles II consistently resisted suggestions that he divorce his queen and remarry in the hope of producing an heir.

Despite the difference in their religions, the Catholic Queen Catherine seems to have been fond of the Duke of Monmouth, Charles II's son by Lucy Walter. There are even reports that the queen herself believed that her husband may have been secretly married to Monmouth's mother.[4] After Charles II's death, when Monmouth attempted to claim the throne and was defeated by his uncle, King James II, it was to Queen Catherine that the young duke appealed for help. The Queen Dowager tried to save Monmouth's life – but to no avail.

The case of Charles II differs from many of the other cases we are considering, in that while a secret marriage is alleged against him, this involves no imputation of bigamy. This is simply a matter of dates. Lucy Walter, whom Charles is alleged to have married secretly prior to his accession, died in 1658, while Charles did not marry his queen, Catherine of Bragança, until four years later. A marriage between Charles and the Infanta Catarina-Henriqueta of Portugal had, indeed, first been proposed by the latter's father, King John IV, in 1644. However, the alliance was at that time rejected by the English court. Thus it was not until after the Restoration, in 1661, that Charles's Portuguese marriage was finally settled. The nuptial mass was celebrated in Lisbon on 23 April 1662. The wedding was re-enacted in Portsmouth on 21 May 1662. Thanks to the chronology of events there is no possible reason to doubt that the marriage between Charles and Catherine was valid, whether or not the king had previously been married to Lucy Walter.

In another respect, however, the case of Charles II shares a feature we have encountered in other instances of disputed royal marriage, in that the allegation of a secret marriage with Lucy Walter did not arise in a vacuum. It must be understood in the context of at least three other reported clandestine weddings in Charles' wider family. The first and most important of these was that of Charles II's younger brother, James, Duke of York [James II], to Anne Hyde. The secret marriage between James and Anne allegedly took place at Breda in the Netherlands, in 1659, and this wedding has been variously dated to either the month of November 1659 or to Christmas Eve of that year. Prior to the supposed marriage Anne had reportedly been James's mistress.[5] It was also in the Netherlands that Charles is usually said to have perhaps married Lucy Walter – possibly in 1648.

The alleged secret wedding of the Duke of York and Anne Hyde was not the only one of its kind in the Stuart royal family. One of the most celebrated of Charles I's army commanders in the Civil War had been the king's nephew, Prince Rupert of the Rhine, one of the numerous children of Charles I's elder sister, Elizabeth (Princess Royal, and subsequently Electress Palatine and Queen of Bohemia). Prince Rupert was unmarried during the war years, but in the early years after the Restoration he formed an alliance with Frances Bard (1646–1708), the daughter of another Civil War veteran. Frances later claimed to have been secretly married to Rupert in 1664. Like his first cousin, Charles II, Prince Rupert denied the secret marriage allegation, although – again like the king – he recognised the son whom Frances bore him in 1666, Dudley Bard, alias 'Dudley Rupert'. Later still Rupert lived with his actress mistress, Margaret Hughes, and there was some talk of the possibility of a marriage between them. However, no such marriage ever materialised, although Margaret bore the prince a daughter, Ruperta (later Ruperta Howe).

Moreover, in 1685, at the very time when the possibility of a marriage between Lucy Walter and Charles [II] was very much on people's lips in England, a third and very famous secret marriage was contracted by Charles II's first cousin, King Louis XIV of France. In the summer of 1683 Louis had lost his royal wife, Queen Marie-Thérèse, and at some point during the winter of 1685–86 he allegedly contracted a secret morganatic marriage with his companion, Françoise d'Aubigné (Mme de Maintenon). Although there is no documentary proof of such a marriage, it was universally credited at the time, and (unlike many of the other secret royal unions which we have been considering) the marriage between Louis XIV and Françoise d'Aubigné is also generally accepted by historians.

✠ ✠ ✠

Various and divergent accounts of Charles [II]'s alleged secret marriage to Lucy Walter exist, and although attention focuses chiefly on the Netherlands in 1648, several other locations and dates have been suggested. In fact, the stories about this alleged wedding are many, varied and mutually inconsistent. In themselves, however, such contradictions do not disprove the notion of a marriage since, as we have seen, even in respect of James [II]'s secret marriage to Anne Hyde a great deal of doubt and uncertainty remains. Thus some authorities doubt whether a secret ceremony between James and Anne ever took place at Breda, believing that Anne Hyde was simply James's mistress until 1660. However, following the Restoration of the Monarchy, there is no doubt that the marriage between James and Anne was privately but officially (re-?)enacted on 3 September 1660, at Worcester House in London, thereby giving their relationship a status beyond question. The London ceremony has been described by one writer as 'a shotgun wedding',[6] Anne being large with child at the time. But of course, if the couple had already married in secret, Anne's pregnancy would have been perfectly legitimate.[7]

The alleged secret marriage between Charles and Lucy could never have been made official in the same way as that of James and Anne, Lucy having died before the Restoration. Nevertheless, the fact of the wedding between James and Anne Hyde, coupled with the uncertainty about when and where their marriage actually took place, the rumours of a secret marriage in the Netherlands and the lack of surviving documentation in relation to that supposed event, all helped to strengthen the notion that, despite the lack of surviving evidence, a similar secret union might possibly have taken place some years earlier, also in the Netherlands, between Charles [II] and Lucy Walter. When similar stories began to circulate in 1664 about Prince Rupert, that only served to fan the flames.

Incidentally, it is interesting to compare the social status of Anne Hyde, Duchess of York, with that of Lucy Walter. Lucy has often had a bad press and was described by the contemporary diarist, John Evelyn, as 'a strumpet' and 'the daughter of some very mean creatures'.[8] While her eventual way of life may have invited censure, Lucy was actually quite well-born – the daughter of gentry and the descendant of aristocrats and kings. As for Anne Hyde, she was the daughter of gentry families on both her father's and her mother's side.[9] At first sight her background appears superficially similar to that of Lucy. Unlike Lucy, however, the Duchess of York enjoyed no known royal descent, and had no family connection with earlier generations of royal consorts.[10]

Lucy Walter, then, was a girl from Wales who had a relationship with the future King Charles II in his youth, during the troubled period of the English Civil War and Commonwealth. She bore Charles a son who, in his early childhood, was known as James Crofts. However, he was later given the surname Scott, and created Duke of Monmouth. Lucy subsequently had a daughter, Mary, but Charles refused to acknowledge paternity of this second child, and took no interest in her. Mary's father was probably Lord Taaffe, who subsequently adopted her. These basic facts are generally accepted.

Despite the increasing use of condoms in the seventeenth century, and the fact that these devices reputedly gained their name from a member of Charles II's household or circle, Charles II is, of course, famous for the number not only of his mistresses but also of his illegitimate progeny.[11] There would therefore be no particular reason for Lucy and her son to stand out above the rest were it not for the fact that in the 1670s and 1680s, when Lucy herself was long dead, the Duke of Monmouth was put forward by the Protestant Whigs as a rival heir to the throne, in opposition to his Catholic uncle, James, Duke of York [James II]. Monmouth's supporters were deeply interested in the question of whether or not his parents had been married to one another. If they had not, Monmouth was simply one of Charles II's many illegitimate children.[12] If, on the other hand, Lucy Walter had been married to Charles then Monmouth was a legitimate son and a valid claimant to the throne. Indeed, he would have been the king's only legitimate child, since his father's subsequent marriage to the Portuguese Infanta produced no offspring.

While those who supported the Duke of Monmouth claimed that Lucy Walter had been not Charles II's mistress but his wife, the rival supporters of Charles' younger brother, the Duke of York, vigorously opposed this claim, and did all in their power to denigrate Lucy. For this reason it is particularly important, in studying Lucy Walter, to distinguish clearly between two kinds of historical sources: those contemporaneous with the events to which they refer, and those which were written later, with hindsight, and with an ulterior motive. Anything written about Lucy and her children in the 1670s, the 1680s or later is almost bound to be slanted, either in favour of the Duke of Monmouth or in favour of the Duke of York. Such material must therefore be used with caution, taking careful note of its likely bias. Material which is contemporary, on the other hand, while not necessarily free from bias of some kind, is more likely to be trustworthy. In historical writing the distinction between contemporary and later source material is always significant. In the case of Lucy Walter, however, this distinction presents itself in a particularly extreme form.

Supporters of the Duke of York did their utmost to undermine Lucy. They described her as of low birth, a brunette of some cunning but of limited wit, a girl who lived by the sex trade and who ultimately also died by it, having contracted a sexually transmitted disease of some kind.[13] However, the legend that Lucy was of low birth is very easily disproved by reference to authentic source material in preference to partisan narrative. Actually, Lucy was born into the Welsh landed gentry. She had relations in the ranks of the aristocracy, and was herself of genuine Plantagenet royal descent, via the dukes of Norfolk (*see Family Tree 3*). It remains to be seen whether the remainder of the partisan, pro-James II account of Lucy's career will stand up any better than the story of her low birth when the spotlight of contemporary sources is turned upon it.

Lucy was probably born in Wales, at Roche Castle, Pembrokeshire, in about 1630.[14] Although no specific evidence seems to exist proving this to have been her birthplace, the assumption is not unreasonable, since her father certainly held Roche Castle (though he also had another house at Ravensdale).[15] Lucy's parents were William Walter and his wife, Elizabeth Prothero. Both belonged to the Welsh gentry. Lucy's mother was the niece of the first Lord Carbery, and on her mother's side she was one of the great-granddaughters of Lady Catherine Howard. Lady Catherine herself had been the daughter of Thomas Howard, second Duke of Norfolk. She was therefore the aunt of Queens Anne Boleyn and Catherine Howard, and a descendant of Edward I and his second wife, Margaret of France. Thus Lucy was by no means the low-born creature that some of her enemies later represented. She was, in fact, a first cousin (albeit at four generations' remove) of Anne Boleyn, one of the subjects of a previous chapter. Lucy also had links with Eleanor Talbot, since Eleanor's sister had been a duchess of Norfolk. Moreover, the mind of a Restoration playwright would draw specific parallels between Lucy's position and that of Eleanor (whose name had, in the seventeenth century, only recently been salvaged from the oblivion into which Henry VII had striven with might and main to cast it).[16] In addition, of course, Lucy and Eleanor shared royal descent from King Edward I.

Although Lucy seems to have received little in the way of formal education, she was brought up in a gentry milieu, with the social graces which would later enable her to mix with people of rank. However, in 1640 her parents parted, and the following year a long separation dispute between them commenced in the House of Lords.[17] Lucy left both Wales and her father, travelling with her mother to an England which was then on the brink of Civil War. With her mother she settled in London. According to the later accounts of James II and his father-in-law, Lord Clarendon,[18] Lucy is rumoured to have embarked on a love affair with Algernon Sidney, an officer in the Parliamentary army. Subsequently, she is said to have transferred her affections to his younger brother, Robert, who was a Royalist. This account is repeated as fact by Clifton in his recent biographical account of Lucy in the *Oxford Dictionary of National Biography*,[19] but there seems to be no contemporary evidence to support it. Other writers have argued that 'the account of her relationship with Algernon Sidney accords neither with the latter's known movements nor with his character', and James II is known to have had reasons for wishing to disparage Sidney as well as Lucy Walter.[20]

Monmouth supporters later alleged that Lucy met Charles, possibly in the West Country, in about 1645, and that a relationship developed between the young couple (who were then in their mid-teens). It is even suggested that a secret marriage took place between them at that time. Later rumours and publications dating from the nineteenth century have claimed that a record of Charles's marriage to Lucy once existed in the parish register of the church of St Thomas, Haverfordwest, but that the record was destroyed early in the eighteenth century. It is true that the Walter family had a house in Haverfordwest.[21] However, there is no real evidence that such a marriage record ever existed, or that it was destroyed as reported.

Nor does a meeting between Charles and Lucy at that time seem plausible. Charles's movements at that period may be briefly summarised as follows: early in 1645 his father sent him to Bristol to take command of the Royalist forces in the west. On 2 March 1646 he escaped to the Scillies, moving on to Jersey on 16 April. On 26 June 1646 he landed in France, where he remained until the desertion of an English fleet from the Parliamentarian to the Royalist side took him to the Netherlands to assume command of the newly arrived ships. Charles arrived in The Hague on 12 July 1648. Nothing whatever is known of Lucy Walter's movements during the period 1645 to 1647, but there is no solid evidence of any meeting with Charles prior to 1648.

Nevertheless, a letter from Sir Edward Hyde (later Lord Clarendon and father-in-law of James II) to Mr Secretary Nicholas has been cited by one author as possible evidence of such a meeting, and indeed, as evidence of a marriage between Lucy and Charles. Although this letter does not name Lucy, and probably has, in reality, nothing whatever to do with her, the fact that it has been cited elsewhere as evidence of her marriage means that we must review it here. The letter is dated 7 March 1646/47, and in it Hyde states that:

> I am far from secure, for many reasons, that the intelligence from London of the Prince's Marriage may not be true, we were apprehensive of it before he went, and spoke freely to him our opinions of the fatal consequences of it.[22]

This letter has been interpreted as implying Charles' presence in London, but that is clearly an error. In March 1646/47 Charles was not in London, but in France. London is merely cited in Hyde's letter as the source of a marriage rumour in respect of Charles. And the rumour in question referred not to a marriage with Lucy Walter but to a wedding with Charles's French cousin, *la Grande Mademoiselle*.[23] The courtship of these royal cousins had been encouraged by the prince's Catholic mother (and *Mademoiselle*'s aunt), Queen Henrietta Maria, and Hyde's evident disapproval of the match was doubtless occasioned by a combination of the religion and the nationality of the prospective bride. At all events, the marriage rumour was false. In the context of Charles's courtship of Mademoiselle, however, it should also be noted that Charles is on record as having promised his cousin in July 1649 that he would terminate any other attachments if they married.[24] This hardly seems compatible with the notion that Charles was then already married to Lucy Walter.

It is not known how Lucy reached the Netherlands. The suggestion was later made that she came there in company with Robert Sidney. This suggestion may be correct, although there is actually no surviving contemporary evidence to support it. Hyde (who was of course a hostile witness) later wrote that Lucy came to The Hague with the deliberate intention of meeting and seducing Charles, but there is no reason to believe him. 'On balance, however, likelihood lies with the idea that Lucy Walter was introduced to Charles at the Hague by a courtier in July 1648',[25] and that Charles quickly became enamoured of her. Harris suggests that 'Charles met Lucy during a brief visit to The Hague in July 1648, when she was still under the protection of Colonel Robert Sidney (1628–68), and it was during this time that Monmouth was evidently conceived'.[26] At this period the 18-year-old Lucy was described, even by her enemies, as an attractive brunette, and it would be otiose to doubt her charms, since it seems inherently improbable that Charles would have deliberately selected an unattractive partner. The Baronne d'Aulnoy, who had seen her, said of Lucy:

> her beauty was so perfect that when the King saw her in Wales where she was, he was so charmed and ravished and enamoured that in the misfortunes which ran through the first years of his reign he knew no other sweetness or joy than to love her, and be loved by her … He was so very young, and this was his first passion.[27]

For some reason Lucy was known in the Netherlands as 'Mrs Barlow'. Her motives for using this alias are unknown.

> Charles was evidently besotted with the ravishing 'Mrs Barlow', and soon his devotion to her welfare became such a talking point that rumours concerning their relationship sprang up like weeds. It was assumed by many, from the very beginning, that they had secretly married while Charles's passion was overwhelming his judgement, and so firmly established did the belief become that official denials in later years only served to reinforce it.[28]

There seems no possible room for doubt that a sexual relationship rapidly developed between Charles and Lucy. When, in 1649, Lucy bore a baby boy who was christened James, Charles acknowledged his paternity without hesitation.[29] The arguments which James II would later advance to suggest a different father for the boy were clearly specious, and motivated by self-interest.[30] Charles II consistently treated the boy as his son, and there is widespread modern agreement that 'portraits of the two as adolescents show a clear family likeness'.[31] Indeed, Oliver Cromwell, who briefly held the future Duke of Monmouth and his mother in the Tower of London during the summer of 1656, specifically commented at that time upon the boy's resemblance to 'Charles Stuart'.[32] And although, after the Restoration, couplets could sometimes be heard in London denigrating Monmouth's claim to be Charles II's son,[33] modern scientific evidence has now proved beyond any possible doubt that Charles II was Monmouth's father. Y-chromosome DNA tests have shown that Monmouth's direct descendants, 'the Dukes of Buccleuch descend in the male line from the same stock as do the Dukes of Grafton, St Albans and Richmond, which of course is from King Charles II'.[34]

Charles and Lucy can have spent only a short time together before Charles put to sea with the fleet. However:

> most biographers have assumed that Charles resumed his relationship with Lucy when he returned to the Netherlands in September 1648, although the historical record is obscure … John Evelyn later recalled meeting Lucy at St Germain-en-Laye in August 1649, where she had come to be introduced to Charles's mother, Henrietta Maria.[35]

Lucy's introduction to the queen mother in 1649 is another of the intriguing aspects of this story, and it was to have a sequel (see below). However, shortly after the meeting, Charles left for Jersey, so as to be in a better position to monitor developments in Scotland and Ireland, and a year later he embarked for Scotland, in a last-ditch attempt to rescue the royalist cause'.[36]

During Charles' absence Lucy appears to have attached herself to Viscount Taafe, and in 1651 she gave birth to a daughter, Mary, of whom, as we have seen, Taafe was probably the father. At all events, Charles II never extended paternal recognition to Mary, although some have sought to argue that she may have been his daughter.[37] When Charles returned to France following the royalist defeat at Worcester in September 1651, he made no attempt to revive his affair with Lucy.[38] Lucy seems to have taken this badly, but her unpredictable behaviour merely strengthened Charles's motives for dissociating himself from her. She began to create scandals and scenes, and it must have become evident to Charles now (if it had not already been so before) that Lucy had become something of a liability to his cause. By about 1653 at the latest, he seems definitively to have ended his relationship with her.[39] This, Lucy clearly found very hard to accept. If she ever invented a private fantasy of having been married to Charles it may well have been at about this time, for had she believed herself married to him earlier her desertion to Lord Taafe would have been both reprehensible and dangerous, and would have provided good grounds for Charles to set her aside.

During the 1650s we have what has been claimed as possible evidence that Charles' elder sister, the Princess Royal,[40] may have had dealings with Lucy Walter. This evidence comprises three letters from the Princess to her brother, all of which speak of 'your wife'.[41] For example, she wrote to her brother that:

> Your Mothere says that the greatest thankfulness she can show for the honour of your kind remembrance is to have a special care of your wife for feare her husband here may make her forget them that are absent. Your wife thanks you in her own hand and still though she begs me very hard to help her.[42]

However, some authorities have questioned whether the word 'wife' necessarily carried the implication of marriage at this period, or whether perhaps the use of the word in this context might have been some kind of private code.[43] The latter suggestion does certainly seem to be a real possibility, because the extract quoted above is strange in several respects. First, it refers to 'your Mothere' – as though Charles and his sister did not share the same mother. Secondly, it speaks as though the 'Mothere' in question was in The Hague with the Princess Royal when the letter was written. But Queen Henrietta Maria was actually in Paris at that time. The third strange point is the reference to the wife's 'husband here'. This is reinforced in a later letter, which informs Charles that:

> Your wife … thinks of another husband, and does not follow your example of being as constant a wife as you are a husband: 'tis a frailty they say is given to the sex, therefore you will pardon her I hope.[44]

Unfortunately the letters mention no names, so that, as with so much evidence in this case, their testimony remains equivocal. Since a king is usually considered to be married to his kingdom, is it possible that the 'wife' was England, and that the letters were coded to contain some kind of news of political events? Alternatively it has been suggested that they may refer to the Princess Henrietta Catherine of Orange, with whom Charles was then in love.[45]

Nevertheless, those who insist that Lucy Walter was meant can cite direct and indirect supporting evidence from three other quarters which suggests that in the 1650s Lucy may have been describing herself as Charles's wife. The first evidence comes from English Government sources. In 1656, Charles seems to have acted firmly to rid himself of Lucy's embarrassing presence. Supplied with a little money and a pearl necklace, she was embarked with both her children on a ship bound for England, where her arrival soon caught the eye of the Republican Government. It was at this time that Lucy and her children found themselves in the Tower of London – the closest that Lucy ever came to living in an English royal palace!

During the summer of 1656, while Lucy was in detention, she and her son were seen by Oliver Cromwell, who referred to Lucy as the woman who 'passeth under the character of Charles Stuart's wife or mistress'.[46] Cromwell's warrant indicates that Lucy may have represented herself to her captors as married to Charles. Moreover, a later pamphlet produced by Monmouth's supporters claimed:

> That there was in Olivers time, a Letter intercepted from the King to the said Lady, then in the Tower, superscribed, to his Wife. Nor is it unknown with what fear and homage the Kings party in England, at that time paid their Devotion and testified their Obedience to her. For as they addressed her upon the Knee, so by that and many other Symbols, they declared that they esteemed her for no less than the lawful Wife of their King and Master.[47]

These later comments must be treated with some caution, of course, first because we have no direct evidence to support them, and second, because it seems somewhat strange that Charles, who had apparently terminated his active relationship with Lucy in 1651, should have written to her as his wife in 1656, particularly in view of his later very firm denials. Nevertheless it seems probable that the later recollections of those witnesses who recalled Lucy herself as claiming, in the 1650s, to have been married to Charles may have voiced neither more nor less than the truth. It is also alleged that Lucy's own mother referred, at this period, to her daughter's marriage with 'the king'.[48]

Lucy's visit to England with her children in 1656 was of short duration. After a period of detention the government in London clearly saw that she represented no danger to them. At the same time they perceived that she might be used to embarrass the exiled Charles. They therefore shipped her back to the Low Countries.

The second source of evidence for Lucy's married status in the 1650s comes from France, and the exiled court of the queen mother. We have already seen that Henrietta Maria received Lucy in 1469. Subsequently 'she allowed Lucy to be present at her sick bed which was a very great honour indeed'.[49] Moreover, the queen mother, who showed no interest whatever in Charles [II]'s other bastards, also took a unique interest in her grandson, Lucy's son, 'taking him to stay with her outside Paris and treating him with the honour and esteem normally reserved for a prince of the blood. In Paris he had even publicly been greeted as Prince of Wales'.[50]

The third piece of evidence in support of a marriage, dating from the 1650s, is contained in a letter from Daniel O'Neill, Charles' Groom of the Bedchamber. On 8 March 1654 he wrote to Charles that:

> … if he [Ormonde] had been here when he was expected, which was two moneths ago, in all likely hood you might have been at home with your wife and children now peaceably.[51]

As usual, there are no names mentioned, so the precise meaning of this letter is open to interpretation. Possibly 'at home with your wife and children' was merely being used as an idiom in this case, with no specific or personal reference to Charles' matrimonial status. Alternatively it has been suggested that, once again, a code to which the key is now lost was being used in this letter.

Back in Brussels, after her return from England, Lucy tried to make use of her growing son against the boy's father. A prolonged period of strife then ensued, during which Charles sought repeatedly to rescue the boy from his mother's increasingly disorderly and stressful household. Lucy was finally persuaded to surrender the child. This was in 1658, by which time she was already sick. Later reports suggest that she was suffering from a sexually transmitted disease of some kind. However, these accounts are imprecise and unsubstantiated. Towards the end of 1658, Lucy died, apparently in Paris, where she was said to have been buried, but even these final points of her story are the subject of some uncertainty.[52]

Although witnesses may accurately have reported Lucy's claims to be married to Charles, in itself that does not guarantee that those claims were true. It nevertheless constitutes evidence of a kind, seeming to permit three possible explanations. The first is that, while the witnesses were truthfully and accurately reporting what they had heard and seen, Lucy herself had been lying, or fantasising. The second possibility is that Lucy had been telling the truth as she saw it, but that she was in fact mistaken. The third possibility, of course, is that there had indeed been a marriage of some kind between her and Charles.

Rather like the case of the alleged marriage of Eleanor Talbot to Edward IV (see above), which was discussed much more after Eleanor died than it ever was during her lifetime, the alleged marriage of Lucy Walter to Charles II became a major topic of conversation after Lucy's death. Nor is this retrospective reference to Eleanor Talbot's story merely a whim of the present author. During the seventeenth century the first attempts were being made to rescue Eleanor from the oblivion into which Henry VII had cast her, and although her story was still little-known and not entirely understood, possible parallels between her case and that of Lucy Walter were actually noted and commented upon at the time.[53]

Since Lucy had died in 1658, two years before the Restoration of the Monarchy, it was, of course, impossible to invite her comments on the question of her marriage with Charles during the 1670s and 1680s, when this became a very important issue politically. However, Charles II was alive, and he maintained firmly and consistently that he had never been married to Lucy. The king even went to the length of writing out in his own hand, and signing, the following statements:

There being a false and malicious report industriously spread abroad by some who are neither friends to me nor to the Duke of Monmouth, as if I should have been either contracted or married to his mother; and though I am most confident that this idle story cannot have any effect in this age, yet I thought it my duty in relation to the succession of the Crown, and that future ages may not have any further pretence to give disturbance on that score, or on any other of this nature, to declare, as I do declare, in the presence of Almighty God, that I never was married nor gave contract to any woman whatsoever, but to my wife Queen Catherine, to whom I am now married.

In witness whereof, I sett my hand at Whitehall, the sixth day of January, 1678. Charles R.[54]

For the avoiding of any dispute which may happen in time to come concerning the possession of the Crowne, I do heere declare in the presence of Almighty God, that I never gave nor made any contract of marriage, nor was married to any woman whatsoever, but to my present wife Queene Caterine now liveing.

Whitehall the 3 day of March 1678/79. Charles R.[55]

The king's hope that the question would cease to be discussed in the future was to prove utterly vain, despite his very explicit public denials. In point of fact Charles had already made it clear much earlier, that his son by Lucy was a bastard, for shortly after the Restoration he seems to have dallied briefly with the idea of legitimising him.[56]

It is not surprising, therefore, to find that some popular ballards of the 1670s and 1680s castigated the Duke for not accepting his illegitimate status, and for failing to offer his father the filial obedience that was his due:

Advice to the Duke of Monmouth.[57]

Awake, vain man! 'tis time th' Abuse to see;
Awake, and guard thy heedless Loyalty
From all the Snares are laid for it and thee.
No longer let that busie juggling Crew
(Who to their own mis-deeds entitle you,)
Abuse your ear: Consider, Sir, the State
Of our unhappy Isle, disturb'd of late
With causeless jealousies, ungrounded Fear,
Obstinate Faction and seditious Care;
Gone quite distracted for Religion's sake;
And nothing: their hot brains can cooler make
(So great's the deprivation of their sense,)
But the excluding of their lawful Prince:
A Prince, in whose each Act is clearly shown
That Heaven design'd him to adorn a Throne;
Which (tho' He scorns by Treason to pursue,)
He ne'er will quit, if it become His due.
Then lay betimes your mad Ambition down,
Nor let the dazzling lustre of a Crown
Bewitch your Thoughts; but think what mighty care
Attend the Crowns that Lawful Princes wear;
But when ill Title's added to the weight,
How insupportable's the Load of State!

Believe those working Brains your Name abuse;
You only for their Property do use:
And when they'r strong enough to stand alone,
You, as an useless Thing, away'l be thrown.
Think you, how dear you have already paid
For the fine Projects your false Friends had laid.
When by the Rabble's fruitless zeal you lost
Your Royal Father's love, your growing Fortune crost:
Say, was your Bargain, think ye, worth the cost?

Remember what relation, Sir, you bear
To Royal Charles; Subject and Son you are,
Two names that strict Obedience does require;
What Frenzy then does your rash Thoughts inspire,
Thus by Disloyal Deeds to add more cares
To them of the bright Burden that he wears?
Why, with such eager speed hunt you a Crown
You're so unfit to wear, were it your own?

With bows, and leers, and little Arts, you try
A rude unthinking Tumult's Love to buy:
And he who stoops to do so mean a thing,
Shows, He by Heaven was ne're design'd for King.

Would you be great, do things are great and brave,
And scorn to be the *Mobile*'s dull Slave:[58]
Tell the base Great Ones, and the shouting throng,
You scorn a Crown worn in another's wrong.
Prove your high Birth by Deeds noble and good,
But strive not to Legitimate your Blood.

Chiefly because of the king's explicit denials, historians have generally been inclined to dismiss the story of Lucy Walter's marriage to Charles II as a fabrication. However, in this context we should not, perhaps, overlook the fact of the later official denials by George [IV] of *his* marriage to Maria Smythe (Fitzherbert) – which were, in fact, blatant lies motivated by self-interest – or the denials on the part of George V of any relationship with the daughter of Admiral Sir Michael Culme-Seymour – which, in spite of the legal rulings of 1911, seem open to certain questions (see below).

The alleged marriage of Charles [II] to Lucy Walter has been widely seen as part of a propaganda ploy to establish the legitimacy of the Duke of Monmouth's claim to the throne in the 1670s and 1680s. There is absolutely no doubt that attempts were made to use accounts of the marriage for that purpose and at that time. However, it also seems clear that the story of Lucy's marriage to the king was not *invented* in the 1670s, or with the specific aim of supporting her son's candidature for the throne. As we have seen, rumours of a marriage had apparently been current much earlier, in the 1650s.

The fact that Lucy herself apparently claimed during her lifetime to be married to Charles, while it does not, in itself, authenticate the alleged marriage, does tend to refute the notion that the story was simply political propaganda invented by the Duke of Monmouth and his supporters. Indeed, it is probable that some of Monmouth's adherents really believed in the marriage. Even Monmouth himself may genuinely have credited the story – or at least have been in doubt about the truth.

At the same time, however, superficially it seems clear, both from circumstantial evidence and from the direct statements of King Charles II himself, that in reality this particular secret royal marriage was never anything more than a fantasy. Charles II greatly loved his son Monmouth, and did everything in his power to promote the young man's career. In the light of this it seems incredible that the king would have deliberately bastardised his son if the latter had, in reality, been a legitimate heir to the throne.

In fact this very point mystified Monmouth's supporters in the 1680s. At that time a claim was circulating regarding the existence of a Black Box which allegedly contained documentary proof of a marriage between Charles II and Lucy Walter. One of Monmouth's adherents, Robert Fergusson, a Presbyterian from Scotland, who would later draft the duke's disastrous proclamation of his kingship, wrote a pamphlet about this Black Box. It was Fergusson's contention that the story of the box was nothing more than a myth: a myth, moreover, which was designed to discredit the duke's claims. As Fergusson put it to his unnamed correspondent:

> Your Lordship, whose conversation hath given you great advantages of know-ing the reports of the World in relation to the Kings Marriage with the Duke of Monmonths Mother, can easily recollect that there was never so much as a sug-gestion given out, till of late, of any such thing as a Black Box ... For they who judg'd it conducible to their present Interest to have the D. of M's. Title to the Crown not only discredited but exposed, thought it necessary, instead of nakedly enquiring whether he be the Kings Legitimate or only Natural Son; to bring; on the Stage a circumstance no way annex d with it, supposing that this being found a Fable, the Marriage itself of the K. with the said Ds. Mother, would have undergone the same Censure.[59]

In the same pamphlet, however, Fergusson went on to express his astonishment at Charles II's conduct in relation to Monmouth in the following terms:

> A more unaccountable thing yet than all the former is, to see the King so far concern himself in having the Succession declared and determined. For it is not usual to find a Prince appear in favour of a Brother, when so many are in the Belief, that he hath a Legitimate Son of his own. Many Kings have endeavoured the advancement of their Bastard Children, to the exclusion of their nearest Relations of the right Blood; Only Charles the 2d will be the first on the File of History, that when nothing but his bare Word was needful to the settling his Dominions on his Son as Legitimately born. He alone, and in the face of strong suspitions to the contrary would insinuate him to be only his Natural Son.[60]

The dispute regarding the alleged marriage of Charles II and Lucy Walter did not end with the death of the key players in the drama. Arguments continued long after Monmouth's attempt to establish himself as 'King James II' had failed, and long after his head had been brutally hacked from his body. Finally, therefore, we should briefly consider a much later story about the discovery of a record of Charles [II]'s marriage to Lucy Walter amongst the family papers of their descendants, the Dukes of Buccleuch. It was the fifth Duke who was said to have found the paper.[61] After some reflection, it is reported that he decided to burn it, because 'that might cause a lot of trouble'.[62] While some writers have accepted that a document of some kind was found and destroyed, it is, of course, very difficult at this stage to verify the point beyond question. And even if a document was found, its subsequent destruction has unfortunately ensured that there is now not the remotest possibility of assessing its authenticity.

However, it is extremely difficult to believe that whatever was found could have constituted clear and irrefutable proof of a marriage: for how would a copy of the marriage record of Charles and Lucy have entered the Buccleuch family archives, and at what date? The Duke of Monmouth saw his mother for the last time in 1658, when he was about 9 years old. It is highly unlikely that, if Lucy held a document proving her marriage to Charles, she would have surrendered this to her young son just at the point when Charles was about to remove the boy from her custody. Conversely, if such a paper had remained amongst Lucy's documents until the time of her death in Paris, then how would it have reached her son or his descendants? Moreover, it seems incredible that, if Monmouth himself had ever possessed such a document, he would not have produced it, either during his father's reign, or at that fatal moment of his attempted coup in 1685, when he landed at Lyme [Regis] in Dorset and allowed himself to be proclaimed and crowned 'King James II'.

We shall leave the last word on the question of Lucy Walter's marriage, to the poet Dryden. While clearly admiring the Duke of Monmouth, Dryden nevertheless considered him illegitimate and categorised Lucy Walter not as Charles' true wife, but merely as a royal 'slave' or 'concubine':

Absalom and Achitophel (extract)

In pious times, ere priestcraft did begin,
Before polygamy was made a sin;
When man on many multiplied his kind,
Ere one to one was cursedly confined;
When nature prompted, and no law denied,
Promiscuous use of concubine and bride;
Then Israel's monarch[63] after heaven's own heart,
His vigorous warmth did variously impart

To wives and slaves; and, wide as his command,
Scattered his Maker's image through the land.
Michal,[64] of royal blood, the crown did wear,
A soil ungrateful to the tiller's care:
Not so the rest; for several mothers bore
To godlike David several sons before.
But since like slaves his bed they did ascend,
No true succession could their seed attend.
Of all the numerous progeny was none
So beautiful, so brave, as Absalon;[65]
Whether inspired by some diviner lust,
His father got him with a greater gust;
Or that his conscious destiny made way,
By manly beauty, to imperial sway.

John Dryden, 1681

14

DR AND MRS THOMSON

Until recently in Scotland, there was a form of common law marriage called 'marriage by cohabitation with habit and repute'.

The theory behind this law was that if a man and woman cohabited as husband and wife in Scotland for sufficient time and were generally held and reputed to be husband and wife and were free to marry each other, they would be presumed to have consented to marry each other and if this presumption was not overturned, they would be considered to be legally married.

This form of common law marriage has now been abolished by the Family Law (Scotland) Act 2006 which came into force on 4 May 2006.[1]

Monmouth's failure to prove himself legitimate or make good his attempt to seize the Crown left his uncle James, Duke of York [James II], on the throne. But James' Catholicism, coupled with his political insensitivity, combined to bring about his removal in the Glorious Revolution of 1688. From this point a split occurred in the royal family between the reigning (but in terms of blood-right, usurping) Protestant heirs, and the rightful (in terms of bloodline) but exiled Catholic heirs. It is the history of the exiled Catholic Stuarts that we shall follow first, because that presents us with our next example of a disputed royal marriage. Later we shall pick up the Protestant line of descent – which also has stories of disputed royal marriages.

✠ ✠ ✠

Superficially, based on the summary of Scottish marriage law given at the head of this chapter, the alleged marriage of 'Charles III' and Clementina, Countess of Albestroff, actually seems to be potentially one of the clearest disputed royal marriage cases which we have to consider. Nevertheless, this 'marriage' continues to be largely ignored and overlooked by historians, who still persist in describing Clementina as Charles' mistress. The key, of course, as we sought to establish at the beginning of this book, is to look at the marriage law in force at the time when the disputed marriage is alleged to have been contracted. And in this particular case it is not the marriage laws of England, or of the United Kingdom, which concern us, but the marriage laws of Scotland, because Clementina was certainly Scottish, Charles was of Scottish ancestry and (at the time of their meeting) a Scottish (as well as English) prince, and the couple probably met and began their relationship in Scotland.

The principal characters in this story are possibly not so well-known in Britain as some of the other royalty we have been studying, because of the revolution of 1688, and the consequent exile of the male line of the royal house of Stuart. In 1701 an important piece of legislation was enacted which fundamentally affected the order of succession to the throne in England, Scotland and Ireland. This was the Act of Settlement, which debarred from the throne all members of the royal family who were Catholic, or who married a Catholic. It was as a result of this act that 'James III', 'Charles III' and 'Henry IX' – who should have succeeded their father and grandfather, King James II – were excluded from the throne and forced to live in exile. In some ways the act was unfairly enforced, for although 'Charles [III]', or 'Bonnie Prince Charlie', at one stage of his life renounced his Catholic faith and converted to Anglicanism, he did not thereby find himself reinstated in the order of succession. The name Bonnie Prince Charlie is probably familiar to many people, and may be the appellation by which the would-be Stuart king 'Charles III' is best remembered.

Charles Edward Louis John Casimir Silvester Severino Maria Stuart, known to his father as 'Carluccio', was born at the Palazzo Muti in Rome on 31 December 1720. His father was James Francis Edward Stuart, who was recognised in several European countries as 'James III and VIII', rightful King of England and Scotland. Charles' mother was Maria Clementina Sobieska, a Polish princess and the grand-daughter of the late King John III of Poland.

Charles' father, 'James III', had been born on 10 June 1688 at St James's Palace, the son of the reigning king, James II, by his second wife, Mary of Modena. The royal couple's Catholicism was unpopular in late seventeenth-century Britain, and there had been a widespread hope that eventually James II would be succeeded by one of his two surviving Protestant daughters, Mary and Anne, the children of his first wife, Anne Hyde. Under these circumstances, the birth of Prince James had been perceived as a threat that James' Catholicism would be perpetuated indefinitely. As a result, attempts were made to suggest that the newly born Prince was a changeling, substituted for the real royal baby (who had been stillborn) by means of a warming pan inserted in the queen's bed. Within months of his birth Queen Mary, anxious about her son's safety, had taken him to France, leaving James II to try to defend his throne – unsuccessfully as things turned out.

When James II was deposed in favour of his daughter and son-in-law/nephew, Mary II and William III, he joined the queen and the young prince in France, and it was there that the future 'James III' was brought up. When James II died in 1701, France, Spain, the Papal States and Modena recognised the 13-year-old prince as rightful King of England and Scotland, with the titles of 'James III and VIII'.

The accession in Britian of his half-sister, Queen Anne, might have appeared at first to offer some hope that eventually the young James might regain his thrones. Anne had no surviving children, and English Tories might perhaps have been willing to consider recognising the claims of 'James III' had he, in turn, been willing to renounce Catholicism. However, James absolutely refused to abandon his faith, and when Queen Anne died this led to the establishment in England of the Protestant Hanoverian dynasty.

The new king, George I, was very eager to prevent the continuation of the exiled Catholic Stuart line, and when 'James III' was betrothed to the wealthy heiress, Princess Maria Clementina Sobieska of Poland, the Hanoverian sovereign tried hard to prevent their marriage. At his instigation the Holy Roman Emperor Charles VI arrested Maria Clementina and imprisoned her in Innsbruck Castle. However, the intrepid princess escaped and fled to Bologna, where she was married by proxy to 'James III' (who was then in Spain). The royal couple were finally married in person on 3 September 1719, and their first son, Charles, was born just over a year later. Subsequently the couple also had a second son, Henry, later created Duke of York by his father, in the Jacobite peerage.

As for Clementina Walkinshaw, later Countess of Albestroff in Lorraine,[2] she was born in 1720, possibly at Camlachie in Scotland. Some accounts name her birthplace as Rome, but this is unlikely. She was roughly of an age with her future partner, for 'Charles [III]' was born in Rome on 31 December 1720. Of course it is obvious that Clementina was named in honour of Charles' mother, the Polish princess – and the Jacobite English and Scottish 'queen' – Maria Clementina Sobieska. Writers who ascribe Clementina Walkinshaw's birth to Rome also assume that 'Queen' Maria Clementina was her godmother and that this accounts for the baby girl's name. However, this is improbable. There is no evidence that Clementina Walkinshaw was ever in Rome as a child. Moreover, reportedly, other girls born to Jacobite families at that time were also named in honour of the new 'queen'.[3] Incidentally, various versions of Clementina Walkinshaw's name are extant, including 'Clementine' and 'Clemintine', but the version which will be used here is 'Clementina'.

Clementina was the youngest of the ten daughters of Lieutenant Colonel Sir John Walkinshaw of Barrowfield (1671–1731), a wealthy Glasgow merchant, an Episcopalian and a Jacobite who had fought in the 1715 uprising on behalf of the Old Pretender ['James III and VIII']. Her mother was Catherine Patterson, the daughter of Sir Hugh Patterson of Bannockburn. Catherine's date of birth is variously cited as 1677 and 1683. The couple married in 1703, and the eldest of their ten daughters, Barbara Walkinshaw, was born at Barrowfield the following year. Two years later, in 1706, a second daughter, Margaret, made her debut. The dates of birth of the later daughters are only known approximately. Catherine Walkinshaw was born in about 1708, Anne probably in 1709, Elizabeth in about 1711, Mary in 1713, Jean in 1715, Helen in 1717 and Lyonella in 1718.[4]

Clementina's father owned land at Camlachie and also the estate of Barrowhill. He had been captured during the 1715 rebellion and was briefly imprisoned at Stirling Castle, from which he escaped to the European mainland. In 1717 he was pardoned by the British Government and returned to Scotland. Indeed, his third daughter, Catherine, subsequently entered the service of the Hanoverian dynasty in London. In 1736 she was appointed 'sempstress' (seamstress) to Augusta of Saxe-Gotha-Altenburg (1719–72), the consort of Frederick, Prince of Wales (1707–51),[5] and by 1767 she was a woman of the bedchamber to the (by then) dowager Princess of Wales. She remained in Princess Augusta's service until 1772, and her Hanoverian royal employment, together with the curious fact that she was Clementina's sister, was recorded in surviving letters written by Horace Walpole, later fourth Earl of Orford (1717–97).[6]

Clementina was largely educated on the Continent and she was either baptised or – perhaps because she was educated at a convent – brought up as a Roman Catholic. At all events she was a Catholic throughout her adult life. She returned to Scotland in time for the 1745 Jacobite uprising, and was staying at the home of her uncle, Sir Hugh Walkinshaw, at Bannockburn near Stirling, in January 1746, when Sir Hugh received Prince Charles (Bonnie Prince Charlie) there as a guest. This was her first meeting with the Jacobite Prince of Wales. The prince's visit was short, but later in January he came back to Sir Hugh's house so that Clementina could nurse him while he recovered from a bad cold. Obviously Clementina had attracted the prince's notice. This is clear both from his return to Bannockburn, and from later events. The fact that Clementina remained unmarried in the following years has been interpreted as evidence of her love for Prince Charles. However, there is no firm evidence that the relationship between the young couple progressed to a physical level in 1746.

After his disastrous defeat at the battle of Culloden, Prince Charles' stay in Scotland was cut short. He was forced to flee back to France where he had illicit relationships first with his cousin, Louise de Montbazon (whom he deserted when she became pregnant), and then with the Princesse de Talmont. Later, in 1750, during a secret visit to London, Charles nominally forsook his Roman Catholic faith and became an Anglican, in the vain hope that this would help the Stuart cause. During this period Charles fell victim to depression, which subsequently caused him to succumb to alcoholism.

In 1752 Clementina was again on the Continent, at Dunkirk. 'Much against the wishes of her family she had decided to enter one of those religious houses for the daughters of nobility on the Continent … She left Scotland sometime in

1751 and possibly stayed at a convent in Boulogne'.[7] The initiative for renewed contact between her and Prince Charles seems to have come from the prince, who made it clear, even at the cost of some important friendships, that he was planning a sexual relationship with Clementina. First he sent her fifty *louis d'or*. Subsequently he sent Sir Henry Goring to Dunkirk to ask Clementina to come to Ghent and live with him. Many Jacobites were opposed to this relationship and distrusted Clementina because her sister served the house of Hanover. In fact it was widely assumed that Clementina was a spy acting on behalf of the British Government. Nevertheless, the couple was living together by November 1752, and they remained together for the following eight years. After a short time they moved from Ghent to Liege, where on 29 October 1753 their only child, a daughter, was born. Despite her father's nominal change of religion three years earlier, the baby was baptised into the Catholic faith at the church of Ste Marie-des-Fonts. She was given the name of Charlotte. It seems unlikely that the then Anglican Prince Charles attended his daughter's baptism, and neither he nor Clementina was named on the baptismal record in the parish register.

Charles did not treat Clementina well. His increasing dependence on alcohol made his temper very difficult and uncertain, and his behaviour towards Clementina alternated between the violent and the obsessively possessive. Those who knew the couple at this time reported frequent arguments between them. By 1760 they had moved to Basel in Switzerland. Here Clementina decided that she could not cope either with Charles' temper or with their peripatetic lifestyle any longer.

She wrote to Charles' father, the Jacobite 'King James III and VIII', asking for his help. She told him that she wanted to ensure a Catholic upbringing for her daughter, while for her own part she wished to retire to a convent. 'James III' agreed to pay Clementina an annuity of 10,000 livres, and there is evidence that he helped her to escape from Charles, taking her 7-year-old daughter with her. Clementina and Charlotte subsequently took refuge at the convent of the Nuns of the Visitation in Paris. She left Charles a letter explaining what she had done and why. Charles was reportedly furious, and tried to get both of them back, but to no avail. Charles never forgave Clementina for depriving him of 'ye cheild'.

Until the death of 'James III' in 1766, Clementina and Charlotte were able to live safely in various French convents, thanks to the annuity he paid them. But when James died in January 1766 – thus bringing to an end the longest 'reign' in English, Scottish and Irish history[8] – they found themselves in trouble. Appeals to Charles were of no avail. Finally Clementina was forced to approach Charles' younger brother, Cardinal Henry Stuart, Bishop of Frascati, and the Jacobite 'Duke of York'. The Cardinal eventually agreed to pay Clementina a reduced annuity of 5,000 livres, on condition that she sign a statement avowing that she had never been married to Charles. Clementina had little choice. She signed the required affidavit on 9 March 1767 – though later she sought to retract it. Based on the reduced income which Henry paid her, she found herself new and cheaper accommodation at the convent of Notre Dame at Meaux-en-Brie.

✠ ✠ ✠

At various times prospective brides such as the Princess de Bouillon, the Princess de Conti and the Princess of Massa had been considered for Charles, and in the early 1740s he had even sought an alliance with a daughter of Louis XV, but all these projects had come to nothing. In the 1750s 'James III' again urged his son to marry, but no suitable bride could be found. It was not until 1772 that 'Charles III' finally decided to contract a marriage with Princess Louise of Stolberg-Gedern, a relative by marriage,[9] who, at the age of 19, was just one year older than his daughter Charlotte. Louise's subsequent love affair with Count Vittorio Alfieri comprises an interesting story in its own right, but it is one which we shall not explore here, given that our focus is on whether Charles' marriage to Louise may have been bigamous.

Meanwhile Charlotte had been in contact with her father for the first time since 1760. She asked him to allow her to join him in Rome (where Charles was now residing in the Palazzo Muti) and to recognise her as legitimate. After some correspondence the Stuart 'king' agreed to receive her, but only on the condition that she leave her mother. This Charlotte absolutely refused to do. As a result 'Charles III' broke off the correspondence.

However, later the same year Charlotte and her mother made their own way to Rome, though they could ill afford the journey. Charles refused to see them, but Charlotte continued to plead by letter. She felt that the only course for her was to marry as soon as possible. However, her father refused to give her permission either to marry or to become a nun. At this time Charlotte and Clementina were in dire straits, and Charlotte was already ill with the liver complaint (part of her Stuart heritage) which would eventually bring about her early death.

In view of her father's refusal to permit either marriage or a religious life, Charlotte was trapped. She needed a protector and since she could not marry she was more or less forced to enter into an illicit relationship. The protector she ultimately chose was Ferdinand Maximilien Mériadec de Rohan, Archbishop of Bordeaux and Cambrai. She bore the archbishop three children: Marie Victoire, Charlotte and Charles Edward. She kept these children secret from her father, and very little was known about them until last century.

On 23 March 1783 'Charles III' finally legitimised his daughter, who joined him in Florence. Charlotte was accorded the rank of 'Royal Highness', and created Duchess of Albany in the Jacobite peerage of Scotland. The Stuart 'king', now in his sixties, was ailing and it was Charlotte who took care of him in his last years. In order to do this, she left her children in her mother's care.

'Charles III' died on 31 January 1788. His daughter survived him by just under two years, dying in Bologna on 17 November 1789. Charlotte's will, written just before her death, left 50,000 livres to her mother, together with an annual annuity of 15,000 livres. However, the new Jacobite king 'Henry IX' (Cardinal Stuart) took two years to release these moneys, and only did so on the condition that

Clementina sign a 'quittance' renouncing, on behalf of herself and her descendants, any further claims on the Stuart estate. Clementina Walkinshaw survived until 1802, seeking refuge from the French Revolution in Switzerland. In terms of financial support, 'Henry IX' is said to have treated her shamefully and cruelly, and she died 'aged and poor'.[10]

✤ ✤ ✤

So was Clementina married to Charles? No record of a marriage has ever been found. Nevertheless the urgent demands of Cardinal Stuart that Clementina sign an affidavit denying that she was married to his brother show that the rumour was current in Jacobite circles in the 1760s. Indeed, Clementina herself may have believed that, under Scottish law, she had been Charles' wife, even though no formal marriage ceremony had ever taken place between them. Charles' younger brother, the cardinal, who saw himself as the heir to the Stuart claim, was obviously extremely anxious to have any question of such a marriage set aside. Nevertheless, Clementina only signed the cardinal's affidavit because at the time her poverty left her no option. One historian has declared that 'the document was a nonsense',[11] and certainly Clementina later consistently sought to repudiate it and to assert the claim that she had been married to Charles.

It is also interesting to note that Charlotte herself asked, in her letters to her father, to be recognised as his legitimate daughter, and that in the end 'Charles III' granted this request. Until the day of her death Charlotte consistently claimed that her parents were husband and wife, and the basis of her claim was the law of Scotland, which at that time – and indeed up to the present century and the year 2006 – recognised a type of marriage which was officially described as 'marriage by cohabitation with habit and repute'. The chief requirements for such a marriage were that a couple should live together publicly as husband and wife for a number of years, and should be known to others as husband and wife.

There can be little room for doubt that Charles and Clementina's case meets *these* criteria. When Clementina came to live with Charles in Ghent, in 1752, they cohabited 'a preti house' in the Rue des Vernoples, where they were known to their neighbours as 'Count and Countess de Johnson'.[12] Thus we have clear evidence of cohabitation and that they used appellations which gave out that they were husband and wife. Indeed, Charles 'generally presented Clementina in public as his wife'.[13] Their cohabitation led to the birth of their daughter, Charlotte, in 1753, after which they lived together as a family, first in Liege and later in Basel. In Switzerland Charles and Clementina continued to give themselves out to their neighbours as man and wife, this time by calling themselves 'Dr and Mrs Thomson'.[14] It is therefore clear that they cohabited as a married couple and were known as such from 1752 until at least 1756, and probably up to Clementina's flight with Charlotte in 1760. On this basis Charlotte may seem justified in claiming that under Scottish law her parents had been married. Nothing further needed to be demonstrated, and there was, in fact, no need to show evidence of a marriage registration, or to prove that a church ceremony had ever taken place. Unfortunately there is just one flaw in Clementina's case. As the parallel case of MacCullock v. MacCulloch (1759) showed, in order for the Scottish marriage law to apply, the cohabitation had to have taken place *in Scotland*.[15]

15

Review of Alleged 'Tudor' and Stuart Secret Royal Marriages

In theory the period under study in this section might perhaps have been expected to produce clearer outcomes than the medieval period in terms of its disputed royal marriages, since the circumstances under which marriages were contracted in the second half of the sixteenth century and during the seventeenth century were supposedly more precisely regulated in legal terms. In principle not only should weddings have been preceded by the public reading of banns (as indeed had also been theoretically the case in the later medieval period), they should also have been concluded by a formal written record of what had taken place, naming the parties concerned and their witnesses.

In fact, however, as we have seen, the reality was rather different. Secret marriages were still taking place in the sixteenth and seventeenth centuries. Robert Dudley, Earl of Leicester made at least one secret contract in the second half of the sixteenth century, and Charles II's brother and cousin did so, or were suspected of having done so, in the seventeenth century. It is possible that Charles II did likewise, though the king himself denied this.

However, the strong probability which has emerged is that neither Elizabeth I nor Charles II ever contracted secret marriages, despite the fact that this has been alleged against them. There are good grounds for believing that Elizabeth I may have found the whole notion of marriage intimidating, because of her family history. Also, if she ever did contract a secret marriage one would be forced to conclude that she cannot have taken it very seriously. At all events, such a secret marriage (if it ever existed) apparently did not prevent her from contemplating the notion of a different and public marriage, even if she would thereby have been committing bigamy. Of course, this point does not, in itself, completely rule out the possibility of a secret marriage on the part of the queen. We have already seen that neither Elizabeth's father, Henry VIII, not her great-grandfather, Edward IV, seem to have been intimidated by the prospect of bigamy. Nevertheless, the fact remains that throughout her reign Elizabeth I continued to play publicly with the idea of a possible marriage as though she believed herself to be still single; she never lived openly with any man as with a husband, she is not known to have borne any children, and she certainly did not recognise any. Also the favourite candidate for the role of her secret husband, Robert Dudley, Earl of Leicester, himself contracted other unions during the period of his relationship with the queen. Overall, the weight of this combined evidence argues strongly that Elizabeth I never married.

As for Charles II, he certainly was not intimidated by marriage. However, he stated publicly and unambiguously that he only ever had one wife: Catherine of Bragança. Therefore if he had previously married Lucy Walter, Charles must clearly have been telling a deliberate lie. Not only that, but it would have been a lie which completely undermined the life and career of the son whom he adored. This would have been very strange and inexplicable behaviour on the king's part, given that in all other respects he appeared eager to support and promote the Duke of Monmouth. Thus although it is just possible that Charles II's public statements that he was never married to Lucy Walter should be disbelieved, this would confront us with the enormous question of *why* the king told lies. What could his motives possibly have been for such behaviour? After all, many people half expected him to recognise his son by Lucy Walter as legitimate – and may even have hoped that he would do so. Again, therefore, the balance of the evidence in the case of Charles II favours the view that he was never secretly married to Lucy Walter. Of course, this does not mean that the Duke of Monmouth may not have genuinely believed that his mother and father were married. It also does not rule out the possibility that Lucy Walter herself may have imagined that she had been married to Charles. We must also note that it leaves unexplained some evidence dating from the 1650s; evidence which appears to suggest that Charles referred at that time to someone – possibly Lucy Walter – as his 'wife'.

The case of 'Charles III' is very different. First, there is no doubt whatever that he had a sustained relationship with Clementina Walkinshaw, and that this relationship produced a child who was eventually recognised by Charles himself as legitimate and accorded the rank of 'Royal Highness'. There is also no possible question about the fact that Charles and Clementina lived together for a number of years, during which time they were publicly known by appellations which implied very clearly that they were a married couple. Thus 'Charles III' was believed by some to have had a secret wife. This was not as a result of a clandestine marriage ceremony of any sort, but merely due to contemporary Scottish law – a unique survival which permitted and recognised a kind of common law marriage. Belief in their marriage 'by cohabitation with habit and repute' is strengthened by the insistence on the part of their daughter, Charlotte, that she was legitimate. It is also reinforced by the insistence of Charles's younger brother, 'Henry IX', that he would only give Clementina financial support if she signed an affidavit denying that she had been married to Charles, and also by Clementina's reluctant acceptance – and subsequent repudiation – of this affidavit.

'Charles III' could perhaps have contracted a marriage with Clementina Walkinshaw simply by living with her openly in this way, and by giving out to their neighbours that they were husband and wife, by the names and titles they both used. However, for this claim to be valid they would have needed to live together in Scotland, not in the Low Countries or in Switzerland. But in reality, as a result of significant new legislation in Britain itself, 'Charles III's' relationship with Clementina largely took place abroad, and in exile.

This new British legislation comprised the Act of Settlement, which, from the beginning of the eighteenth century, excluded any possibility of a marriage between an accepted member of the English royal family and a Catholic. Under the terms of the new law, if such a marriage took place it would automatically exclude the royal person who contracted it from ever inheriting the Crown. The Act of Settlement produced an immediate and enormous effect. Not only were all surviving legitimate descendants of Charles I excluded from the throne, but so also were a number of the senior heirs of Charles I's sister, Elizabeth, Queen of Bohemia. The Electress Sophia of Hanover and her son, the future George I – who were eventually recognised as the heirs of Queen Anne as a result of this new law – were very far indeed from being the next in line to the throne simply by right of blood.

Subsequently the eighteenth century witnessed further legislation which impinged on marriage in general and upon royal marriages in particular. First, the Marriage Act in England introduced further rules about how and by whom marriages could be conducted; rules which made it much more difficult than it had previously been to contract a secret marriage. Later the mad and unattractive George III introduced the Royal Marriages Act, which prohibited any British descendant of George II from marrying without the explicit approval of the reigning sovereign. Why was the last of these laws introduced? And did these new laws in combination succeed in ruling out completely the clandestine royal marriage? We shall discover this in the next section.

Four

The Act Of Settlement, The Marriage Act And The Royal Marriages Act

16

QUEEN HANNAH
AND PRINCESS OLIVE

I am happy at being able to say that I never was personally engaged in such a transaction.

George III, writing about the extra-marital affairs of his eldest son[1]

Following the Act of Settlement of 1701, which, as we have already seen, regulated the English (and British) succession to the throne, a second significant law was enacted in 1753. This was the Marriage Act, which – irrespective of their religious beliefs – obliged all English people except Jews and Quakers to marry in Anglican churches, and to have their marriages formally registered by an Anglican clergyman acting on behalf of the State. Some twenty years later, in 1772, a third new Act of Parliament followed, which impinged specifically upon *royal* marriages. This was a draconian piece of legislation which has controlled the choice of British royal marriage partners from the reign of George III up until the twenty-first century. In the present chapter we shall explore the background which led to this third piece of legislation.

The Royal Marriages Act of 1772 was the culmination of several interconnected events involving sons of Frederick Prince of Wales and his wife Augusta (whom we met in the last chapter). The first episode comprises the story of George [III]'s reported love for a beautiful Quaker called Hannah Lightfoot, which we shall examine in detail in this chapter. The second story was the secret marriage of George III's younger brother, William, Duke of Gloucester and Edinburgh (1743–1805) to Maria Walpole, dowager Countess of Waldegrave. This marriage was privately contracted in 1766, and it only became more widely known five years later. Maria was not really acceptable as a royal spouse, because, despite her title and her Walpole ancestry, she was a widow, and also of illegitimate birth. Nevertheless, because no legislation existed to debar the Duke of Gloucester from marrying her in 1766, Maria automatically became a princess and a royal duchess once the marriage was made public, despite the fact that her brother-in-law the king refused to receive her. Our third incident is the secret marriage of George III's youngest brother, Henry Frederick, Duke of Cumberland (1745–90). It was this last event which led directly to the enactment of new legislation governing marriages of members of the royal family – legislation which is still in force at the time of writing. For although it was recently earmarked for repeal, this plan seems now to have been shelved by the current government.

Our understanding of the complex cases of George III and his brothers has evolved over the years, but in the first and third cases the whole truth still remains unclear. The first of these three stories received very little publicity during the life-times of its key figures. In this respect it recalls somewhat the relationship of Edward IV and Eleanor Talbot. However, contrary to the outcome in the case of Edward IV and Eleanor Talbot (where the evidence, when finally made public, apparently convinced the royal council, and later Parliament), the subsequent legal assess-ment of the case of George III and Hannah Lightfoot, together with the Duke of Cumberland's alleged fathering of Olive Wilmot (Serres), merely seemed to expose flaws in the supporting evidence as presented in court. Thus one nineteenth-century historian, reviewing the situation, resoundingly concluded that the whole story of George [III]'s royal love affair with a Quakeress was a myth, while the royal status claimed by the descendants of 'Princess Olive' Wilmot was rejected in court.

Subsequently, however, historical research has revisited these cases. As a result, it is now clear that, even if some of the evidence produced in the nineteenth-century was fabricated, the story of George [III]'s royal romance cannot be entirely dismissed. Research has proved that Hannah Lightfoot and her Quaker family were real people – a point which had previously been questioned. Moreover, evidence has emerged to show that contemporary rumours existed in the 1760s and 1770s, linking George [III] with a beautiful Quakeress. As for Princess Olive, although she unwisely filled gaps in her story with fanciful inventions which ultimately undermined her case, recent investigations suggest that she really was a daughter of the Duke of Cumberland.

✤ ✤ ✤

George [III], the eldest son of Frederick, Prince of Wales and his wife, Augusta of Saxe-Gotha, was born at Norfolk House in London on 4 June 1738 (the first sovereign of the new Hanoverian dynasty born in England). In 1751 his father died suddenly, at which point Prince George became the heir to the throne of his grandfather, George II. The boy was brought up under the influence of his mother, who maintained a strict moral code.

In 1758, when Prince George was 20 years old, the 13-year-old Lady Sarah Lennox appeared at his grandfather's court, and reportedly infatuated the heir to the throne. Sarah was a daughter of Charles Lennox, second Duke of Richmond, Lennox and Aubigny. Her father was the grandson of Charles II by his mistress,

Louise de Kerouaille, Duchess of Portsmouth. For the next two years Sarah's family cherished hopes that she might become the next Queen of England, but Lord Bute, friend and advisor of the dowager Princess of Wales, counselled against this match which, had it taken place, would have brought a new dose of Stuart blood into the veins of the house of Hanover. In the event, it was not until the twentieth century that Lennox descendants would finally marry into the reigning dynasty. (The first Duke of Lennox was an ancestor of Diana, Princess of Wales, of Camilla, Duchess of Cornwall and of Sarah, Duchess of York.) Nevertheless, it is interesting to find that such a marriage for an heir to the British throne was contemplated in the eighteenth century. Like Lord Bute, however, King George II opposed the idea of a marriage between his grandson and Sarah Lennox. The king sought instead to betroth the young prince to Sophie Caroline Marie of Brunswick-Wolfenbüttel. However, the prince and his mother resisted this suggestion, and plans for the prince's marriage remained unresolved.

Thus, George III was ostensibly still single when he succeeded to his grandfather's throne in October 1760. In the following year, in the Chapel Royal of St James's Palace, he married Princess Charlotte of Mecklenburg-Strelitz – having met his bride for the first time on their wedding day. Despite this, the royal marriage proved generally successful. George III was apparently faithful to his consort. No royal mistress was ever in evidence and, despite earlier gossip, it was not until after George III's death, in 1820, that serious discussion arose of another relationship in his life.

In April 1821 a letter by a correspondent calling him- (or her-) self simply 'B.' was published in the *Monthly Magazine*. The letter referred to 'the attachment of the late King to a beautiful Quakeress of the name of Wheeler'.[2] Three months later a much fuller account of the story, which corrected some of the points made in the first version, was published in the same journal, in the form of a letter by a writer from Warminster in Wiltshire. This second writer asserted that the name:

> of the fair Quaker who once engaged the affections of Prince George … was not WHEELER, but HANNAH LIGHTFOOT. She lived with her father and mother at the corner of St James' Market, who kept a shop there (I believe a linendrapers). The Prince had often noticed her in his way from Leicester House to St. James', and was struck with her person. Miss Chudleigh, late Duchess of Kingston, became his agent.[3]

Warminsteriensis, as the writer of the second letter called him- (or her-) self, went on to explain that the royal family, alarmed at the young prince's growing affections for the 'fair Quakeress' had bribed a young man called Isaac Axford to marry Hannah. Isaac Axford was reported to have been a 'shopman to Barton the grocer on Ludgate Hill'.[4] Subsequently a third correspondent asserted that the marriage between Isaac and Hannah had taken place in 1754.[5]

William Thoms, the librarian at the House of Lords in the 1860s, who investigated these published accounts, was extremely sceptical of every aspect of Hannah's story. Indeed, he doubted Hannah's very existence, claiming that even the name of George [III]'s alleged 'fair Quaker' girlfriend was in doubt. He also claimed that there were also conflicting accounts of where her family came from, when and where she attracted the attention of Prince George and when precisely she married.

In many respects Thoms greatly overstated his case. It is true that various versions of Hannah's name were reported in the published nineteenth-century correspondence about her, but there appears to be an explanation for that, as we shall learn shortly. Thoms also suggested that there were conflicting reports regarding the date of Hannah's marriage to Isaac Axford, but this was incorrect. The published nineteenth-century accounts of Hannah's marriage to Isaac consistently referred to 1754. There were also references to a marriage of Hannah in 1759, but these related, not to her marriage with Isaac, but to her alleged union with Prince George [III].

Thoms' scepticism notwithstanding, modern research has verified that Hannah Lightfoot and Isaac Axford did indeed both exist. Moreover, they were indisputably married to each other on 11 December 1753 – just a month or two earlier than the nineteenth-century *Monthly Magazine* correspondence later suggested.[6] The couple's marriage was celebrated at a Nonconformist chapel. In the marriage register Hannah is listed as a parishioner of St James, Westminster, while Isaac was from St Martin's parish, Ludgate: details which are entirely consistent with the geographical locations reported for this couple by *Warminsteriensis* in 1821.

The account published by *Warminsteriensis* and other early nineteenth-century writers is complicated, and in some respects contradictory. We shall need to return to one further important aspect of the story presently. For the moment, however, we should note that *Warminsteriensis* stated in July 1821 that after their marriage, Isaac lost his wife to Prince George [III]. 'Many years after Hannah was taken away, her husband, believing her dead, was married again to a Miss Bartlett of Keevel (N. Wilts)'.[7] Once again confirmation exists. The marriage of Isaac Axford to his cousin, Mary Bartlett, was celebrated at Erlestoke, Wiltshire in 1759.[8] Moreover, the record of this second marriage also supplies the additional information that Isaac had been born in 1731.

Assuming that Hannah was probably of a similar age, this information allows us to seek to verify her own date of birth. It transpires that Hannah Lightfoot, daughter of Mathew and Mary Lightfoot of Stepney, Barking and Ratcliff, was baptised on 12 October 1730. Moreover the Nonconformist marriage of her father, Matthew Lightfoot (son of Matthew and Ruth Lightfoot), to Mary Wheeler had taken place in Westminster in August 1728.

The fact that the maiden name of Hannah's mother was Wheeler takes us back to the initial report of Hannah's relationship with George III, published in April 1821. It offers a plausible explanation of why the writer 'B.' should have mistakenly suggested that Hannah's *own* surname was Wheeler. It also indicates that 'B.' was genuinely familiar with Hannah's family background. We must remember that the 1821 accounts were penned more than sixty years after the events to which they referred. Under these circumstances the mistaken substitution of Hannah's mother's maiden surname for 'Lightfoot', and the error which attributed Hannah's Axford marriage – which actually took place in December 1753 – to the year 1754, can both be easily understood.

So Hannah Lightfoot did exist, and she was indeed the daughter of a Quaker family. Hannah's family lived in Westminster, and in 1753 Hannah married Isaac Axford. Moreover, rumours of Hannah's relationship with George [III] seem to have been current in the 1760s, and hints of this relationship first appeared in print in 1770–71.[9] Moreover, alleged portraits of Hannah seem to have been commissioned from Sir Joshua Reynolds by the future George III in July 1757.[10] They show a girl with a round face, dark hair and blue eyes. The writers of 1821 described Hannah as short in stature, beautiful, and 'rather disposed to *embonpoint*'.[11]

What became of Hannah after her marriage to Isaac Axford is difficult to ascertain. Since Isaac married a second wife in 1759, it is obvious that he had somehow lost Hannah in the intervening six years. No record of her death has been found under the surname 'Axford', but it is possible that she used some other name after leaving Isaac.

The first accounts of the love affair between Hannah and George [III], published in 1821, merely claimed that Hannah deserted Isaac Axford to become the prince's mistress. *Warminsteriensis*, for example, stated that after living with Isaac for only a short time Hannah had left her husband in order to become the mistress of George [III], by whom she had a child or children. A daughter, later married to a cavalry officer in the service of the East India Company (Bengal Presidency), is alleged. Other writers later spoke of sons of Hannah and her royal partner, and the prince was said to have maintained Hannah in an establishment at either Lambeth or Knightsbridge.[12] Incidentally, the alleged secrecy surrounding the identity of these royal bastards is a new feature in English history, not encountered prior to the eighteenth century. However, from the eighteenth century up to the last (twentieth) century such secrecy seems to have been the norm.

A significant new twist was added to the story in 1824, and it was ascribed to Caroline of Brunswick, then nominally Queen of England, and the estranged German consort of George III's eldest son, George IV. Caroline is a lady whom we shall meet again later in the context of another disputed royal marriage. Queen Caroline was said to have stated that she believed her own 'husband' to have been married to Maria Smythe (Mrs Fitzherbert – see below). She was also reported to have thought that 'previous to his marriage with Queen Charlotte',[13] her father-in-law and uncle, King George III, had married Hannah Lightfoot. On this basis Hannah Lightfoot, rather than Charlotte of Mecklenburg, might have been George III's true wife. Like Elizabeth Woodville in the 1470s, Queen Charlotte is rumoured to have been anxious about the legitimacy of her own marriage with the king. 'It has been suggested that these matters preyed on her mind to such an extent that when she got hold of yet another whisper that Hannah had really died in early 1765, she persuaded George that they should go through a remarriage ceremony as soon as possible.'[14]

Subsequent versions of Hannah's story claimed that documentary evidence existed of a clandestine marriage in 1759 between Hannah and the prince. Since this was six years *after* Hannah's marriage to Isaac Axford, even if such a royal marriage took place, it would presumably have been of questionable validity. There is no evidence of a divorce between Hannah and Isaac, and Isaac was still living in 1759.

The documentary evidence of Hannah's alleged royal marriage was in the hands of a lady who is the second leading character in our investigation: 'Princess Olive of Cumberland, Duchess of Lancaster'. We shall return to the complex story of 'Princess Olive' presently. But the documents which she held purported to record that the marriage between George [III] and Hannah was celebrated by an Anglican clergyman and Oxford don, Dr James Wilmot, who, according to various versions of Princess Olive's story, was either her uncle or her grandfather. Two different versions of Hannah's marriage certificate were subsequently published. The first reads:

April 17th, 1759

The Marriage of These Parties was this Day duly Solemnised at Kew Chapel, according to the Rites and Ceremonies of the Church of England, by myself,
J. Wilmot
George P.
Hannah

Witness to this marriage –
W. Pitt.
Anne Taylor

The second version reads as follows:

May 27th, 1759

This is to certify that the marriage of these parties, George, Prince of Wales to Hannah Lightfoot, was this day duly solemnised this day according to the rites and ceremonies of the Church of England, at their residence at Peckham, by myself,
J. Wilmot
George Guelph
Hannah Lightfoot

Witnesses to this marriage
of these parties –

William Pitt
Anne Taylor

The royal signature on the first document was in the correct form for 1759. Moreover, it was subsequently authenticated by two of George III's sons: the Duke of Clarence (later William IV), and the Duke of Sussex. The royal signature on the second document is in a form which George is never known to have used, and the second marriage certificate definitely appears to be a forgery. The reason for its fabrication may have been that the first certificate omitted Hannah's surname. However, in 1759 Hannah's real and legal surname seems to have been not Lightfoot but Axford.[15]

The final version of Hannah's story claimed that Isaac Axford had been bribed by the royal family to take Hannah away from Prince George, but that nevertheless Hannah's *first* attachment had been to the prince. Thoms was probably right to dismiss this version of the story out of hand. First, there is no genuine evidence to support it, and second, this revised version of the story – which proclaims Miss Lightfoot as *Hannah Regina* – clearly runs counter to the real evidence which has now been found to show that Hannah married Isaac in 1753.

But while a *marriage* between Hannah Lightfoot and Prince George appears improbable, this does not mean that no *relationship* ever existed between them. Despite the evidence of George [III]'s morality, he certainly fell in love with Sarah Lennox, and it is conceivable that he also fell in love with Hannah. Whether this love was ever given physical expression it now seems impossible to say, but various nineteenth-century individuals subsequently claimed to be descended from Hannah and George III. Thoms later asserted that at least some of these putative royal descendants must have been lying, because the various families who advanced such claims were apparently unknown to – and unconnected with – one another. In fact, however, this point proves nothing, as we shall shortly see.

✠ ✠ ✠

When did Hannah Lightfoot (Axford) die? If her marriage to Isaac Axford was legitimate, logic suggests that she must have died prior to Isaac's second marriage in 1759. However, it could simply be that Isaac, having somehow 'lost' Hannah, simply decided to contract a second marriage without verifying that his first wife was dead. Moreover the situation is further complicated by the fact that Caroline of Brunswick reportedly believed that Hannah's true marriage had been to Prince George [III]. No evidence has so far been found to support this view, but if it was correct then *Isaac Axford's* marriage to Hannah would have been bigamous (on Hannah's side), so that Isaac would actually have been free to marry Mary Bartlett in 1759 even if Hannah was then still alive.

Queen Caroline reportedly believed that Hannah died after the birth of George III's second son, the Duke of York (16 August 1763), but before the birth of his next son, the Duke of Clarence (William IV – 21 August 1765). No precise record of Hannah's death has in fact been located, and the search is complicated by the fact that we have no idea what surname she might have been using at the time of her death. However, there is some evidence that Hannah died in or just before 1759. In December 1759 Lady Sophia Egerton wrote to her uncle, William Bentinck (later Duke of Portland) that Prince George had 'kept a beautiful young Quaker for some years, that she is now dead and that one child was the produce of that intrigue'. Hannah is rumoured to have died on 27 May 1759, and to have been buried in Islington churchyard under the name of Rebecca Powell.[16] If Hannah did die in 1759, that would explain the date of Isaac Axford's second marriage.

✤ ✤ ✤

Whether or not George [III] contracted a secret marriage with Hannah Lightfoot, there is absolutely no doubt about the fact that both of his younger brothers contracted clandestine marriages with non-royal spouses. There is also no doubt that, whatever the truth of his own amorous history may have been, the king proved extremely intolerant of the marital escapades of his brothers. Subsequently he also showed similar intolerance regarding the love affairs of his sons (as we shall see in the next chapter). But despite George III's anger, the elder of his two brothers, the Duke of Gloucester, married the illegitimate granddaughter of Sir Robert Walpole, Britain's first prime minister, while his younger brother, the Duke of Cumberland, has been accused of contracting *two* secret marriages.

We have already noticed that some of the documentation purporting to relate to the story of 'Queen Hannah' seems subsequently to have been in the possession of one who claimed to be George III's niece, 'Princess Olive of Cumberland, Duchess of Lancaster'. The story of this lady is, if anything, even more extraordinary than that of Hannah Lightfoot, and the truth behind it is harder to ascertain. Since several women called 'Olive' figure in the story we shall henceforth refer to 'Princess Olive' as Olive (iii).

Olive (iii) Wilmot (later Mrs Serres) was brought up as their daughter by Robert Wilmot and his wife, Anna Maria Brunton (or Burton). Robert Wilmot was the brother of Dr James Wilmot, the clergyman whose signature appears on the marriage certificate of George [III] and Hannah Lightfoot. However, Olive (iii) later claimed to be the daughter of Henry Frederick, Duke of Cumberland – the younger brother of King George III. This claim has been treated with scorn by some researchers but it has been taken seriously by others. The most recent investigation, by Miles Macnair, strongly suggests that Olive (iii) really was Cumberland's daughter. During her lifetime, her claim was certainly taken seriously by significant members of the royal family, most notably the Duke of Kent, son of George III and eventual father of Queen Victoria, who always addressed Olive as his cousin.

Macnair's study is thorough, and it is not necessary to repeat all his findings here. Olive (iii) certainly possessed a 'birth certificate' attesting Cumberland's paternity, and this document appears to be authentic. Unfortunately it confused the name of Olive (iii)'s mother, and this confusion seems to have led Olive (iii) into complex fantasy realms which, in the end, undermined the whole credibility of her story. After initial speculation that her real mother might have been Olive (i) Wilmot, sister of Robert Wilmot, and of Dr James Wilmot, Olive (iii) finally surmised that her mother was Olive (ii) Wilmot – the daughter of Dr James Wilmot by 'Princess Poniatowski' (the sister of King Stanislas II of Poland). Olive (iii) claimed that Olive (ii) had been the Duke of Cumberland's alleged true legal wife.

In fact, Olive (ii) never existed, and Olive (iii)'s real mother was Anne Luttrell (Horton), the Duke of Cumberland's undoubted wife (despite George III's disapproval). There is absolutely no doubt that Prince Henry, Duke of Cumberland, did contract a non-royal marriage with the widowed Anne Luttrell (Horton). This was in 1771, and it infuriated the king, his brother. Indeed, it was the immediate cause of the Royal Marriages Act, which legislated that descendants of George II (except via those princesses who had married into foreign royal houses) could not contract valid marriages without the explicit permission of the reigning monarch.

Curiously, Princess Olive (iii) subsequently gave the name 'Horton' to one of her own children. The elder of her two daughters was named Lavinia Janetta Horton Serres. This point seems previously to have passed largely unnoticed. However, it strongly suggests that in fact Olive (iii) had at some point been aware of her real mother's identity. Lavinia Serres was later to become Mrs Ryves, and she and her son pursued a well-publicised but ultimately unsuccessful case for recognition as royalty in the British courts in 1866.

The fact that Olive (iii) is alleged by Macnair to have had a brother, who was brought up by another branch of the Wilmot family, and whom she did not know, suggests that Thom's earlier assertion about the alleged descendants of Hannah Lightfoot and George III is worthless, for it suggests that the royal house of Hanover may, in fact, have farmed out its bastard children to various families, with the result that siblings really could grow up in ignorance of each other's existence. In short, we have a situation in which members of the Hanoverian dynasty in the second half of the eighteenth century unquestionably contracted secret and non-royal marriages. Some of these marriages may have resulted in the birth of children whom George III wished to have brought up as non-royal persons, without any recognised claim to the throne. It appears that Princess Olive of Cumberland may have been one of these children – and a victim of George III's policy to keep such semi-royal offspring out of the royal family. George III also unquestionably sought to pre-empt future problems of this nature by enacting the Royal Marriage Act, which prohibited heirs to the throne from marrying without the consent of the reigning monarch.

In this context, a loving, but clandestine, relationship between George III and Hannah Lightfoot is by no means incredible. It is also possible that such a relationship produced a child or children who was or were subsequently fostered or adopted. However, the allegation that George [III] *married* Hannah seems difficult to reconcile with other aspects of the chronology.

17

PRINCESS FITZ

I'd crowns resign to call her mine,
Sweet lass of Richmond Hill.

❦

There is no sacrifice, my beloved wife,
yt I will not make for thee.

George [IV], Prince of Wales, to Maria Smythe (Fitzherbert), 1785

❦

... I hear from everybody that her character is irreproachable, and her manners
most aimiable.

Charles James Fox, MP, 1785

❦

to a most amiable and justly valued female character, whom I conclude to be in
all respects, both legally, really, worthily, and happily for this country, Her Royal
Highness the Princess of Wales.

J. Horne Tooke, *A Letter to a Friend on the Reported Marriage of the Prince of
Wales*, London 1787, p. 3

❦

One point which emerged very clearly from the last chapter is the fact
that in the second half of the eighteenth century princes of the royal
house of Hanover began to engage in secret marriages with spouses
who were of less than royal birth. Whatever the truth about the alleged marriage of George [III] and 'Queen Hannah', or the invented 'marriage' of Henry
Frederick, Duke of Cumberland, and the mythical Olive (ii) Wilmot, there is no
doubt that Cumberland *did* contract a marriage with Anne Luttrell (Horton).

Moreover, if Princess Olive (iii)'s accounts of Cumberland's earlier marriage to the invented 'Olive (ii) Wilmot' had been true, then the Luttrell (Horton) marriage would have been bigamous. As a result of Cumberland's matrimonial escapade his brother, King George III, brought in the Royal Marriages Act, to enable the sovereign to police future weddings within the royal family. It is against the background of these real and alleged events – and the public speculation which resulted from them – that we must now explore the marriages of George III's own sons, and most particularly, the alleged bigamy of his eldest son, the Prince of Wales, Prince Regent, and future George IV.

The marital history of George III's numerous children, like that of his brothers, once again undermines thoroughly Fiona Macdonald's contention, that English (or British) royal marriages have followed a consistent pattern of arranged marriages with foreign royalty throughout history.

The eldest son of George III and Queen Charlotte was the future George IV, Prince of Wales, and Prince Regent during his father's later illness. He and his marital history comprise the main subject of this chapter. George [IV]'s next brother was Frederick, Duke of York, who in 1791 dutifully married a Prussian princess. However, that marriage was not a success. The couple soon separated, and their union remained childless. Next came William, Duke of Clarence (later King William IV), who first fell in love while he was serving in the navy, with a girl called Sarah Martin (later the authoress of *Old Mrs Hubbard and her Dog*). Prince William proposed to Sarah but her family would not allow her to accept the proposal. Later, William lived happily for many years with his Anglo-Irish actress mistress, Dorothea Bland (better known under her stage name as Mrs Jordan). By Dorothea, William had no less than ten illegitimate children, from one of whom the present British prime minister, David Cameron, is descended. The relationship was even grudgingly countenanced by William's father, King George III. Only very late in life did William abandon his mistress for a royal marriage, which, however, produced no living children. After William, George III's next son was Edward, Duke of Kent, whom we encountered earlier, because he formally recognised 'Princess Olive' (iii) as his cousin. Like William, Edward only made a royal marriage very late in life (thereby becoming the father of the future Queen Victoria).

As for the future King George IV, he was born on 12 August 1762 at St James's Palace. In his youth he was a very attractive young prince, and his elegance earned him the accolade of 'the first Gentleman of England'. However, gradually his extravagant lifestyle made him unpopular in the country at large. His relationship with his parents was strained, and his father had great difficulty in persuading him into a suitable royal marriage.

The most notable impediment to such a royal union was the relationship that developed between the prince and a Catholic widow, Maria Smythe (Fitzherbert).

As we shall see, George [IV] repeatedly pressed Maria to marry him, and eventually she consented. Of course, their marriage was officially regarded as illegal in England, because of the recently enacted Royal Marriages Act, which required the sovereign's consent for marriages within the royal family. Moreover, if the marriage had been publicly acknowledged, it would have debarred George from succeeding to the throne, because of the terms of the Act of Succession of 1701. Consequently, when gossip about the relationship became widespread, Prince George had the marriage officially denied in Parliament. In the light of this action (which infuriated Maria) it is interesting to reconsider the public denials issued by Charles II, just over a hundred years earlier, of *his* alleged secret marriage to Lucy Walter: for there is no question but that George [IV] *had* married Maria, so that his public denial was a lie. In the previous chapter we discovered that the existence of a marriage certificate may not constitute absolute proof of the authenticity of a marriage. We now see that public statements by sovereigns and governments are also not absolute proof of the validity or otherwise of an alleged secret royal marriage. We must keep this in mind later, when we consider the case of George V. Certainly George [IV] had an excellent motive for lying about *his* secret marriage. On the other hand, Charles II, as we saw earlier, had no such motive.

✠ ✠ ✠

The lady generally known to posterity as Mrs Fitzherbert was actually born with the surname Smythe, and although she would later be known as Maria, she was baptised Mary Anne. She was born into a family of Catholic gentry at a time when Catholicism in Britain was still subject to persecution, and her religion – together with her fidelity to it – was to prove one of the key factors determining the course of her life.

Mary Anne Smythe was born on 26 July 1756, reputedly in the Red Room at Tong Castle, Shropshire. She was the first of the seven children of Walter Smythe and Mary Anne Errington, who had been married at Walton in Lancashire on 11 September 1755:[1]

> As the crow flies, Tong Castle is some seventeen miles north-east of the [Smythe] family seat at Acton Burnell. The young baby was probably baptised at Acton Burnell by Dom Edward Ambrose Elliot. From her mother she got not only her name but her good looks. From her father she inherited her aquiline nose which would become one of her most famous – and most frequently caricatured – features.[2]

The fact that Mary was baptised by a Catholic priest rather than in an Anglican parish church means that no written record of the event appears to survive.

We saw earlier that Lucy Walter was linked by ties of blood to Anne Boleyn and Eleanor Talbot, and that in popular perception her case was considered to be in some ways analogous with that of Eleanor. It is curious, therefore, to find that Mary or Maria Smythe also has a distant family connection with Eleanor, via the Catholic Turville family.[3] It is possible that she may also have a distant connection with the Boleyns, and with Henry VIII's reputed bastard son, Lord Hunsdon.[4] One episode in Mary (Maria's) career, when she frequented the court of the house of Orange in the Netherlands, also reminds us of Lucy Walter's similar connection with the same court more than a century earlier.

From the age of 12, Maria was educated at an English convent in Paris. The young Catholic girl probably narrowly missed meeting the common-law wife and daughter of the younger Stuart Pretender, who, as we have already seen, had been residing at another Paris convent until about two years before Maria's arrival in the French capital. However, by the time Maria reached Paris the Countess of Albestroff and her daughter, Charlotte, had moved to Meaux-en-Brie.

On her return to England, when her education in Paris had been completed, the 18-year-old Maria married Edward Weld, a Catholic landowner in his mid-forties, whose home was at Lulworth Castle in Dorset. Their marriage was celebrated on 16 July 1775, ten days before Maria's nineteenth birthday. But a mere three months later, on 23 October, Edward died as a result of a riding accident, leaving Maria a very young widow. Three years later she married a second Catholic landowner, Thomas Fitzherbert of Swynnerton in Staffordshire, and it is his surname, rather than her own, which Maria has made famous. Thomas was younger than Edward Weld – in his thirties when he married Maria – and he also lasted longer than Maria's first husband. However, her second marriage also proved to be of relatively short duration, and it ended in May 1781, when Thomas Fitzherbert died of tuberculosis in Nice. Once again Maria was a young and still childless widow.

According to Maria's own version of events it was during the period of her marriage to Thomas that she first encountered the Prince of Wales. She reported that in 1780, when she and her husband were driving in a carriage near Chiswick, Prince George [IV] passed them on horseback, and paused to gaze at Maria, though he did not speak. There is an alternative popular tradition that the couple first met on Richmond Hill, and that the song *Sweet Lass of Richmond Hill* commemorated this. Despite the apparent appropriateness of the lyrics, however, it seems that in actual fact the song was not originally connected with Maria and her royal lover.

The widowed Maria was not really a Society figure. Generally speaking she preferred to live a quiet life. Most of her personal friends were Catholics, and Maria herself certainly took her religion seriously. For example she later built the Brighton church in which her body was subsequently laid to rest. On the contentious issue of Catholic emancipation, however, Maria was never outspoken.

In politics she seems to have favoured the Whig party, although here again she seems to have been reluctant to voice her opinions very loudly. She was friendly with Sheridan, though for reasons which will emerge presently she was not close to Charles James Fox.

In terms of her physical appearance, during her late teens and her early twenties she was short and somewhat plump. (Later in her life – like her third husband himself – she became obese.) She was generally considered a good-looking woman, and was said to have a good, smooth skin. Certainly, when the Prince became properly acquainted with the widowed Maria, he found her very attractive. Caricaturists, however, as we have already noted, liked to emphasise her large Roman nose. They also enjoyed depicting her capacious bosom.

One of Maria's most constant companions in London society was her maternal relative, Isabella, Countess of Sefton. One day in spring 1784, Maria accompanied Lady Sefton to the opera. The audience also included the Prince of Wales and this opera visit led to the prince's first proper meeting with Maria.[5] Prince George was enchanted with her and captivated by her. Perhaps predictably, at first he seems to have simply expected Maria to become his mistress. This is a scenario with which we are already familiar, from the earlier relationships of Edward IV with Eleanor Talbot and Elizabeth Woodville, and of Henry VIII with Anne Boleyn. However, like Eleanor, Elizabeth and Anne, Maria refused to enter into such an illicit – and from her point of view, immoral – relationship. Prince George then followed the examples of Edward IV and Henry VIII, by offering to marry Maria. Like Anne Boleyn, however, Maria declined the royal proposal. It is true that, unlike Henry VIII when he first made his offer to Anne Boleyn, George [IV] was not already married when he proposed to Maria. However, as Maria was very well aware, colossal legal impediments stood in the way of a marriage between a non-royal Catholic widow and a Hanoverian prince.

Pursued relentlessly by the prince, Maria decided to leave the country, and made plans to travel on the Continent. When Prince George heard what she had in mind, he made a dramatic feigned attempt at suicide, stabbing himself in Carlton House. Maria, accompanied by the Duchess of Devonshire, was induced to visit him, and during her visit he made renewed threats of suicide, which he proposed to carry into effect unless Maria would agree to marry him. Worn down by the hysterical scene, Maria finally consented, and the prince pressed a ring on to her finger as a sign that they were now betrothed.

Once she had left Carlton House, however, Maria immediately began to regret her decision. Maria's own surviving correspondence records her feeling that she had only agreed under pressure. As the Duchess of Devonshire later wrote, 'we went there [Carlton House] & she promis'd to marry him at her return [from her Continental holiday] but she conceives as well as myself that promises obtain'd in such a manner are entirely void'.[6] Maria therefore pressed ahead with her original plan, and departed, with companions, for the Continent.

During her travels Maria was subjected to a continuous torrent of correspondence from Prince George, urging his love for her and seeking repeatedly to make
their marriage a reality. Eventually, he overcame her scruples, and towards the end
of 1785 she returned to England. As she then told her friend, Lady Anne Lindsey,
'I have told him I will be his'.[7] Prince George consulted with Maria's maternal
uncle, Henry Errington, about the details of the marriage, and the couple was
married very secretly on the evening of 15 December 1785, in Maria's draw-
ing room in her Park Street house.[8] The ceremony was conducted according to
Anglican rites (as was then normal for Catholics resident in England) by one of
the prince's chaplains. His name was Rev. Robert Burt, and he had been in prison
for debt, but the prince had paid off Burt's debts in return for his conducting of
the marriage service. A record of the marriage was written out by the prince,
and was signed by himself, Maria, and the witnesses. This is an interesting new
development which we have not found in any previous alleged secret marriage.
The document reads:

> We the undersigned do witness that George Augustus Frederick, Prince
> of Wales, was married unto Maria Fitzherbert this 15th of December, 1785.
> John Smythe
> Henry Errington
> George P.
> Maria Fitzherbert [9]

As we have already seen, Errington was Maria's mother's brother. John Smythe
was one of Maria's own brothers. The couple honeymooned at Ham Common,
near Richmond.

After their honeymoon the couple did not actually live together, though the
prince bought Maria a house in Pall Mall, not far from his own residence at
Carlton House. Nevertheless they were frequently seen together, and speculation
and gossip about their relationship became rife. This caused Maria some problems.
Apart from her own immediate birth family, no one was aware of the marriage.
Consequently the families of Maria's two previous husbands assumed that she
had become the prince's mistress, and began to shun her.

Maria and George began to visit Brighton together. This was then a small fish-
ing village which had first been visited by the prince's uncle and aunt. Later
George himself had gone there to experiment with sea bathing, and found that
he liked the place. At first the couple used (separate) rented accommodation, but
after a couple of years George began building a home of his own – then called
'the Marine Pavilion' (now the Royal Pavilion).

Through this and other aspects of his lavish lifestyle George acquired large debts,
and in 1787 the prince began to seek the help of notable politicians in resolv-
ing his financial embarrassment. In return for such help George was required to

issue a public denial of his marriage to Maria. Charles James Fox, in particular, made in Parliament a very strong statement that no such marriage existed, and never could have existed. This upset Maria very much, and she never forgave Fox for his words. Despite the fact that George subsequently had Richard Brindsley Sheridan make a much milder parliamentary speech about the affair, Maria was not conciliated. She left her husband, and for a while she would have nothing to do with him. Only a further attempt at suicide on his part finally induced her to return to him.

Nevertheless, Maria's experiences at this period were not all negative. One outcome of the parliamentary discussion of her relationship with Prince George was that she became very much a public figure, and where previously she had been shunned, many people now made a point of visiting her. Perhaps inevitably, her life was never destined to be easy. In 1788–89 the crisis over the prince's regency for his sick father brought forth more parliamentary denials of Maria's marriage to George, together with hints in newspapers that her Catholicism must inevitably be linked with disloyalty. For example, she was accused of acting as an agent of the French Government.

Also, despite being the prince's wife, Maria was never the sole object of his attentions. Gradually George reverted to having mistresses, and on 8 April 1795 he also entered into a second, royal and politically expedient marriage with his cousin, Caroline of Brunswick.[10] In England this marriage was regarded as legal, but of course, in Maria's eyes it was bigamous. Rather like Louise of Stolberg after her marriage with 'Charles III', Caroline of Brunswick has been accused of later having lovers. She and George parted within a year of their marriage, and he later sought to divorce her on grounds of adultery, but was unable to prove anything against her.

Meanwhile the prince and Maria were no longer really an item. However, Maria behaved very well, refusing to use the record of their marriage (which she held), or the prince's many letters to her, against him. George was appreciative in his own way, and in 1796, when he was ill, and thought that he might die, he drafted a will in which Maria was named as almost his sole beneficiary.

After his recovery, George tried to persuade Maria to return to him, and although she would not immediately agree to do so, in 1799 she sought the advice of her confessor, Fr John Nassau. At his own suggestion, Fr John was sent to canvas papal opinion regarding the validity of Maria's marriage, and probably he took with him her marriage certificate. Maria herself declared that if the pope did not accept her union with the prince, then she would leave Britain for good and never see George again. The result, however, was unequivocal. Pope Pius VII declared that she was George's true wife in the eyes of God and the Church.[11] Once she had received this answer, Maria hesitated no longer. In 1800 she returned to her husband, and for the next eight years their relationship was a very happy one.

During this period, Maria acquired a 'daughter'. Mary ('Minnie') Seymour was ostensibly the child of Lord Hugh Seymour and his wife, Horatia (though the claim has also been advanced that in actuality she was the daughter of Maria herself, by the prince). When the little girl's official parents died in 1801, Maria virtually adopted Minnie, and finally, with her husband's help, a legal accommodation was agreed, whereby the child could stay with her. Minnie remained in Maria's care until her own marriage, in 1825.

Towards the end of 1806 the prince started an affair with Isabella, Lady Hertford, and his relationship with Maria suffered greatly as a result. Sometimes George – who was now in love with Lady Hertford – treated Maria with little respect. Matters between them reached crisis point on 18 December 1809, when Maria declined an invitation to join her husband at the Pavilion in Brighton on the grounds that she had been subjected to 'very great incivilities' there.[12] Thereafter, their relationship continued to worsen until, a year and a half later, in plans for a reception at Carlton House Maria was denied her usual seat at the prince's table. She therefore declined the invitation, and from that point onwards she rarely saw her husband. Maria was now living most of the time at Brighton, where she was still accorded quasi-royal status by the local population.

In 1813 Maria acquired a second 'daughter'. This was Marianne Smythe, who was ostensibly the illegitimate daughter of Maria's brother, Jack. The little girl was then aged 6, while Maria's elder 'daughter', Minnie (see above) was just 15. Inevitably, perhaps, there was speculation – both at the time and subsequently – about Maria's 'daughters'. The suggestion has been raised that one – or possibly both of them – was in reality Maria's child by the Prince of Wales. There are also rumours of a possible son of Maria's royal marriage:

> It is possible that Maria had a child or children by the Prince of Wales. A small boy who was adopted and taken to America may have been theirs. However Minnie Seymour, said to be the youngest child of great friends, or Marianne Smythe, said to be the illegitimate child of her brother Jack, both of whom Mrs Fitzherbert brought up, could also have been theirs. Certainly she divided her jewellery and possessions between them.[13]

However, the truth of this matter is difficult to determine.

In 1820 George IV succeeded to his father's throne upon the old king's death. His royal 'wife', Caroline of Brunswick, was excluded from his coronation ceremony, and later that same year George put her on trial for adultery. Maria is reputed to have expressed some sympathy for Caroline's situation – though she was very careful to ensure that she herself remained in Paris throughout Caroline's trial, lest Caroline's lawyer should make any attempt to call her as a witness.

Ten years later, in 1830, when George IV lay dying, Maria wrote to her husband for the last time. No answer is extant, and the king was probably too ill when he received her letter to respond to it. Even so, George was seen to be wearing a miniature portrait of Maria round his neck during his illness, and subsequently, at his own request, this portrait was buried with him.

After George IV's death, most of Maria's letters to him were burned by the Duke of Wellington and William Charles Keppel, fourth Earl of Albemarle – apparently with Maria's agreement, However, she preserved a few items, which were deposited at Coutts Bank. These included her marriage certificate of 1785 and also the text of George's will of 1796.

The new king, William IV (formerly Duke of Clarence), treated Maria with respect. Indeed, in general her relationship with the wider royal family had been good. She had been particularly close to Frederick, Duke of York, with whom she frequently corresponded. Shortly after his accession, William IV even offered to raise Maria to the rank of duchess. However, her answer to him was that 'she had borne through life the name of Mrs Fitzherbert; that she had never disgraced it, and did not wish to change it'.[14]

In her old age, Maria travelled a good deal, reputedly for health reasons, and as late as 1835 paid a visit to Paris. She died at her home, 55 The Steyne, Brighton, on 27 March 1837, and she was buried in St John the Baptist's Church, Brighton (which she had built) on 6 April of that year. Her body lies in a vault beneath the church. Her white marble mural funerary monument in the church itself depicts Maria kneeling in prayer. On the fourth finger of her left hand three gold wedding rings are conspicuously displayed.

18

MRS BROWN

John Brown stands out as a striking figure of a man in my boyhood memories. Often as I was playing with other children on the green slopes in the castle grounds Queen Victoria would come along in her chair drawn by a pony. A groom sometimes attended the pony, but by the Queen's side there always seemed to be John Brown with his rich Scots brogue.[1]

'Mrs Brown', or even 'the Empress Brown', was how journalists seeking sensational headlines sometimes referred to Queen Victoria during the period from roughly 1865 to 1883. As is well known, Victoria (reigned 1837–1901), who ascended the throne at the age of 18 and enjoyed the second longest reign in British history (if one counts that of 'James III' – see above), married the German Prince Albert of Saxe-Coburg-Gotha. This was a very successful marriage, and the couple had a large family. The marriage ended in December 1861, with Prince Albert's death from typhoid. The death was a shock to the queen and plunged her into a prolonged period of mourning. Naturally, no question has ever been raised as to the validity of Victoria's marriage to Albert.

It appears to have been in September 1849 that Queen Victoria first became aware of the existence of a Scottish servant called John Brown. At least, that was when his name was first recorded in her journal. Queen Victoria was 30 years old in September 1849, while Brown was then approaching his twenty-third birthday. At that time, of course, Prince Albert was still alive, and the royal family was just developing its interest in Balmoral. The Browns lived at Crathie, and John and some of his brothers were employed on the staff of the Balmoral estate. At about this time John was described by the Hon. Eleanor Stanley, one of the queen's maids of honour, as 'the most fascinating and good-looking young Highlander'.[2]

Despite later attempts by the queen to elevate his social status, Brown's ancestry was by no means distinguished. His family of tenant farmers was Presbyterian, but in the course of the eighteenth century they had espoused the cause of the exiled Catholic Stuarts. John Brown's great-grandfather had served under Lord Airlie in the army of Bonnie Prince Charlie in 1745, and was fortunate enough to survive the bloodbath at Culloden in April 1746.

Throughout the 1850s Brown served both the queen and her husband. In October 1852, for example, he attended the entire royal family at the cairn-building ceremony which marked the royal acquisition of the Balmoral estate, and a year later he was attending on them again at the laying of the foundation stone for Prince Albert's new Balmoral Castle. In fact, it seems to have been Prince Albert who initially marked out John Brown for promotion. In 1860 the prince – with his wife's full approval – chose Brown to ride on the box of the queen's carriage. Brown was also detailed to look after the queen while the prince was hunting the Highland deer. As the queen herself reported to her eldest daughter:

> Brown has had to do everything for me, indeed had charge of me and all, on all those expeditions, and therefore I settled that he should be specially appointed to attend on me (without any title) and have a full dress suit.[3]

It was in the late 1850s, while the Prince Consort was still living, that some have suggested that the queen became infatuated with John Brown. 'My Heart's in the Highlands', she wrote, quoting a poem by Robert Burns. 'Yes that is my feeling and I must fight and struggle against it'.[4] These words have been interpreted to imply that Brown was the focus of her affections. Certainly she already felt very dependent upon him. When her son, Prince Arthur, requested that Brown attend him on an excursion, the queen, who spoke German, replied that this was *unmöglich* (impossible), asking 'what should I do without him?'[5]

However, the death of the Prince Consort, in December 1862, changed the queen's life completely. Victoria did not attend her husband's funeral publicly, but watched the service from Catherine of Aragon's closet at St George's Chapel, Windsor. Subsequently she bemoaned her sense of loneliness and desolation. She needed a man about her, and in the long run it was Brown who was to supply this need. There is no doubt that he came to occupy a place of very great importance in her life, and his influence was sometimes astounding. Yet as Victoria herself made clear, riding her favourite pony, *Lochnagar*, with John Brown to escort her was, to her mind, no substitute for the company of her dead husband. It was merely 'a sad alternative for the delightful long walks with my beloved one'.[6]

Examples of the very considerable power and influence John Brown exerted over the royal household, and even over the queen herself, are not hard to find. Queen Victoria even tolerated Brown's drinking, and although she was normally utterly opposed to tobacco, Brown persuaded her to smoke on occasions, on the pretext of fending off the midges.

Of course, Brown's role in the queen's life did not pass unnoticed. On 7 July 1866 *Punch; or the London Charivari* published a celebrated spoof Court Circular, focusing entirely on Brown's activities:

Court Circular

Balmoral, Tuesday

MR JOHN BROWN walked on the slopes. He subsequently partook of haggis. In the evening MR JOHN BROWN was pleased to listen to a bagpipe. MR JOHN BROWN retired early.[7]

At the same time cartoons began to appear in the press, criticising Brown's role in the queen's life (*see Plate 28*). There was even speculation that the queen was married to him. Many have believed this story, both at the time and subsequently, while others have argued forcefully that the notion of such a marriage was impossible. In the final analysis it is hard to settle this question. On the one hand the idea of such a marriage seems preposterous. Yet what was the alternative? The queen's own children – who hated Brown – nevertheless referred to him as 'Mama's Lover', while the Earl of Derby recorded in his diary that Brown and Victoria slept in adjoining bedrooms, a practice which he abhorred as 'contrary to etiquette and even decency'.[8] *WHY? MR. BROWN WAS A HUMAN BEING LIKE VICTORIA.*

If Queen Victoria *was* married to John Brown, in what manner would they have married? Since Brown was Scottish, and the couple met, and partly lived, in Scotland, would theirs have been a marriage like that of 'Charles III' and his Clementina – a marriage 'by cohabitation with habit and repute'? Clearly, it did not fully satisfy the requirements for such a marriage under the then-existing law of Scotland, because the couple did not use married names. The appellation 'Mrs Brown' was merely an invention of the press. Also they did not openly live together as a couple. At the same time, however, their relationship did not conform to the requirements of the eighteenth-century English Marriage Act, since apparently no documentary record of a marriage exists – despite the fact that the case of George [IV] and 'Princess Fitz' (and possibly also the case of George [III] and Hannah Lightfoot) had already demonstrated that a secret marriage could be documented in this way.

Modern belief concerning a marriage between the queen and John Brown is based partly upon the supposed evidence of one of the queen's chaplains. A diary written by Lewis Harcourt, and only quite recently discovered, reports that one of Queen Victoria's chaplains, the Rev. Norman Macleod, confessed on his deathbed that he had personally officiated at the marriage of Brown and the queen. Macleod's confession was ostensibly an act of repentance for the role he had played on this occasion – a role which he had subsequently come to regret.

Unfortunately, while Harcourt probably genuinely believed what he wrote, the evidence of his diary is far from being 'the horse's mouth'. He was only 9 years old when the Rev. Macleod died, and he received the account from his father,

Sir William Harcourt (sometime Home Secretary), who in his turn had the tale from Henry Ponsonby, Queen Victoria's private secretary. Ponsonby derived his information from his wife, who had been Rev. Macleod's sister. With four individuals intervening between Rev. McLeod and Lewis Harcourt, it is very difficult to know exactly how much faith to place in the latter's account.

However, another piece of recently discovered evidence does clearly show that Queen Victoria had very deep feelings for Brown. Indeed, there was never really any reason to doubt this. The new evidence is the more forceful in that it comes directly from the queen's own pen. Following John Brown's death, Victoria wrote to Viscount Cranbrook:

> Perhaps never in history was there so strong and true an attachment, so warm and loving a friendship between the sovereign and servant … Strength of character as well as power of frame – the most fearless uprightness, kindness, sense of justice, honesty, independence and unselfishness combined with a tender, warm heart … made him one of the most remarkable men. The Queen feels that life for the second time is become most trying and sad to bear deprived of all she so needs … the blow has fallen too heavily not to be very heavily felt.[9]

The last sentence quoted here, with its reference to 'the second time', appears to equate the queen's sense of loss at Brown's death to the grievous loss she had previously felt at the death of her consort, Prince Albert. On this basis it has been argued that Victoria must have been married to John Brown – or that at the very least they were lovers.

The final piece of evidence, which shows the strength of the queen's feeling for her 'Highland servant', came at the very end of her life, when Brown himself was already dead and buried. On the queen's own specific instructions, following her death in 1901, various mementoes and keepsakes were placed with her body in her coffin, prior to her burial at Windsor. Naturally these included souvenirs of Prince Albert, comprising one of his dressing gowns and a plaster cast of his hand, both placed in the queen's coffin, at her side. But in the dead queen's *left* hand was placed a lock of John Brown's hair, together with some of the letters he had written to her and his photograph, wrapped in white tissue paper. All these souvenirs of John Brown were carefully concealed from view beneath a bunch of flowers. In addition, on the third (ring) finger of her *right* hand, the hand which in times past had traditionally received the wedding ring, Victoria wore – and still wears in her tomb – the wedding ring of John Brown's mother, which Brown himself had given to the queen in 1883.[10]

19

MURDERS IN WHITECHAPEL
AND MYSTERIES IN MALTA

Seek a cosy doorway in the middle of the night.

'Jack the Ripper' verse, 1888

I tell you at once that there is not the faintest vestige of truth in these statements.

The Attorney General, 1 February 1911

Queen Victoria's long reign had an impact on her heirs. Her son, Edward VII, had a lengthy wait before succeeding to the throne, and both he and Victoria herself outlived the next heir, Edward [VII]'s eldest son, the Duke of Clarence. As a result, when Edward VII died in 1910, he was succeeded by his second son, George V, who was born in 1865 and reigned from 1910 until 1936. As a child George had not been in the direct line of succession. Only in 1892 – when his elder brother, the Duke of Clarence, died – did he become second in line for the throne. When Clarence died, George [V] also inherited his elder brother's prospective bride, Princess Mary of Teck.

The future George V is said to have had several sexual partners prior to his marriage with Mary of Teck, which took place in 1893. These relationships appear mostly to have been ephemeral. However, at the time of the prince's marriage there were widespread rumours regarding one reported liaison, with a Miss Culme-Seymour, the daughter of an admiral. George [V] was reported to have had a relationship with Miss Culme-Seymour during the period from approximately 1889 to 1891. Not only was George said to have fathered children by this lady, but it was also rumoured that he had contracted a morganatic marriage with her. According to a later account, published in 1910, the relationship with Miss Culme-Seymour was alleged to have taken place while George was serving in Malta (see below). However, it is important to note that neither

Malta nor any other location for the relationship seems to have been specified in 1893.

The year in which reports of this alleged relationship first became public was 1893 – just at the time when the future George V was on the point of marrying Mary of Teck. On 25 April of that year George [V] wrote to his father's private secretary:

> The story of me being already married to an American is really very amusing. Cust has heard the same thing from England … and that my wife lived in Plymouth, why there I wonder?[1]

George's letter puts the story in a light-hearted way, suggesting that the tale existed in various versions, all of them ridiculous. But of course if the prince *had* been secretly married, there is no reason to suppose that he would have frankly revealed that fact to his father when he was on the point of contracting an official marriage. The mention of a naval base as the possible location for the relationship may possibly have been more significant than the prince's tone suggests. Plymouth has a name which sounds very similar to Portsmouth, and we know that George was in Portsmouth in 1891 (see below).

Just over a week after the prince's letter, on 2 May 1893, a Guernsey newspaper, the *Star*, stated that 'the rumour is persistently going round Naval circles that the Duke of York has lately married secretly the daughter of an English Naval Officer at Malta.[2] We should note that the mention of Malta in the *Star's* account refers only to the location in 1893 of the *appointment* of the Naval officer who was the bride's father. It implies nothing about where George was alleged to have met, or married, that officer's daughter. However, this and similar accounts may have later become the source of misunderstandings as to where the relationship took place. Of course, the *Star's* report was published on the very eve of the prince's engagement to Mary of Teck.

The tale resurfaced seventeen years later in a much fuller and more serious form. This was towards the end of 1910, soon after George V's accession. An account of the alleged relationship then appeared in a republican magazine called *The Liberator*, which was published in Paris, but which had a British editor – Edward F. Mylius – and which circulated in Britain. The article in *The Liberator* led to a court case, a full report of which was published on 2 February 1911 in the *New York Times*. This refers to 'the report, oft repeated, that King George, while a cadet in the Royal Navy, made a morganatic alliance with a daughter of Admiral Sir Michael Culme-Seymour'.[3]

The article in *The Liberator* had appeared under the title 'Sanctified Bigamy' and had claimed that:

> during the year 1890, in the Isle of Malta, the man who is now King of England was united in lawful and holy wedlock with the daughter of Sir Michael Culme-Seymour, an admiral of the British Navy. Of this marriage offspring were born.[4]

Flirting with a high-ranking naval officer.

Mylius clearly assumed (perhaps from a misreading of earlier accounts such as that published in the *Star*) that the liaison itself had taken place in Malta. This was probably an error on his part – and one for which he later paid dearly, since it could apparently be proved that Prince George had not been in Malta during the key period. The first name of the alleged wife was not supplied. The article continued:

> In order to obtain a woman of the royal blood for his pretended wife, George Frederick [*later George V*] foully abandoned his true wife, the daughter of Sir Michael Culme-Seymour, of the British Navy, and entered into a sham and shameful marriage with the daughter of the Duke of Teck in 1893. The said George Frederick not having been divorced, his first wife, by the common law of England, and by the law of the Christian Church, remains – and, if she still lives is – the true wife. He committed the crime of bigamy, and he committed it with the aid and complicity of the prelates of the Anglican Church.[5]

Admiral Sir Michael Culme-Seymour was a baronet descended from a cadet line of the Seymour family. He was thus a relative of the Duke of Somerset, of Queen Jane Seymour (wife of Henry VIII), and of her son, King Edward VI. The admiral actually had two daughters in 1890. The elder daughter was Mary, and although she was not specifically named as George [V]'s morganatic wife in 'Sanctified Bigamy', for some reason it subsequently seems to have been generally assumed throughout the court case of 1911 that she was the daughter referred to in that article. In 1899 Mary had married the future Admiral Sir Trevelyan Napier. However, Sir Michael Culme-Seymour also had a younger and rather more mysterious daughter: Laura Grace Culme-Seymour. It was reported that Laura had died in 1895, and was therefore not available to be questioned in 1911. We shall have more to say about Laura presently.

Sir Michael was called as a witness in the 1911 court case, and he testified that he had assumed command of the British Fleet in the Mediterranean in 1893, and that his wife and daughters had then joined him in Malta. He further stated that prior to 1893 none of these three women had ever set foot on that island. This undermined a key point in Mylius' published account – but we have already noted that Mylius' reference to Malta as the location for the relationship may simply have been based upon a misunderstanding of his sources in this respect. Sir Michael also claimed that Laura had never in her life so much as spoken to George [V]. Mary, on the other hand had met the future king in 1879, when she was a mere child of 8. Thereafter, her father stated, she had not encountered him again until 1898. Mary Culme-Seymour (Napier) and her three brothers, Michael, John and George, also gave testimony, which corroborated that of their father. However, their mother, Lady Seymour, was reported to be suffering from indifferent health. Consequently she neither gave evidence nor attended the trial.[6]

Evidence was also presented in court to show that between 1888 and 1901 George [V] had not visited Malta. In spite of this evidence, however, George certainly seems to have had a connection with the island at some point, for he served under the command of his uncle, Prince Alfred, Duke of Edinburgh, who was stationed in Malta. Moreover, he was known to have fallen in love with his uncle's elder daughter, Princess Marie of Edinburgh, and he had at one time sought to marry her. His own father, together with Marie's father and their joint grandmother, Queen Victoria, had all favoured this alliance. However, it had been opposed by the Princess of Wales (Alexandra of Denmark) and by the Duchess of Edinburgh (Grand Duchess Marie of Russia). Influenced by her mother, Princess Marie had therefore refused George's proposal, and she subsequently married the King of Romania in 1893. Perhaps it had been this earlier connection of George's love-life with a Maltese location, coupled with mentions like that in the *Star*, which misled Edward Mylius in his published account.

During the trial in 1911, all the marriage registers for the island of Malta – Catholic, Protestant, Greek Orthodox and civil – covering the period 1886 to 6 July 1893 (the date of George's marriage to Mary of Teck) were produced in court. Apparently not one of them showed any record of a marriage which could possibly have referred to George [V] and a Miss Culme-Seymour.

However, there is one further aspect of the evidence of the Culme-Seymour family which must be highlighted, because it could be very significant. 'Admiral Sir Michael Culme-Seymour, giving evidence, said he had five children – three boys and two girls … The younger [daughter], Laura Grace, died in 1895, unmarried'.[7] Subsequently this point was reinforced by the admiral's elder (and surviving) daughter, Mary Culme-Seymour (Napier). Mary's interrogation by the Attorney General produced the following exchange:

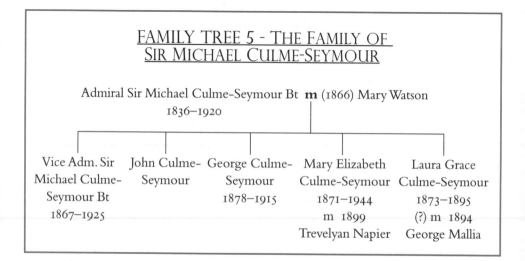

FAMILY TREE 5 - THE FAMILY OF SIR MICHAEL CULME-SEYMOUR

Admiral Sir Michael Culme-Seymour Bt **m** (1866) Mary Watson
1836–1920

| Vice Adm. Sir Michael Culme-Seymour Bt 1867–1925 | John Culme-Seymour | George Culme-Seymour 1878–1915 | Mary Elizabeth Culme-Seymour 1871–1944 m 1899 Trevelyan Napier | Laura Grace Culme-Seymour 1873–1895 (?) m 1894 George Mallia |

Would you know if your sister had contracted any marriage?
Yes, certainly.
Did she ever marry?
No.[8]

Again, we shall return to this point presently.

✣ ✣ ✣

Edward Mylius was found guilty of libel, and was sentenced to a year's imprisonment. Subsequently, however, he returned to the offensive, publishing a pamphlet on *The Morganatic Marriage of George V* in New York in 1916. Interestingly, in this second publication Mylius produced some new evidence, aimed at showing that the Culme-Seymours had committed perjury. He demonstrated that when Mary Culme-Seymour (Napier) had sworn under oath in 1911 that she did not meet George [V] between 1879 and 1898 she had, at the very least, been guilty of a terminological inexactitude. The archives of the *Hampshire Telegraph and Sussex Chronicle* proved that on 21 August 1891 Mary had opened the ball at Portmouth Town Hall by dancing with Prince George. While Mary's error seems, in itself, insufficient to overturn the verdict of 1911, or to prove the allegation of royal bigamy:

> it is difficult to believe that it was a mere mistake. Opening the dancing at a ball with the Prince of Wales (*sic*) is not the kind of thing a young lady of her background would ordinarily forget. For the purposes of her testimony in the criminal libel trial it may have been an inconvenient truth best forgotten.[9]

Mylius did not apparently have access to any further evidence to discredit the testimony of the Culme-Seymours. Nevertheless, had he but known it, other indications exist to show that the family may have lied. We have seen that both the Admiral and his surviving daughter, Mary, insisted that Laura Culme-Seymour had never been married. Yet the present author has found some evidence to the contrary – evidence which seems previously to have been overlooked. A website entitled Maltagenealogy, and subtitled *Libro d'Oro di Melita*, explores the descendants of a Maltese nobleman, Salvatore Mallia Tabone, first Marchese di Fiddien, whose title was created in 1785. The list of Salvatore's descendants includes:

> 6.2.2. George Mallia, (1875–1966 Ohio USA)., married (1) 1894 Civil at Valletta to Laura Grace Culme-Seymour (d. Valletta 1895) (daughter of Admiral Sir Michael Culme-Seymour, 3rd Bt), married (2) 1899 London to Laura Lopes, with issue.[10]

An enquiry to the owner of this website revealed that 'a lot of the data on the Marchese di Fiddien was provided through private donors' and has not necessarily been confirmed from official documentary sources.[11] Nevertheless, the information regarding Laura's official date of death does appear to be correct, in so far as this can be checked (but see below). If the account of her marriage to George Mallia is also true, then when the Culme-Seymours declared unequivocally in 1911 that Laura had died unmarried, they would have been lying. However, there now appears to be no surviving record of any marriage of Laura Culme-Seymour in the Public Registry in Valletta.[12] Since she allegedly married George Mallia in Valletta in 1894, her name should have been recorded in the Maltese marriage registers for that year. Interestingly, the Maltese registers presented in court in 1911 covered only the period to 1893. Was history perhaps being edited for the trial?

What is even more curious is the fact that attempts by the present writer to find an official record documenting the allegation that Laura died in Malta in 1895 encountered many difficulties. The British General Register Office appears to have no record of this event, either under the surname Culme-Seymour or under the surname Mallia. Likewise no record of Laura's death is available in response to an in-person enquiry at the Maltese Public Registry under either of these surnames. Attempts both by myself and by a Maltese colleague to order a full death certificate from the Maltese Public Registry online also received the response that no such record was available. It subsequently transpired, however, that an *extract* death certificate could be ordered online. The resulting statement of death describes Laura as a spinster and gives the date of her death as Friday 22 November 1895. Because it is only an extract and not a full certificate, key items of information are omitted. No cause of death is stated, nor is it specified by whom the death had been officially notified. Details of the attempt to obtain Laura's death certificate are given in Appendix 4.

Meanwhile, the Ta' Braxia cemetery in Malta certainly contains a grave inscribed:

IN LOVING MEMORY OF
LAURA GRACE
DAUGHTER OF ADMIRAL SIR MICHAEL
AND LADY CULME SEYMOUR

BORN JULY 18 1873
FELL ASLEEP NOVEMBER 22 1895
WHEN I AWAKE UP AFTER THY LIKENESS
I SHALL BE SATISFIED WITH IT[13]

The grave (vault Z 11) was once surmounted by a cross, which has collapsed, and which now lies on the surface of the gravestone. The monument is situated beside the wall on the southern side of the cemetery. It is interesting to note that the inscription on the gravestone gives no information regarding Laura's surname at the time of her death. It merely records the surname of her parents.

✠ ✠ ✠

The king himself did not appear in court in 1911, despite the fact that Mylius would have liked to subpoena him (and sought to do so). In fact it is very clear that the whole trial epitomised what one recent writer on the subject has described as 'legal and constitutional realpolitik ... [for] the prosecution of Mylius is an example of the legal process having been intentionally constructed to help secure a particular outcome ... [Moreover] as an exercise of the Attorney General's powers it was arguably an abusive prosecution'.[14] Evidently the government of the day – including the Home Secretary, Winston Churchill – took a very heavy hand in the proceedings. In addition, in a curious sequel to the problems encountered in locating the record of Laura Culme-Seymour's death in Malta (not to mention the confusion surrounding her relationship – if any – with George Mallia), we should also note that the surviving records of the 1911 court case, both in the British National Archives and in the Royal Archives at Windsor, now appear to be incomplete, implying that they may subsequently have been tampered with.[15]

✠ ✠ ✠

Although the king was not present at the trial, after the verdict had been given a statement on his behalf was made by the Attorney-General, who said:

> I am authorised by His Majesty to state publicly that he was never married except to the Queen and that he never went through any ceremony of marriage except with the Queen.[16]

This is as clear and precise as the statements which we saw earlier from King Charles II (see above), and in the light of the overall evidence presented at the trial it would seem that we must accept it. Questions remain, however. First, if Mary Culme-Seymour lied under oath about her meetings with George [V], and if she and her father both lied about Laura's marriage to George Mallia, can we have any confidence that they, or the other members of her family who testified, told the truth, the whole truth and nothing but the truth in other respects? Second, why was it apparently assumed throughout the court case that the daughter who was alleged to have had a relationship with George [V] was *Mary* Culme-Seymour? No Christian name had been published in any of the accounts of the liaison. Thus, the story could well have referred not to Mary, but to her younger sister, Laura (who was apparently unavailable to be questioned in 1911). If it did refer to Laura, even if there was no evidence of a marriage between her and George [V], it is nevertheless possible that she enjoyed a relationship of some kind with the future king, and perhaps bore him a child or children. Most curious of all are the problems which seem to surround both records of Laura's life and death and the official records of the 1911 court case. Do Laura's remains really lie under the gravestone at Ta' Braxia?

✠ ✠ ✠

Even more scandalous allegations of secret marriage have been published involving George V's elder brother, Albert Victor, Duke of Clarence, known as 'Eddy'. These allegations link the Duke of Clarence with the Whitechapel murders of Jack the Ripper. The allegations have appeared in various forms, but the most recent and colourful version claims that the Whitechapel murders were an attempt by the royal family's doctor to protect the reigning dynasty from the consequences of the Duke of Clarence's secret and illicit marriage to a Catholic girl called Annie Elizabeth Crooks. This alleged marriage reputedly produced a daughter called Alice Crooks, whose potential claim to the throne was thought to pose a threat to the future of the dynasty.

The Duke of Clarence is an unfortunate prince who has been harshly handled, both by his contemporaries and by some historians. His early death has been described as fortuitous for the future of the royal house, and he has been accused of immorality and homosexuality. It is difficult to offer a fair assessment of his true character.

There is no doubt whatever that he did seriously contemplate marriage with a Catholic, but the consort he had in mind was no commoner but Princess Hélène of France, daughter of the Orléanist pretender to the French throne, who was then living in exile in the United Kingdom. After initial opposition from his grandmother, 'Eddy' and Hélène did eventually succeed in convincing Queen Victoria that they were in love, and the queen was then willing to countenance the alliance. However, Princess Hélène's father and Pope Leo XIII proved harder nuts to crack, and eventually the planned alliance was abandoned.

As for the Whitechapel murders, of course these did really take place in 1888. However, it is easy to demonstrate that they could not possibly have been committed by the Duke of Clarence in person, because he had clear alibis for all the traditionally accepted Jack the Ripper murders. Nevertheless, as we have seen, the case against Clarence, as most recently presented, does not argue that Eddy committed the murders himself, but rather that they were carried out by Queen Victoria's physician, Dr Gull, in an attempt to protect the royal family from the possible consequences of the Duke's secret marriage to Annie Crooks.

It was said that Annie, who had been hospitalised and driven – or at least certified – insane by Gull, had left her royal daughter Alice in the care of Mary Jane Kelly, her co-religionist, and the last of the traditionally accepted Ripper victims. The Ripper murders were allegedly designed to intimidate – and ultimately to get rid of – all those of Annie's friends who had knowledge of her royal marriage and of the birth of her royal daughter.

Like George III's alleged bride, Hannah Lightfoot, Annie Elizabeth Crook was undoubtedly a real person. Moreover, she did give birth to a daughter called Alice Crook, at Marylebone Workhouse on 18 April 1885. Alice's birth certificate names no father. A link has been proposed (though not proved) between Annie Elizabeth Crook and a woman called 'Elizabeth Cook' who was living at 6 Cleveland Street in the 1880s. Annie was said to have met the Duke of Clarence for the first time at 15 Cleveland Street – at the studios of artist William Sickert, where Annie was working part-time as a model.

The story of Clarence, Annie, Alice, Dr Gull and Jack the Ripper sounds exciting and has naturally attracted wide interest, but unfortunately – like the case of the 'Tudor Rose/Tudor Prince' theory which we examined earlier – real evidence to substantiate the 'Clarence/Ripper' hypothesis seems to be completely lacking. Moreover, assuming that Annie Crook's pregnancy was of the normal duration, then the Duke of Clarence could not possibly have been Alice's father because he had been in Germany in July and August 1884. Moreover, there is absolutely no evidence to substantiate the claim that Annie Crook was a Catholic – although her alleged religion was supposedly one of the key elements in the secret marriage allegation against the Duke of Clarence.

20

REVIEW OF SECRET MARRIAGE ALLEGATIONS IN THE MODERN MONARCHY

The situation governing marriage in general – and royal marriage in particular – in the final section of our study was very different from that pertaining previously, and it shows enormous changes when compared with the situation in the medieval period. The cases of George [III] and Hannah Lightfoot, and of George [IV] and 'Princess Fitz', show clearly that, even in an alleged secret marriage, the need for documentary evidence was now accepted, and an attempt could be made to meet it. At the same time, however, religious bigotry had now become a matter of legislation, as had the requirement for the formal consent of the reigning monarch. The consequence of such legislation was that royal marriage was now something unique – a thing set apart from the marriage of the general public. Thus, if George [IV] had not been royal, his marriage to Maria – even though it had been clandestine, and had not been preceded by the publication of banns – would probably have been universally accepted as legal and binding.

The set of royal marriage regulations in force from the eighteenth to the twentieth centuries is one which has – quite wrongly – been seen until recently as typical of royal marriage throughout history, leading to misleading generalisations such as the one which was quoted in our first chapter. Thus for many years there was the expectation that English royalty would marry foreign, Protestant, virginal, royal brides in public ceremonies arranged – or at least approved – by the reigning sovereign.

But our exploration of the past has already shown us very clearly that such rules did not always apply. In the later Middle Ages Plantagenet princes – whether Lancaster or York – actually experienced very little difficulty in marrying non-royal brides: even brides who had been married previously and who already had children. Likewise the so-called 'Tudor' monarchs and their family felt the same freedom, so that Henry VIII and his sisters married – and his daughter Elizabeth considered marrying – English commoners just as readily as they considered marrying foreign royalty. And during the sixteenth century there was still no requirement for the consort to have been previously unmarried.

Later, the Stuarts showed similar flexibility. Mary Queen of Scots, James II and 'Charles III' chose spouses for love, not status, as did many of the children of Charles I's sister, Queen Elizabeth of Bohemia – including, as we have seen, her son, Prince Rupert. Moreover, throughout this very long period, and even after the Reformation, no questions were asked about the religion of potential royal spouses. Elizabeth I cheerfully considered the claims of Catholic suitors, while her Catholic cousin, Mary Queen of Scots, could marry a Protestant. And Elizabeth's Stuart successors mostly married Catholics – though their children were then brought up as Anglicans.

It is only with the 'Glorious Revolution' of 1688 that the element of bigotry was introduced into the selection of English – or British – royal consorts. From this time onwards religious conditions had to be met by prospective royal spouses. And it is only in the days of 'mad king' George III (who sadly seems to have been thwarted in his own choice of a bride for love) that we finally encounter the introduction of draconian rules which preferred foreign (preferably German) 'princesses' to the fairest, most moral and most accomplished native-born potential royal marriage partners. Moreover, these German 'princesses' were frequently not princesses in the usual English meaning of that word. That is to say, they were not the daughters or granddaughters of kings or emperors.

Fortunately the rules governing royal marriage have recently been interpreted with much greater flexibility. Indeed they may now, at last, be approaching their legal end. Thus the late twentieth century witnessed, for the first time since the troubled episode of 'Princess Fitz', the appearance of Catholic spouses in the British royal family. The notion that a royal consort should be of royal – and hence probably foreign – birth had been questioned even a little earlier, and during the course of the twentieth century the selection of spouses who were clearly not royal by birth once again became acceptable. Even so, in 1936 a virgin bride was apparently still considered a requirement. Also, following the abdication of his brother, Edward VIII, the accession of George VI (whose wife was non-royal) was initially questioned. Some politicians expressed a preference for a younger son of the late George V – the Duke of Kent, whose wife, Marina of Greece, was a foreign princess, rather than the daughter of a British peer.

So what is our final verdict on the allegations of secret marriages involving George III and his brothers, George IV, Queen Victoria and the sons of Edward VII? George III's brothers definitely contracted secret and non-royal marriages. Moreover, it is at least possible that the bizarre 'Princess Olive' was Cumberland's legitimate daughter – though she was excluded from the royal family because King George III disapproved of her mother. As for George III himself, it seems unlikely that he could have married Hannah Lightfoot – the chronology seems not to fit. However, he may well have loved her, and she might have borne him a child or children.

The love of George [IV] for Maria Smythe cannot be questioned. Nor can the fact that he contracted a secret marriage with her. In their case the problem (and it is a new problem which we did not encounter in any of the earlier cases) was simply the *legality* of their situation. In an earlier period – even as recently as one generation earlier – it would probably have been impossible to deny their marriage, and hopefully today no one would even try to keep them apart. But under the new legislation current in their day they had a problem.

As for Queen Victoria, there seems no possible reason for denying her affection for John Brown. Moreover, since she was the reigning monarch she could, had she so wished, have approved her own marriage to Brown. In fact, however, there is no surviving evidence of a marriage between them. The same is true in the cases of her two grandsons. There is no surviving proof that Eddy married Annie Crook, or that George [V] married Miss Culme-Seymour. As for relationships in these two cases, we cannot say. Eddy may perhaps have had a brief fling with Annie – though it seems unlikely that he fathered her daughter. George may well have had a relationship with Laura, but the allegation that she bore him children cannot be judged, because no clear evidence on this point has yet come to light.

Indeed, as we have seen, even such basic facts as Laura's date and place of death have proved difficult to verify. This is a very strange situation. In this context it might, perhaps, be relevant to recall a precedent – namely the fact that in 1468, following the death of Eleanor Talbot, the government appears to have taken deliberate action to edit the official record in respect of Eleanor's death in such a way as to conceal evidence of her relationship with King Edward IV. Eleanor's inquisition *post mortem* avoided any examination of her tenure of estates which had probably been given to her by the king.

21

CONCLUSIONS:
THE QUEENS-THAT-
MIGHT-HAVE-BEEN

Since, for chronological reasons, we have, on the whole, dismissed the idea that Elizabeth I was secretly married, and since strong doubts remain about the notion that Queen Victoria may have gone through a form of marriage with John Brown, there seems to be no strong case for English or British male consorts-who-might-have-been. On the other hand, in the case of female consorts, there are several serious possibilities to consider, as well as some contenders for whom the case seems less convincing.

The first 'might-have-been' queen is Eleanor Talbot. The idea that she was secretly married to Edward IV has been dismissed far too easily in the past – and chiefly by writers who had taken very little trouble to seek real evidence about Eleanor and her relationship with Edward. Eleanor was a high-born lady. Her family was very well accustomed to exercising power and influence and bestowing patronage. Her younger sister proved well able to do this in her capacity of Duchess of Norfolk (as surviving Paston Letters testify), and her first cousin, Anne of Warwick, took on first the role of Princess of Wales and subsequently that of queen. There is therefore no reason to suppose that Eleanor would have experienced any particular difficulty in assuming the consort's Crown. Not being a *parvenue*, she would have had no need to indulge in the nepotism and financial sharp practices which subsequently tended to make her rival, Elizabeth Woodville, unpopular. Eleanor was also a moral and devout lady, which might perhaps have helped her to be a good queen. However, she suffered from one very big drawback as a candidate for the role of queen consort: she seems to have had difficulty in conceiving children. Eleanor was never recognised as queen during her lifetime, and she never sought such recognition. However, her marriage to the king was officially – and probably uniquely – recognised in an Act of Parliament. She therefore has a strong claim not to be continually denigrated as Edward IV's 'mistress' – a title which would unquestionably have shocked and offended her.

Clementina Walkinshaw was also a religious lady. She came from a gentry background and seems to have been able to cope even with rather difficult situations, and to have been a kind person. She bore a daughter and heiress who also seems to have had good qualities in terms of character, though she suffered from ill health. Perhaps Clementina could have made a good queen. We know from her conduct during her lifetime that she would have wished to be remembered by history as a wife, and not as a mistress. But in her case, of course, to have become a queen she would have needed to overcome not only questions about her marriage, but also the exclusion of the Catholic Stuart dynasty from the British throne.

Maria Smythe also seems to have been a promising candidate for a consort's Crown, and at least some contemporaries so described her. She too was a moral and religious lady, and we know from her behaviour that she objected very much to any suggestion that she was not married to George [IV]. She was admired by many in her day for her upright character and her charm, and she tried to curb her husband's expenditure. In Maria's case there is no possible question about the *fact* of her royal marriage. The only problem is that on several grounds that marriage contravened the British succession law as then enacted. If we are considering Maria as a potential queen, we are also left with some uncertainty about her capacity to produce heirs to the throne. Although it has been suggested that she did produce a child or children by George [IV], this remains open to dispute, and it is certain that her first two marriages had remained childless.

Little information is available about Laura Culme-Seymour. Like several of our other contenders she had an ancestral relative who had previously worn the consort's Crown, and her family background may have meant that she would have been able to take on a public role without too much difficulty. But in her case, despite some new evidence which has now been revealed, a great deal of uncertainty about the facts remains. It must now be considered possible that she had a relationship with the future George V, just as a widespread contemporary rumour suggested, even though both Laura's family and the king later publicly denied this in a court of law. I have suggested that the confused state of the evidence today recalls, in some ways, the official action on the part of the government of Edward IV to hide evidence of his relationship with Eleanor Talbot at the time of *that* lady's demise. Unlike the case of Edward IV and Eleanor, however, it is by no means certain that there was ever any form of *marriage* between George [V] and Laura. Moreover, Laura, like Eleanor Talbot and perhaps Maria Smythe, may not have been well equipped to produce heirs to the throne. In addition, her early death (if true) means that she might not, in any case, have survived long enough to wear the consort's Crown which her distant cousin, Jane, had briefly assumed in the reign of Henry VIII.

Anne Boleyn was officially demoted by Henry VIII, but history has treated her more kindly than he did. Whatever the truth about the technicalities of her marriage, she has consistently been remembered by history as a Queen of England. Also, despite her lack of living sons, she did produce an heir to the throne – an heir, moreover, who, despite the questions about her birth, ultimately became one of England's most celebrated monarchs.

As for Lucy Walter, her relationship with the future King Charles II is beyond doubt, and by him she produced a son, and a line of descendants of whom she could have been proud. However, Charles himself consistently denied that he had ever been married to her, and no real evidence has been found to undermine his official statements. Fortunately, perhaps, Lucy died before the Restoration of the Monarchy, so there was never any question of her making a bid for the role of queen – a role for which her suitability seems in some respects to have been questionable.

Finally we come to Hannah Lightfoot, a mystery figure about whom so little is known that her suitability for a consort's Crown is impossible to evaluate. In the past Hannah's very existence was questioned, but recent research has shown that this was unjustified. Nevertheless, the question of a marriage between her and George [III] remains very open. Although it now appears possible that there really was a relationship between them, on balance it seems improbable that they ever married.

APPENDIX 1

MONARCHS OF ENGLAND AND THEIR CONSORTS

Controversial consorts examined in this book are included, with question marks.

'Foreign' royal consorts (children or grandchildren of a foreign monarch) are marked in bold. Only nineteen out of forty-nine monarchs or heirs listed here (abut 39 per cent) married such 'foreign' royal consorts. Most of the Lancastrian and Stuart sovereigns did so, but since the Hanoverian accession there have only been two such 'foreign' royal marriages.

William I	Matilda of Flanders
William II	[none]
Henry I	**Matilda (Edith) of Scotland**; Adeliza of Louvain
Stephen/	Matilda of Boulogne
Matilda (civil war)	**Emperor Henry V**; Geoffrey, Count of Anjou
Henry II	Eleanor of Aquitaine
[Henry the Young King	**Margaret of France**]
Richard I	Berengaria of Navarre
John	Isabel (Hawise) of Gloucester; Isabelle of Angoulême
Henry III	Eleanor of Provence
Edward I	**Eleanor of Castile**; **Margaret of France**
Edward II	**Isabelle of France**
Edward III	Philippa of Hainaut
[Edward the Black Prince	Joan of Kent]
Richard II	**Anne of Bohemia**; **Isabelle of France**
Henry IV	Mary de Bohun; **Joanna of Navarre**
Henry V	**Catherine of France**
Henry VI	**Margaret of Anjou**
Edward IV	?Eleanor Talbot; ?Elizabeth Woodville

Edward V	[?none]
Richard III	Anne Neville
Henry VII	Elizabeth of York
Henry VIII	**?Catherine of Aragon**; ?Anne Boleyn; Jane Seymour; ?Anne of Cleves; ?Catherine Howard; Catherine Parr
Edward VI	[none]
[Jane	Guildford Dudley]
Mary I	**Philip II of Spain**
Elizabeth I	?none; ?Robert Dudley, Earl of Leicester
James I	**Anne of Denmark**
Charles I	**Henrietta Maria of France**
interregnum	
Charles II	?Lucy Walter; **Catherine of Bragança**
James II	Anne Hyde; Mary of Modena
William III and Mary II	(married couple)
Anne	**George of Denmark**
[*James III*	*Maria Clementina Sobieska*]
[*Charles III*	*?Clementina Walkinshaw; ?Louise of Stolberg*]
[*Henry IX*	*none*]
George I	Sophia Dorothea of Celle
George II	Caroline of Ansbach
[Frederick, Prince of Wales	Augusta of Saxe-Gotha-Altenburg]
George III	?Hannah Lightfoot; ?Charlotte of Mecklenburg
George IV	?Maria Smythe; ?Caroline of Brunswick
William IV	Adelaide of Saxe-Meiningen
Victoria	Albert of Saxe-Coburg-Gotha; ?John Brown
Edward VII	**Alexandra of Denmark**
[Albert Victor, Duke of Clarence	?Annie Elizabeth Crook]
George V	?Laura Culme-Seymour; ?Mary of Teck
Edward VIII	Bessie Wallis Warfield
George VI	Elizabeth Bowes-Lyon
Elizabeth II	**Philip of Greece and Denmark**

APPENDIX 2

LIST OF ROYAL EXTRAMARITAL AFFAIRS

For marriage partners and alleged marriage partners see Appendix 1.

William I
No recorded mistress

William II
No recorded mistress

Henry I
Gieva de Tracy
Ansfride …
Sybil (*or* Adela *or* Lucia) Corbet
Edith Fitzforne
Nest ferch Rhys, daughter of Rhys ap Tewdwr, last King of South Wales
Isabel de Beaumont.

Stephen
No recorded mistress

Henry II
Ykenai (or Hikenai), described as a 'prostitute'
Ida de Toesny, Countess of Norfolk, was very likely a daughter of Ralph V de
Tosny (died 1162) and his wife Margaret (born circa 1125 and living in 1185), a
daughter of Robert de Beaumont, 2nd Earl of Leicester.
Nest(?), wife of Ralph Bloet
Alys of France, Countess of the Vexin
Rosamund Clifford

Richard I
No recorded mistress

John
Clemence d'Arcy [Pinel] – mother of Joan of Wales
… de Warenne

Henry III
No recorded mistress

Edward I
No recorded mistress

Edward II
Male lovers: Piers Gaveston; Hugh Despenser – no recorded mistress, but one illegitimate son

Edward III
Alice Salisbury (Perrers; Windsor), lady-in-waiting to Queen Philippa
?Catherine Montacute (or Montagu), Countess of Salisbury

John of Gaunt
Catherine de Roët (Swynford)

Richard II
No recorded mistress

Henry IV
No recorded mistress

Henry V
No recorded mistress

Henry VI
No recorded mistress

Edward IV
Elizabeth Wayte (Lucy)
Elizabeth Lambert

Richard III
No mistress as king, but ?Catherine Haute before his marriage

Henry VII
No recorded mistress as king, but unnamed mother of Sir Roland de Velville before his marriage

Henry VIII
Ann Stafford [Hastings] Countess of Huntingdon (niece of Elizabeth Woodville)
Elizabeth Blount
Mary Boleyn
Elizabeth Bryce
Anne Bassett
Elizabeth Bryan (Carew)
Elizabeth Browne (Somerset) Countess of Worcester
Margaret Shelton
[Mary Shelton]

Edward VI
No recorded mistress

Mary I
No recorded lovers

Elizabeth I
?Thomas Seymour, ?Edward de Vere, Earl of Oxford

James I
Male lovers but no recorded mistress

Charles I
No recorded mistress

Charles II
Barbara Palmer
Moll Davis
Nell Gwynn
Hortense Mancini
Catherine Pegge
Louise De Kerouaille
Elizabeth Killigrew, Viscountess Shannon
Lucy Walter
Winnifred Wells

James II
Arabella Churchill
+ 10 other short-lived affairs
Catherine Sedley, Countess of Dorchester, Countess of Portmore

William III
Elizabeth Villiers
Elizabeth Hamilton, Countess of Orkney

Mary II
None

Anne
None but relationships with
Sarah Churchill, Duchess of Marlborough
Abigail, Baroness Masham

[James III
None

Charles III
Marie-Louise de la Tour d'Auvergne and others

Henry IX
None]

George I
Ehrengard Melusine Baroness von der Schulenburg, Duchess of Kendal and
Duchess of Munster

George II
Henrietta Howard
Amalie Sophie Marianne von Wallmoden, 1st Countess of Yarmouth

Frederick, Prince of Wales
None

George III
None

George IV
Mary Robinson
Grace Elliot
Frances Countess of Jersey
Marchioness of Hertford
Marchioness Conyngham

William IV
Dorothea Bland [Mrs Jordan]

Victoria
None

Edward VII
Alice Keppel and others

George V
Several prior to his marriage – names unknown

Edward VIII
Thelma, Lady Furness and others

George VI
None

ORIGINAL DOCUMENTS

1. Text of the 'Remarriage of Widowed Queens' statute of 1427.[1]
Original in French.

Item, it is ordered and established by the authority of this parliament for the
preservation of the honour of the most noble estate of queens of England that
no man of whatever estate or condition make contract of betrothal or matrimony to marry himself to the queen of England without the special licence
and assent of the king, when the latter is of the age of discretion, and he who
acts to the contrary and is duly convicted will forfeit for his whole life all his
lands and tenements, even those which are or which will be in his own hands
as well as those which are or which will be in the hands of others to his use,
and also all his goods and chattels in whosoever's hands they are, considering
that by the disparagement of the queen the estate and honour of the king will
be most greatly damaged, and it will give the greatest comfort and example
to other ladies of rank who are of the blood royal that they might not be so
lightly disparaged.

**2. Extract from the Petition to Richard, Duke of Gloucester, 26 June
1483 (as quoted in the Act of Parliament (*titulus regius*) of January 1484.**[2]

Over this, amonges other thinges, more specially we consider howe that the
tyme of the raigne of Kyng Edward IV, late-decessed, — after the ungracious,
pretensed marriage (as all England hath cause so say) made betwixt the said
King Edward and Elizabeth (sometyme wife to Sir John Grey, Knight), late
nameing herself (and many years heretofore) "Queene of England", — the
ordre of all politeque rule was perverted ... unto the grete sorrowe and heavy-
nesse of all true Englishmen.

And here also we considre howe the said pretensed marriage betwixt the above-named King Edward and Elizabeth Grey was made of grete presumption, without the knowyng or assent of the lordes of this lond, and alsoe by sorcerie and wichecrafte committed by the said Elizabeth and her moder, Jaquett, Duchess of Bedford (as the common opinion of the people and the publique voice and fame is through all this land; and hereafter — if, and as, the case shall require — shall bee proved suffyciently, in tyme and place convenient).

And here also we considre how that the said pretensed marriage was made privatly and secretly, without edition of banns, in a private chamber, a profane place, and not openly, in the face of church, aftre the lawe of Godds churche, but contrarie thereunto, and the laudable custome of the churche of England. And howe also that at the tyme of contract of the same pretensed marriage (and bifore, and longe tyme after) the said King Edward was, and stoode, marryed, and trouth-plyght, to oone Dame Elianore Butteler (doughter of the old Earl of Shrewesbury) with whom the saide King Edward had made a precontracte of matrimonie longe tyme bifore he made the said pretensed mariage with the said Elizabeth Grey in manner and fourme aforesaide.

Which premises being true (as in veray trouth they been true), it appeareth and followeth evidently that the said King Edward (duryng his lyfe) and the said Elizabeth lived togather sinfully and dampnably in adultery, against the lawe of God and his church. And therefore noe marvaile that (the souverain lord and head of this londe being of such ungodly disposicion and provokyng the ire and indignation of oure Lorde God) such haynous mischiefs and inconvenients as is above remembered were used and committed in the reame amongst the subjects.

Also it appeareth evidently, and followeth, that all th'issue and children of the said king beene bastards, and unable to inherite or to clayme anything by inheritance, by the lawe and custome of England.

3. Title to the throne (*titulus regius*) – Act of Henry VII, November 1485.[3]

To the pleasure of Almyghty God, the welthe, prosperitie and suertie of this realme of Englond, to the synguler comforth of all the kynges subgettes of the same, and in avoydyng of all ambiguyties and quescions, be it ordeyned, establisshed and enacted, by auctorite of this present parliament, that thenheritaunce of the corounez of the realmes of England and of Fraunce, with all the preemynence and dignytie roiall to the same perteynyng, and all other seigneuriez to the kyng belongyng beyond the see, with thappurtenaunces therto in eny wise due or perteynyng, be, rest, remayne and abyde in the most royall person of our nowe soverain lord Kyng Henry the .vij.ᵗʰ, and in the heires of his body laufully comyng, perpetuelly with the grace of God so to endure, and in noon other.

4. Henry VII's unquoted repeal of Richard III's Act naming Eleanor Talbot as Edward IV's true wife – November 1485.[4]

Where afore this tyme, Richard, late duke of Glouc', and after in dede and not of right kyng of Englond, called Richard the third, caused a falce and sedicious bill of false and malicious ymagynacions, ayenst all gode and trewe disposicion, to be put unto hym, the begynnyng of which billeys thus:
'Please it youre noble grace to understond the consideracions, eleccion and peticion underwryten', etc.

Wheche bill, after that, with all the contynue of the same, by auctorite of parlement, holden the first yere of the usurped reigne of the seid late Kyng Richard the thirde, was ratified, enrolled, recorded, approved and auctorised, as in the same more playnly apereth. The kyng, at the speciall instance, desire and prayer of the lordes spirituall and temporall and of the comons in thys present parlement assembled, woll it be ordeyned, stablisshed and enacted, by thadvyce of the seid lordes spirituall and temporall and the comons in this present parlement assembled, and by auctorite of the same, that the seid bill, acte and ratificacion, with alle the circumstances and dependauntes of the same byll and acte, for the false and cedicious ymagynacion and untrouth therof, be voide, adnulled, repelled, irrite and of non effecte nor force. And that it be ordeyned by the seid auctorite that the seid byll be cancelled, destrued and that the seid acte, recorde and enrolling shalbe taken and avoided oute of the rolle and recordes of the seid parlement of the seid late kyng, and brent and utterly destroyed. And over this, be it ordeyned by the same auctorite that every persone havyng any copy or remembrauncez of the seid bill or acte brynge unto the chaunceller of Englond for the tyme beyng the same copies and remembrauncez, or otherwise utterly destrue theym, afore the fest of Ester next commyng, upon payne of emprisonement and makyng fyne and rawnsom to the kyng at his wyll, so that all thynges seid and remembred in the seid bill and acte therof may be for ever out of remembraunce and forgete. And over this, be it ordeyned by the seid auctorite that this acte, ne any thyng conteyned in the same, be hurtfull or prejudiciall to the acte of stablisshement of the corowne of Englond to the kyng and to the heires of his body bygoton.

5. Extract from Henry VIII's First Succession Act 1533 (passed in 1534).[5]

… your said most humble and obedient subjects, the nobles and Commons of this realm, calling further to their remembrance that the good unity, peace and wealth of this realm, and the succession of the subjects of the same, most especially and principally above all worldly things consists and rests in the certainty and surety of the procreation and posterity of your highness, in whose most royal person, at this present time, is no manner of doubt nor question; do therefore most humbly beseech your highness, that it may please your majesty, that it may be enacted by your highness, with the assent of the lords spiritual and temporal, and the Commons, in this present Parliament assembled, and by the authority of the same, that the marriage heretofore solemnized between your highness and the Lady Katherine, being before lawful wife to Prince Arthur, your elder brother, which by him was carnally known, as does duly appear by sufficient proof in a lawful process had and made before Thomas, by the sufferance of God, now archbishop of Canterbury and metropolitan and primate of all this realm, shall be, by authority of this present Parliament, definitively, clearly, and absolutely declared, deemed, and adjudged to be against the laws of Almighty God, and also accepted, reputed, and taken of no value nor effect, but utterly void and annulled, and the separation thereof, made by the said archbishop, shall be good and effectual to all intents and purposes; any licence, dispensation, or any other act or acts going afore, or ensuing the same, or to the contrary thereof, in any wise notwithstanding; and that every such licence, dispensation, act or acts, thing or things heretofore had, made, done, or to be done to the contrary thereof, shall be void and of none effect; and that the said Lady Katherine shall be from henceforth called and reputed only dowager to Prince Arthur, and not queen of this realm; and that the lawful matrimony had and solemnized between your highness and your most dear and entirely beloved wife Queen Anne, shall be established, and taken for undoubtful, true, sincere, and perfect ever hereafter, according to the just judgment of the said Thomas, archbishop of Canterbury, metropolitan and primate of all this realm, whose grounds of judgment have been confirmed, as well by the whole clergy of this realm in both the Convocations, and by both the universities thereof, as by the universities of Bologna, Padua, Paris, Orleans, Toulouse, Anjou, and divers others, and also by the private writings of many right excellent well-learned men; which grounds so confirmed, and judgment of the said archbishop ensuing the same, together with your marriage solemnized between your highness and your said lawful wife Queen Anne, we your said subjects, both spiritual and temporal, do purely, plainly, constantly, and firmly accept, approve, and ratify for good and consonant to the laws of Almighty God, without error or default, most humbly beseeching your majesty, that it may be so established for ever by your most gracious and royal assent.

... And also be it enacted by authority aforesaid, that all the issue had and procreated, or hereafter to be had and procreated, between your highness and your said most dear and entirely beloved wife Queen Anne, shall be your lawful children, and be inheritable, and inherit, according to the course of inheritance and laws of this realm, the imperial crown of the same, with all dignities, honours, pre-eminences, prerogatives, authorities, and jurisdictions to the same annexed or belonging, in as large and ample manner as your highness at this present time has the same as king of this realm; the inheritance thereof to be and remain to your said children and right heirs in manner and form as hereafter shall be declared, that is to say:

First the said imperial crown, and other the premises, shall be to your majesty, and to your heirs of your body lawfully begotten, that is to say: to the first son of your body, between your highness and your said lawful wife, Queen Anne, begotten, and to the heirs of the body of the same first son lawfully begotten, and for default of such heirs, then to the second son of your body and of the body of the said Queen Anne begotten, and to the heirs of the body of the said second son lawfully begotten, and so to every son of your body and of the body of the said Queen Anne begotten, and to the heirs of the body of every such son begotten, according to the course of inheritance in that behalf; and if it shall happen your said dear and entirely beloved wife Queen Anne to decease without issue male of the body of your highness to be begotten (which God defend), then the same imperial crown, and all other the premises, to be to your majesty, as is aforesaid, and to the son and heir male of your body lawfully begotten, and to the heirs of the body of the same son and heir male lawfully begotten; and for default of such issue, then to your second son of your body lawfully begotten, and to the heirs of the body of the same second son lawfully begotten, and so from son and heir male to son and heir male, and to the heirs of the several bodies of every such son and heir male to be begotten, according to the course of inheritance, in like manner and form as is above said.

And for default of such sons of your body begotten, and of the heirs of the several bodies of every such sons lawfully begotten, that then the said imperial crown, and other the premises, shall be to the issue female between your majesty and your said most dear and entirely beloved wife, Queen Anne, begotten, that is to say: first to the eldest issue female, which is the Lady Elizabeth, now princess, and to the heirs of her body lawfully begotten, and for default of such issue, then to the second issue female, and to the heirs of her body lawfully begotten, and so from issue female to issue female, and to the heirs of their bodies one after another, by course of inheritance, according to their ages, as the crown of England has been accustomed, and ought to go, in cases where there be heirs females to the same; and for default of such issue, then the said imperial crown, and all other the premises, shall be in the right heirs of your highness for ever.

And be it further enacted by authority aforesaid, that on this side the first day of May next coming, proclamation shall be made in all shires within this realm, of the tenor and contents of this Act.

6. *The **Second Succession Act** of Henry VIII's reign was passed by the Parliament of England in June 1536, removing both Mary and Elizabeth from the line of the succession. The act was formally titled 'An Act concerning the Succession of the Crown'. It is also known as the **Succession to the Crown: Marriage Act 1536** (citation 28 Henry VIII c.7), or as the **Act of Succession 1536**.*

7. Extract from Henry VIII's Third Succession Act passed in July 1543.[6]

WHERE in the parliament held at Westminster the eighth day of June in the twenty-eighth year of the reign of our most dread sovereign lord King Henry the Eighth an act was had and made for the establishment of the succession of the imperial crown of this realm of England, by which act among divers other things it was enacted, that the imperial crown of this realm with all dignities, honours, preeminences, prerogatives, authorities and jurisdictions to the same annexed or belonging should be to the king's majesty and his heirs of his body lawfully begotten, that is to say, to the first son of his body between His Highness and his then lawful wife Queen Jane, now deceased, begotten, and to the heirs of the body of the same first son lawfully begotten, and for default of such heirs, then to the second son of His Highness' body and of the body of the said Queen Jane begotten, and to the heirs of the body of the same second son begotten ... since the making of which act, the king's majesty hath one only issue of his body lawfully begotten betwixt His Highness and his said late wife Queen Jane, the noble and excellent prince, Prince Edward, whom Almighty God long preserve; and also His Majesty hath now of late, since the death of the said Queen Jane, taken to his wife the most virtuous and gracious Lady Katherine, now queen of England, late wife of John Neville, knight, Lord Latimer deceased, by whom as yet His Majesty hath none issue, but may have full well when it shall please God ... recognizing and acknowledging also that it is in the only pleasure and will of Almighty God how long His Highness or his said entirely beloved son, Prince Edward, shall live, and whether the said prince shall have heirs of his body lawfully begotten or not, or whether His Highness shall have heirs begotten and procreated between His Majesty and his said most dear and entirely beloved wife Queen Katherine that now is, or any lawful heirs and issues hereafter of his own body begotten by any other his lawful wife ... His Majesty therefore thinketh convenient afore his departure beyond the seas, that it be enacted by His Highness with the assent of the lords spiritual and temporal and the commons in this present parliament assembled and by authority of the same, and therefore be it enacted by the authority aforesaid, that in case it shall happen the king's majesty and the said excellent prince his yet only son Prince Edward and heir apparent, to decease without heir of either of their bodies lawfully begotten (as God defend) so that there be no such heir male or female of any of their two bodies, to have and inherit the said imperial crown and other his dominions, according and in such manner and form as in the aforesaid act and now in this is declared, that then the said imperial crown and all other the premises shall be to the Lady Mary, the king's Highness' daughter, and to the heirs of the body of the same Lady Mary lawfully begotten, with such conditions as by His Highness shall be limited by his letters patents under his great seal, or by His Majesty's last will in writing signed with his gracious hand; and for default of such issue the said imperial crown and other the premises shall be to the Lady Elizabeth, the king's second daughter, and to the heirs of the body of the said Lady Elizabeth lawfully begotten, with such conditions as by His Highness shall be limited by his letters patents under his great seal, or by His Majesty's last will in writing signed with his gracious hand; anything in the said act made in the said twenty-eighth year of our said sovereign lord to the contrary of this act notwithstanding.

8. Extract from the Will of Henry VIII.

We will by these presents that, immediately after our departure out of this present life, our said son Edward shall have and enjoy the said imperial crown and realm of England and Ireland, our title to France, with all dignities, honours, pre-eminences, prerogatives, authorities, and jurisdictions, lands and possessions, to the same annexed or belonging to him and to his heirs of his body lawfully begotten. And for default of such issue of our said son Prince Edward's body lawfully begotten, we will the said imperial crown and other the premises, after our two deceases, shall wholly remain and come to the heirs of our body lawfully begotten of the body of our entirely beloved wife, Queen Katherine, that now is, or of any other our lawful wife that we shall hereafter marry. And for lack of such issue and heirs ... the said imperial crown and all other the premises shall wholly remain and come to our said daughter Mary and the heirs of her body lawfully begotten; upon condition that our said daughter Mary, after our decease, shall not marry nor take any person to her husband without the assent and consent of the Privy Councillors and others appointed by us to our dearest son Prince Edward aforesaid to be of council ... We will that, after our decease, and for default of issue of ... our daughter Mary, the said imperial crown and other the premises shall wholly remain and come to our said daughter Elizabeth and to the heirs of her body lawfully begotten; upon condition [etc.] ...

9. Edward VI's Devise for the Succession to the Crown.[7]
My deuise for the succession.

1. For lakke of issu (masle) of my body (to the issu (masle) cumming of thissu femal, as i haue after declared). To the L Frau[n]ceses heires masles, For lakke of (if she have any) such issu (befor my death) to the L' Janes (and her) heires masles, To the L Katerins heires masles, To the L Maries heires masles, To the heires masles of the daughters wich she shal haue hereafter. Then to the L Margets heires masles. For lakke of such issu, To th'eires masles of the L Janes daughters. To th'eires masles of the L Katerins daughters, and so forth til yow come to the L Margets (daughters) heires masles.

2. If after my death theire masle be entred into 18 yere old, then he to have the hole rule and gouernau[n]ce therof.

3. But if he be under 18, then his mother to be gouuernres til he entre 18 yere old, But to doe nothing w[i]t[h]out th'auise (and agreme[n]t) of 6 parcel of a counsel to be pointed by my last will to the nombre of 20.

4. If the mother die befor th'eire entre into 18 the realme to be gouuerned by the cou[n]sel Prouided that after he be 14 yere al great matters of importaunce be opened to him.

5. If i died w[i]t[h]out issu, and ther were none heire masle, then the L Fraunces to be (gouuernres) rege[n]t. For lakke of her, the her eldest daughters, and for lakke of them the L Marget to be gouuernres after as is aforsaid, til sume heire masle be borne, and then the mother of that child to be gouuernres.

6. And if during the rule of the gouuernres ther die 4 of the counsel, then shal she by her letters cal an asse[n]ble of the counsel wtin on month folowing and chose 4 more, wherin she shal haue thre uoices. But after her death the 16 shal chose emong themselfes til th'eire come to (18 erased) 14 yeare olde, and then he by ther aduice shal chose the[n].

10. Extracts from the Act of Settlement, 1701.[8]

Given that the reigning King, William III, and his sister-in-law and cousin, Princess (later Queen) Anne had no living descendants it was enacted:

… That the most excellent Princess Sophia, Electress and Duchess Dowager of Hanover, daughter of the most excellent Princess Elizabeth, late Queen of Bohemia, daughter of our late sovereign lord King James the First, of happy memory, be and is hereby declared to be the next in succession, in the Protestant line, to the imperial Crown and dignity of the said Realms of England, France, and Ireland, with the dominions and territories thereunto belonging, after His Majesty, and the Princess Anne of Denmark, and in default of issue of the said Princess Anne, and of His Majesty respectively:

…

Provided always, and be it hereby enacted, That all and every person and persons, who shall or may take or inherit the said Crown, by virtue of the limitation of this present act, and is, are or shall be reconciled to, or shall hold communion with, the See or Church of Rome, or shall profess the popish religion, or shall marry a papist, shall be subject to such incapacities, as in such case or cases are by the said recited act provided, enacted, and established; and that every King and Queen of this Realm, who shall come to and succeed in the imperial Crown of this Kingdom, by virtue of this act, shall have the coronation oath administered to him, her or them, at their respective coronations, according to the Act of Parliament made in the first year of the reign of His Majesty, and the said late Queen Mary

...

[and] That whosoever shall hereafter come to the possession of this Crown, shall join in communion with the Church of England, as by law established.

11. Extract from the 1753 Marriage Act.[9]

Except between Jews or Quakers, marriages in England [10] must henceforth be celebrated in an Anglican Church, following the due publication of banns or the obtaining of a license, and

... in order to preserve the evidence of marriages, and to make the proof thereof more certain and easy, and for the direction of ministers in the celebration of marriages and registering thereof, be it enacted, That from and after the twenty-fifth day of March in the year one thousand seven hundred and fifty-four, all marriages shall be solemnized in the presence of two or more credible witnesses, besides the minister who shall celebrate the same; and that immediately after the celebration of every marriage, an entry thereof shall be made in such register to be kept as aforesaid; in which entry or register it shall be expressed, That the said marriage was celebrated by banns or licence; and if both or either of the parties married by licence, be under age, with consent of the parents or guardians, as the case shall be; and shall be signed by the minister with his proper addition, and also by the parties married, and attested by such two witnesses; which entry shall be made in the form or to the effect following; that is to say:

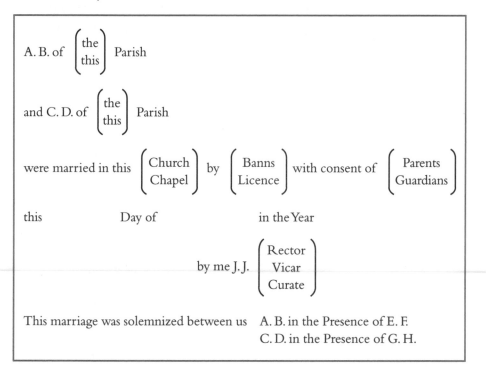

A. B. of (the / this) Parish

and C. D. of (the / this) Parish

were married in this (Church / Chapel) by (Banns / Licence) with consent of (Parents / Guardians)

this   Day of   in the Year

by me J. J. (Rector / Vicar / Curate)

This marriage was solemnized between us   A. B. in the Presence of E. F.
C. D. in the Presence of G. H.

12. Extract from the Royal Marriages Act 1772.[11]

… No descendant of the body of his late Majesty King George the Second, male or female, (other than the issue of princesses who have married, or may hereafter marry into foreign families,) shall be capable of contracting matrimony without the previous consent of his Majesty, his heirs or successors, signified under the great seal, and declared in council (which consent, to preserve the memory thereof, is hereby directed to be set out in the licence and register of marriage, and to be entered in the books of the Privy Council); and that every marriage, or matrimonial contract, of any such descendant, without such consent first had and obtained, shall be null and void to all intents and purposes whatsoever.

Provided always that in case any such descendant of the body of his late Majesty King George the Second, being above the age of twenty-five years, shall persist in his or her resolution to contract a marriage disapproved of, or dissented from, by the King, his heirs or successors; that then such descendant, upon giving notice to the King's Privy Council, which notice is hereby directed to be entered in the books thereof, may, at any time from the expiration of twelve calendar months after such notice given to the Privy Council as aforesaid, contract such marriage; and his or her marriage with the person before proposed and rejected, may be duly solemnized, without the previous consent of his Majesty, his heirs or successors; and such marriage shall be good, as if this Act had never been made, unless both Houses of Parliament shall, before the expiration of the said twelve months, expressly declare their disapprobation of such intended marriage.

Appendix 4

The Mystery of Laura Culme-Seymour's Death Certificate

The following correspondence was received from the Public Registry in Malta:

Acknowledgement of the author's request for a full death certificate

Sent: Monday, August 20, 2012 6:16 AM
Subject: Confirmation of order received by Ċertifikati.gov.mt

Dear Customer,
Thank you for ordering with Ċertifikati.gov.mt.
This email is an acknowledgement of receipt of your order which has been passed to our Civil Status staff to be processed.
Please keep the following order information as reference of your order.

Order Reference: 46866

Reference: 46866-71660-49115
Certificate: Death
Details: Laura Grace Culme-Seymour
Format: Full
Item Price: € 9.32
Quantity: 1
App. Cost: € 9.32

Delivery Method: Europe – Post

Delivery Cost: € 1.30

A total of € 10.62 will be deducted from credit/debit card.

Transaction Ref.:T46866

If you have any queries in relation to the above order please contact us at:
https://secure2.gov.mt/certifikati/Contact.aspx
Please note that by receiving this email, you are accepting our payment terms
and conditions, a copy of which can be found on the website at:
https://secure2.gov.mt/certifikati/Conditions.aspx

Rejection of the author's request for a full death certificate

Sent:Tuesday, August 21, 2012 8:51 AM
Subject: Ċertifikati.gov.mt – Application Rejected

We are sorry but your application with reference #46866-71660-49115 has
been rejected for the following reason: No certificate could be found matching
the details as entered by the applicant from the year 1895 to the year 1896.
regards

iii)   Rejection of a colleague's request for a full death certificate
Date: 11 October 2012 11:21:40 GMT+02:00
Subject: Ċertifikati.gov.mt – Application Rejected

We are sorry but your application with reference #48953-61144-51366 has been
rejected for the following reason: No certificate could be found matching the
details as entered by the applicant from the year 1894 to the year 1896.
Regards

iv)   Acceptance of a colleague's request for an 'extract' death certificate
Date: 05 October 2012 10:15:59 GMT+02:00
Subject: Ċertifikati.gov.mt – Order Settled

Your order for certificates with reference #48696 has been processed and payment has been settled by the Public Registry.Your certificate copies have been
sent by mail.

v)   Contents of 'extract' death certificate 0247941 received from the Maltese Public Registry

Name and surname of the deceased	Whether married or unmarried, widower or widow	Occupation and age (years)	Place of birth	Name and surname of parents	Place and date of death
LAURA GRACE CULME-SEYMOUR	SPINSTER	NO OCCUPATION 21	BLETCHINGTON OXFORDSHIRE ENGLAND	MICHAEL CULME-SEYMOUR (ALIVE) MARY CULME-SEYMOUR NEE WATSON (ALIVE)	SLIEMA MALTA Fri 22 NOVEMBER 1895

NOTES

INTRODUCTION

1. William II (Rufus), Edward V (assuming he died *c*.1483), Edward VI and perhaps Elizabeth I. The Stuart pretender, 'Henry IX' (Cardinal Duke of York and Bishop of Frascati), was also unmarried.
2. Reputedly homosexual English monarchs include William II, Richard I, Edward II, Richard II, and James I. Homosexual preferences have also been alleged in the case of 'Henry IX'. But with the exceptions of William II and 'Henry IX', all of these kings married. Robert Mills and Randolph Trumbach argue, for cogent reasons, that it is inappropriate to call them 'gay' (M Cook et al., *A Gay History of Britain*, Oxford 2007, Chapter 1). But while the word 'gay' and its modern connotations are certainly anachronistic in a medieval context, these kings seem to have enjoyed – and perhaps preferred – same-sex relationships.
3. In modern English the titles 'prince' and 'princess' are generally applied to the children and grandchildren of a sovereign. This usage dates only from the early eighteenth century. (Previously the styles 'lord' and 'lady' were used instead.) However, 'prince' and 'princess' are applied here to earlier periods, even though strictly speaking that is an anachronism.
4. J. Ashdown-Hill, *Eleanor the Secret Queen*, Stroud, The History Press, 2009.
5. This study is mainly concerned with English legislation and practice in respect of marriage. In one case, however, Scottish law will be the key element.
6. This point was stated very clearly many years ago by the great nineteenth-century historian James Gairdner in his *History of the Life and Reign of Richard the Third*, Cambridge, CUP, 1898, p. 91.

1 THE EVOLUTION OF MARRIAGE

1. http://oxforddictionaries.com/definition/marriage?q=marriage (January 2012).
2. http://dictionary.reference.com/browse/marriage (January 2012).

3. http://en.wikipedia.org/wiki/Marriage (January 2012). Present writer's emphasis.
4. 97 per cent.
5. http://blog.theukweddingshows.co.uk/wedding-industry/2008-uk-wedding-industry-statistics-43/ (January 2012).
6. The legitimacy of royal offspring is probably also still important – though the issue has not yet been put to the test.
7. Quoted in http://www.bbc.co.uk/news/magazine-12744146 (January 2012). The marriage of Edward IV and Elizabeth Woodville is explored in much more detail below – see Chapter 9.
8. 14 November 1501.
9. Pre-sixteenth-century English sovereigns were Catholics. From the mid-sixteenth century they have been Anglicans. Since the end of the seventeenth century marriage with Catholics has been forbidden to members of the royal family, and this remains the case today. During the seventeenth century, however, although the Stuart kings were generally Anglican, Catholic consorts were acceptable – even normal. All the Stuart queens consort of England were Catholic. Anne of Denmark, wife of James I, is thought to have converted to Catholicism. So did James II's first wife, Anne Hyde – though she died before becoming queen.
10. There were public processions, but the nuptial mass itself was private.
11. This is no longer the case today. Under Catholic canon 1081 a priest must now be present at the marriage.
12. Though by this date there was beginning to be a clear ecclesiastical trend in favour of making it so, precisely because experience had proved the prevailing lack of formal regulation to constitute very dangerous ground. See below.
13. L. Stone, *The Family, Sex and Marriage in England 1500–1800*, Harmondsworth, Penguin, 1979, 1990, p. 383.
14. A present tense promise: 'I marry you'.
15. A future tense promise: 'I shall marry you'.
16. C.N.L. Brooke, *The Medieval Idea of Marriage*, Oxford 1989, p. 169; P. Coss, *The Lady in Medieval England*, Stroud 1998, p. 87.
17. Stone, *Family, Sex, Marriage*, p. 386.
18. Notice of a couple's intention to marry.
19. Coss, *The Lady in Medieval England*, p. 87. The Catholic Church abolished banns in 1983, but they are still published in the Anglican Church.
20. Stone, *Family, Sex, Marriage*, p. 383.
21. Anglican canon B 31.
22. Catholic canon 109.1.
32. In the Middle Ages similar rulings were sometimes specified – as for example in the case of Eleanor of Aquitaine (see Chapter 3).

2 MEDIEVAL MARRIAGE PRACTICE

1. B.J. Harris, *English Aristocratic Women, 1450–1550*, Oxford 2010, p. 45.
2. *Catholic Encyclopedia*, http://www.newadvent.org/cathen/04264a.htm (February 2012).
3. The sixpenny piece was reduced to 50 per cent silver content in 1920. In 1946

minting of silver coins ceased, silver being replaced by cupro-nickel. In 1967 decimal coinage was introduced and the sixpenny piece was discontinued.

4. See illustrations.
5. See illustrations.
6. J. Ashdown-Hill, ' "Al ful of fresshe floures whyte and reede": The Jewellery of Margaret of York and Its Meaning', *Ricardian* 17 2007, 56–72.
7. The picture of the wedding of Edward III's daughter shows the bride with her head covered.

3 ROYAL MARRIAGES 1050–1330

1. This split was recent. The Great Schism (1054) divided the Church into two halves – Orthodox in the east and Catholic in the west.
2. Dowry was money or property settled on the bride by her birth family at the time of her marriage. Jointure refers to the provision which the groom's family agreed to make for the bride if and when she became a widow.
3. William was drowned in the White Ship.
4. At 14, Count Geoffrey would have been too young, in the eyes of the Church, to consummate his marriage immediately. The medieval Church normally required a minor to be 16 years old before a marriage could be consummated.
5. The only children having been two daughters: Marie (b. 1145) and Alix (b. 1151).
6. Richard had two elder brothers, William, Count of Poitiers and Henry 'the Young King'.
7. A similar situation is reported to have arisen in the case of Richard II, who also possibly preferred men to women. Richard II is said to have formally recognised as his heir his young cousin, Roger Mortimer, despite the fact that at the time Richard II himself was young, and married. See below.
8. Isabel is also called Hawise by some sources. She was the granddaughter of Robert Fiztroy, Earl of Gloucester, bastard son of Henry I.
9. http://en.wikipedia.org/wiki/Arthur_I,_Duke_of_Brittany (June 2012). The burial place referred to is the Abbey of Bec.
10. http://www.geni.com/people/Ranulf-de-Blundeville-4th-Earl-of-Chester/6000000002043244300 (June 2012).
11. See, for example, the illustration of the marriage of Edward II and Isabelle of France; BL, Royal 15 E iv f. 295v. Also Chaucer, *Canterbury Tales*, General Prologue, The Wife of Bath, line 460:'Housbondes at chirche dore she hadde fyve [She had five husbands at the church door]' http://chschaucer.wetpaint.com/page/The+Wife+of+Bath+Translation (January 2012).
12. BL, MS Royal 14 C. vii, f. 124v.
13. A representation of this ritual can be seen in the film *Le Retour de Martin Guerre*. There, however, the ring is slipped on to the middle finger of the bride's right hand, the word 'Amen' being omitted.
14. D. Anderson et al., *Exploring the Middle Ages*, New York 2006, pp. 420–21.
15. This is also the case in the *Martin Guerre* film (see above).
16. Eleanor was a granddaughter of Richard I's sometime fiancée, Alys of France.
17. The church (cathedral from 1567) was destroyed in the French Revolution, when

the miraculous image of Our Lady was burned. Later the nineteenth-century
Basilica of Notre Dame was erected on the same site. This enshrines a small
surviving fragment of the medieval image. Only the Romanesque crypt of the
original cathedral still exists, and this houses a plaque commemorating the marriage
of Edward II and Isabelle of France.

18. G.G. Sury, 'Guillaume Ier (d'Avesnes) comte de Hainaut et sa fille Philippe', in G.G.
Sury, ed., *Bayern Straubing Hennegau: la Maison de Bavière en Hainaut, XIVe – XVe s.*,
Bruxelles, 2010 (2nd edition), p. 55 ; G. Wymans, *Inventaire analytique du chartrier de la
Trésorerie des comtes de Hainaut*, Bruxelles, 1985, pp. 130, 131.

4 SUITABLE STATUS

1. Quoted in http://www.bbc.co.uk/news/magazine-12744146 (January 2012).
2. Henry I, Matilda, Henry the Young King, Richard I, Edward I and Edward II.
3. See Appendix 1. N.B. Some monarchs married more than once.
4. English existed in the Middle Ages; however, it was not the modern form of the
language, but Old English (the language of Beowulf) in the case of the Norman
Kings, gradually evolving into Middle English (the language of Chaucer) by the
reign of Edward III.
5. Adeliza's original tomb was destroyed during the French Revolution, but her
remains were found and reinterred in the restored abbey church in the nineteenth
century.
6. She was originally interred at the Abbey of Bec-Hellouin, but her remains were
transferred to Rouen Cathedral in 1847.
7. His undiscovered remains now lie somewhere in the vicinity of Pugin's early
nineteenth-century Norman-style Catholic Church of St James in Reading.
8. The existence of the Holy Roman Emperor, the unquestioned precedence which
he notionally enjoyed over all European kings and the idea that he represented a
continuation of the Roman Empire, of which the whole of Europe was still, in
some sense, part, reflected at this period a somewhat muddled but nevertheless real
perception of a common European history and heritage.
9. The marriage took place *c.*1204.
10. See below, Chapter 7.
11. All the children of Edward IV by Elizabeth Woodville were officially declared
illegitimate by Parliament in 1484. See Chapter 9.
12. A. Carson, *Richard III: The Maligned King*, Stroud, The History Press, 2008, 2012, pp.
259–62; J. Ashdown-Hill, *The Last Days of Richard III*, Stroud, The History Press,
2010, p. 28 *et seq.*
13. In January 1121.
14. Edward I had seven surviving children by Eleanor of Castile. His second wife,
Margaret of France, gave him three more surviving children.
15. She was the first consort not to be crowned since the Norman Conquest.
16. The Fitzalan-Howard family, Dukes of Norfolk, hold Arundel Castle to this day.
17. See Chapters 10 and 13.

5 IRREGULAR ROYAL AFFAIRS

1. http://oxforddictionaries.com/definition/mistress?q=mistress (February 2012).
2. *Collins World English Dictionary*, quoted in http://dictionary.reference.com/browse/mistress (February 2012).
3. C. Humphery-Smith in Beauclerk-Dewar & Powell, *Royal Bastards*, p. 260.
4. See, however, Cook et al, *A Gay History of Britain*, pp. 48–49, on dual desire.
5. Wardrobe account of 1322, quoted in http://en.wikipedia.org/wiki/Adam_FitzRoy (February 2012).
6. An Edith with no recorded surname is also mentioned as one of Henry I's sexual partners, but she may be identical with Edith Fitzforne as her daughter was born in the same decade as Edith Fitzforne's royal bastards.
7. A similar pattern can be seen in the cases of Richard III and Henry VII. See below.
8. See Chapter 3.
9. Most – though not all – of Henry I's illegitimate children bore the surname Fitzroy.
10. C. Humphery-Smith in Beauclerke-Dewar & Powell, *Royal Bastards*, p. 257.
11. *Gesta Stephani*, quoted in http://en.wikipedia.org/wiki/Robert,_1st_Earl_of_Gloucester (February 2012).
12. For the case of James, Duke of Monmouth, son of Charles II, see Chapter 11.
13. See Chapter 2.
14. Alys did ultimately become an ancestress of the English royal family – through her granddaughter, Eleanor of Castile, first wife of Edward I.
15. Rosamund's mother was Margaret Isabel de Tosny.
16. Other illegitimate children have been ascribed to him, but on very questionable evidence.
17. Geoffrey, Bishop of Lincoln, later Archbishop of York, Morgan, Provost of Beverley and Bishop-elect of Durham at the time of his death, and Matilda, Abbess of Barking.
18. John, the youngest son of Henry II and Eleanor of Aquitaine, was born in 1167. Rosamund de Clifford was born before 1150 and died in 1176 – at about the same time as the birth of William Longspee.
19. The executed body of Hugh Despenser was recently identified as a set of mutilated remains excavated from the site of Hulton Abbey, Staffordshire. http://www.telegraph.co.uk/news/uknews/1579006/Abbey-body-identified-as-gay-lover-of-Edward-II.html (February 2012).
20. W.M. Ormrod, 'Alice Perrrers and John Salisbury', http://ehr.oxfordjournals.org/content/CXXIII/501/379.full (February 2012).
21. *Ibid*.
22. John de Southeray (born *c.*1364, died after 1383, knighted 1377, married Matilda Percy; Joan (married Robert Skerne) and Jane (married Richard Northland).
23. F.G. Hay, *Lady of the Sun: The Life and Times of Alice Perrers*, London 1966, p. 7.
24. In France, there was arguably something of a tradition of popular dislike of royal mistresses – an animosity which ran the risk of rebounding on the queen in a case where a king had no mistress (as with Louis XVI and Marie Antoinette).
25. J. Bothwell, 'The Management of Position: Alice Perrers, Edward III and the Creation of a Landed Estate, 1362–1377', *Journal of Medieval History*, 24 (1998), pp. 31–51 (p. 31).

26. J. Taylor & W.R. Childs, eds., & L. Watkiss trans., *The St Albans Chronicle: The Chronica Maiora of Thomas Walsingham 1376–1394*, Oxford 2002, p. 45.
27. *The St Albans Chronicle*, p. 47.
28. O. di Simplicio, *Autunno della stregoneria*, Bologna 2005, p. 63; evidence in the case of Lorenzo di Giovanni Lancellotti, 1583, 1591.
29. *The St Albans Chronicle*, p. 47.
30. http://theroyaluniverse.com/royal-witches/ (March 2012).
31. The foundation of the Order of the Garter was said to be based on an incident at a royal ball when the Countess of Salisbury dropped her garter and the king retrieved it for her. The countess in question is not named and could have been either Catherine or Joan.

7 THE LOVE-MATCHES OF EDWARD III'S CHILDREN

1. In fact the Black Prince never succeeded to the throne, because he died before his father.
2. C. Given-Wilson, ed., *The Chronicle of Adam of Usk 1377–1421*, Oxford 1997, p. 63.
3. These three sons were Sir Roger de Clarendon, whose mother was Edith de Willesford, and a boy called Edward (who died young) and Sir John Sounder, the identity of whose mother (or mothers) is unknown.
4. Blanche died in 1388–89.
5. Stories claimed that Edmund Crouchback was actually the elder brother of Edward I and had a superior claim to the throne. These stories were pure invention, but later Henry IV (son of John of Gaunt and Blanche of Lancaster) based his claim to the throne upon them. See J. Ashdown-Hill, 'The Lancastrian Claim to the Throne', *Ricardian* 13 (2003), pp. 27–38.
6. Constance's mother, Maria de Padilla, had been secretly married to Pedro, but later Pedro was forced to repudiate this marriage, and keep Maria only as his mistress. The legitimacy of Constance and her younger sister was therefore debatable. The question mark over the marriage of Pedro the Cruel shows that problematic royal marriages were not only a feature of English history.
7. Catherine's marriage also gave the future Castilian – and later Spanish – monarchs a good claim to be heirs of the house of Lancaster. Their claim was only bettered by the descendants of Catherine's elder half-sister (the daughter of Blanche of Lancaster), who married into the Portuguese royal family. When these two Lancastrian lines of descent were united in the person of Philip II of Spain, they formed the basis of his claim to the English throne – a claim which led, in 1588, to the launching of the Spanish Armada.
8. Her married name was Swynford.
9. The precise date is not recorded, but they were certainly married by 1365. J. Lucraft, *Katherine Swynford the history of a medieval mistress*, Stroud 2006, 2010, pp. 5–6.
10. Possibly as early as 1365 – though some historians prefer a date of 1368. As with many aspects of this story, the precise date is not recorded.
11. Again, there are differing interpretations of the date at which their liaison started. However John and Catherine themselves both specifically declared, in their request to the pope to confirm their marriage in 1396, that their relationship postdated the deaths of Hugh Swynford and Blanche of Lancaster: Lucraft, *Katherine Swynford*, p. 11.

12. The reason for this has been said to be that they were all born at the Castle of Beaufort in France, but this appears implausible – see Lucraft, *Katherine Swynford*, p. 24.

13. Lucraft is unsure about this. See *Katherine Swynford*, p. 12.

14. By a papal bull in September 1396 and by royal patent in February 1396/97.

8 SECRET WEDDINGS AND WITCHCRAFT IN THE HOUSE OF LANCASTER

1. L.B. Campbell, ed., *The Mirror for Magistrates*, New York 1960, p. 435.

2. The royal mistress was Elizabeth Lambert (aka 'Jane Shore'), last mistress of Edward IV.

3. The house of Lancaster was briefly restored to the throne in 1470–71, before finally disappearing completely.

4. See Chapter 9, below.

5. di Simplicio, *Autunno della stregoneria*, p. 67.

6. di Simplicio, *op. cit.*, p. 65. See also King James VI's *Newes from Scotland*, London 1591, pp. 21–23, which describes the attempted use of pubic hair for a love spell; also Francesca Matteoni, *Blood Beliefs in Early Modern Europe*, unpublished PhD thesis, University of Hertfordshire 2009, p. 206 for the use of pubic hair in love charms.

7. Matteoni, *Blood Beliefs in Early Modern Europe*, p. 204.

8. Matteoni, op. cit, p. 208.

9. di Simplicio, *op. cit.*, p. 63–67. The gradual evolution of St Martha from the patron saint of Christian households to a powerful and demonic voodoo figure is fascinating.

10. From the *Encyclopedia of 5000 Spells*, cited on http://gypsymagicspells.blogspot.com/2011/06/medieval-fish-spell-for-love.html (April 2012).

11. http://thewriteplaceatthewritetime.org/explorationoftheme.html (April 2012).

12. Ashdown-Hill, 'The Lancastrian Claim to the Throne', *Ricardian* 13 (2003), pp. 27–38.

13. Eleanor is referred to as Humphrey's wife in, for example, a memorandum in the Close Rolls dated 20 May 1441.

14. Humphrey had two illegitimate children, but probably by unnamed French mothers rather than by Eleanor Cobham. They were Arthur of Gloucester (d. 1447) and Antigone (who is an ancestress of Queen Elizabeth II on her mother's side).

15. Elsewhere Bolingbroke was described as a 'gret and konnyng man in astronomye' and 'renowned in all the world'. Quoted in http://en.wikipedia.org/wiki/Margery_Jourdemayne,_%22the_Witch_of_Eye%22 (April 2012).

16. Fabyan's *Chronicle*, ed. 1811, p. 614, quoted in H. Ellis, *Original Letters Illustrative of English History*, London 1827, Vol. 1, p. 106.

17. 'Eye' is an old version of Edbury, a district not far from the modern Catholic Cathedral of Westminster, in the vicinity of Victoria Station.

18. J. Ashdown-Hill, *Mediaeval Colchester's Lost Landmarks*, Derby 2009, p. 161. Jeweyn Blakecot appears in the Colchester records for 1466–67.

19. Apparently neither Margery nor Jeweyn foresaw their own future misfortunes.

20. http://en.wikipedia.org/wiki/Margery_Jourdemayne,_%22the_Witch_of_Eye%22 (April 2012).

21. *Ibid.*

22. Ellis, *Original Letters*, p. 107. In this letter the king insultingly refers to his aunt merely as 'Alianore Cobham late called Duchesse of Gloucestr'.

23. J.A. Giles, ed., *Incerti scriptoris chronicon Angliae de regnis trium regum Lancastrensium*, London 1848, part 4, p. 17, cited in *ODNB*, M. Jones, 'Catherine of Valois' (consulted online March 2012).

24. *ODNB*, C. Richmond, 'Edmund Beaufort, First Duke of Somerset' (consulted online May 2012).

25. Leicestershire Record Office B. R. II/3/3, and PRO C 49/16/11.

26. *ODNB*, M. Jones, 'Catherine of Valois' (consulted online March 2012).

27. Rather as Richard Woodville was a member of the household of John of Lancaster (see above).

28. Edmund and Jasper Tudor, a daughter, Margaret, who probably became a nun and died young, and possibly a third son called Owen Tudor (although the existence of the last-named is somewhat doubtful).

29. Ashdown-Hill, *Eleanor*, p. 22.

30. *CPR* 1436–1441.

31. The precise date of this secret marriage is unknown, but by the end of 1437 Edmund and Eleanor were married.

32. He even fathered a bastard son, David, in about 1459. *ODNB*, R.A. Griffiths, 'Tudor, Owen' (consulted online, March 2012).

33. J. Gairdner, ed., *The Historical Collections of a Citizen of London in the Fifteenth Century*, CS, new series, vol. 17, 1876, p. 211.

34. Richmond, 'Edmund Beaufort', *ODNB*.

35. http://www.cherwell.org/news/academic/2012/05/31/tudor-name-is-misnomer-claims-don (consulted June 2012). I am grateful to Annette Carson for calling my attention to Davies' research.

36. Shakespeare, *Henry VI*, Act II, scene iv.

9 TALBOT'S DAUGHTER AND THE GREY MARE

1. J. Ashdown-Hill, 'The Elusive Mistress: Elizabeth Lucy and her Family', *Ricardian* 11 (June 1999), pp. 490–505 (p. 498).

2. Jacquette, of the house of Luxembourg, was a high-born lady, but Richard Woodville was a nobody (see above).

3. In reality Bona (daughter of the Duke of Savoy and sister of the Queen of France) was not exactly a 'princess'.

4. The reasons for suggesting this date are explored below.

5. Stillington was chancellor 1467–70 and 1471–73.

6. For full details see J. Ashdown-Hill, *Richard III's 'Beloved Cousyn': John Howard and the House of York*, Stroud 2009, p. 9 *et seq*.

7. The other 'Prince in the Tower' was Edward V's younger brother, Richard, Duke of York. There is no proof that the two boys were murdered. If they were, then the identity of their alleged murderer is still a historical hot chestnut – but that is another story! Here our focus is on the question of their father's marriage.

8. This was the start of the so-called 'Wars of the Roses' – though that name was only invented in the nineteenth century.

9. The Lancastrian dynasty owed the Crown only to the usurpation of Henry IV, who deposed Richard II in 1399 and seized power. Henry IV himself, and his son Henry V, had both viewed the ancestors of Richard Duke of York with suspicion, knowing that the descendants of Lionel, Duke of Clarence might have a claim to the throne superior to their own.

10. See A. Sutton and L. Visser-Fuchs, *The Royal Funerals of the House of York at Windsor*, London 2004, pp. 113–24.

11. The king acknowledged one illegitimate son, Arthur, Lord Lisle (later surnamed 'Plantagenet'). We also hear of two illegitimate daughters, Grace and Elizabeth. Elizabeth and Arthur were probably borne to the king by Elizabeth Wayte (Lucy). The identity of Grace's mother is unknown. There are much later rumours of a child called Edward of Wigmore, borne to the king by Eleanor Talbot, but there is no contemporary evidence that such a person ever existed and there are excellent reasons for doubting the story, since such a son could have claimed to be heir to the throne, as Charles II's son Monmouth later did.

12. See original source material published in Ashdown-Hill, *Eleanor*, pp. 192, 195, 205–207.

13. Gairdner, *Richard the Third*, p. 91.

14. Henry VII's Act of Parliament of 1485: *RP*, vol. 6, p. 289.

15. E.g. Muriel de Dunham *v.* John Burnoth and Joan, his 'wife': N. Adams and C. Donahue, eds., *Select Cases from the Ecclesiastical Courts of the Province of Canterbury, c.1200–1301*, London 1981, p. 337 and *passim*.

16. Ashdown-Hill, *Eleanor*, pp. 125–26; 129.

17. Corpus Christi College, Cambridge, Parker Library, Ms. XXXI. 121.

18. More than 45 per cent of such women remarried: Harris, *English Aristocratic Women*, p. 10.

19. Beaune and d'Arbaumont, *Mémoires d'Olivier de la Marche*, vol. 3, pp. 106–107. Eleanor was formerly represented amongst the mourners depicted on her mother's tomb at old St Paul's Cathedral in London, but of course this was destroyed in the Great Fire of London.

20. A fine portrait by Petrus Christus of one of Eleanor's nieces shows an attractive brunette with an aquiline nose.

21. For a detailed report on this skeleton, see Ashdown-Hill, *Eleanor*, pp. 174–75.

22. Warwickshire County Record Office, L 1/82. See also J. Ashdown-Hill, "The Inquisition *Post Mortem* of Eleanor Talbot, Lady Butler, 1468', *Ricardian* 12 (2000–02), pp. 563–73.

23. In August 1460 he was at Higham and Stratford St Mary, in Suffolk, in company with the Duke of Norfolk's cousin, John Howard, of Stoke-by-Nayland, Suffolk. Ipswich Record Office, HA 246/B2/498. John Howard himself later became Duke of Norfolk (1483).

24. Her sister, Countess Warenne, her late husband's cousin, Sir Thomas Montgomery, and her uncle, the Earl of Warwick, would all have been well placed to help Eleanor into the royal presence.

25. M. Jones, ed., P. de Commynes, *Memoires*, Harmondsworth 1972, pp. 352–54, 397. These words were penned with hindsight. Commynes wrote down his account in about 1490. In 1460–61 Robert Stillington had not yet become a bishop.

26. Before Edward IV seized the throne Stillington had been in the service of King Henry VI.

27. Jones/Commynes, *Memoires*, p. 354.

28. As already noted, Eleanor was the granddaughter of Thomas Beauchamp, Earl of Warwick, and the niece of Henry Beauchamp, Earl (later Duke) of Warwick, and of Richard Neville, Earl of Warwick.

29. C.A.J. Armstrong, ed., D. Mancini, *The Usurpation of Richard the Third*, Gloucester 1989, pp. 96–97.

30. For Cecily's disapproval of Elizabeth Woodville, see *ODNB*, M. Jones, 'Elizabeth (née Woodville)' (consulted online March 2012). However, the story of her disapproval of the relationship with Elizabeth Lucy is later, and could be merely an invention.

31. P. Maddern, 'Honour among the Pastons: gender and integrity in fifteenth-century English provincial society', *Journal of Medieval History*, 14 (1988) p. 358.

32. Maddern, 'Honour among the Pastons', p. 359.

33. For a fuller discussion of the evidence in this matter, see J. Ashdown-Hill, 'Lady Eleanor Talbot: new evidence; new answers; new questions', *Ricardian* 16 (2006), pp. 113–32. It is also possible that Eleanor's Coldecot estate was part of Caldicot in Monmouthshire – a royal estate inherited by the Lancastrian kings from the de Bohun family: see O. Morgan and T. Wakeman, *Notes on the Architecture and History of Caldicot Castle,* Monmouthshire, Newport 1854. I am grateful to Mary Friend of the Richard III Society (Worcestershire Branch) for the suggestion regarding Caldecot, which, however, remains speculative.

34. Ashdown-Hill, *Eleanor,* p. 147 *et seq.*

35. *CPR 1461–1467*, p. 72.

36. 30 May 1462. *CPR 1461–1467*, p. 191.

37. The patent rolls record commissions in July 1461, March and October 1462, June, October and December 1464, August 1466, February 1468 and November 1469. There were later appointments in 1470, but these, presumably, were made by the government of the restored Henry VI.

38. Ashdown-Hill, *Eleanor,* p. 209.

39. Ashdown-Hill, 'The Elusive Mistress', p. 498.

40. For the chronology of this relationship see *ibid.*

41. P.M. Kendall, *Richard the Third*, London 1973, p. 52.

42. The medieval English calendar year was different, starting not on 1 January, but on 25 March.

43. Suggestions that she is identical with 'Dame Isabella Gray' – one of the attendants of Queen Margaret of Anjou (consort of Henry VI) – are doubtful: *ODNB*, M. Hicks, 'Elizabeth, née Woodville' (consulted online, March 2012).

44. Thomas Grey, later Marquess of Dorset, and Richard Grey.

45. *ODNB*, M. Hicks, 'Elizabeth, née Woodville' (consulted March 2012).

46. Easter Sunday 1464 was 1 April.

47. Even today, marriage during Lent tends to be discouraged by the Catholic Church, and if a church wedding does take place during this penitential season then flowers are not permitted. Some Anglican priests also oppose marriage during Lent.

48. *ODNB*, Hicks, 'Elizabeth, née Woodville' (consulted March 2012).

49. *Ibid.*

50. *Ibid.* Hicks states specifically that while the details of the story of Edward IV's Woodville marriage may be believable, they cannot actually be confirmed, and some of them may be fictional.

51. *Ibid.*

52. *Ibid.*; J. Ashdown-Hill and A. Carson, 'The Execution of the Earl of Desmond', *Ricardian* 15 (2005), pp. 70–93.

53. The Act of *titulus regius* of 1484 maintained the validity of Edward IV's marriage to Eleanor Talbot. Thus, according to that Act, if Eleanor had borne Edward a child, that child would have been legitimate and the heir to the throne. However the same act also stated specifically that 'all th'issue and children of the said king (Edward IV) beene bastards, and unable to inherite or to clayme anything by inheritance, by the lawe and custome of England' (see below: Appendix 4). Although George Buck later suggested that Eleanor may have borne Edward a son (A.N. Kincaid, ed., G. Buck, *The History of King Richard the Third*, Stroud 1979, pp. 176, 181) there is no other evidence to support this belief.

54. Jones/Commynes, pp. 354, 397.

55. R.H. Helmholz, 'The Sons of Edward IV: A Canonical Assessment of the Claim that they were Illegitimate', in P.W. Hammond, ed., *Richard III: Loyalty Lordship and Law*, London, 1986, pp. 91–103. Also Brooke, *The Medieval Idea of Marriage*, p. 169.

56. Harris points out (*English Aristocratic Women*, p. 15) that noblewomen 'were at a particular disadvantage when they disagreed or quarrelled with their husbands'. If the man in question was the king, the disadvantage would have been greater.

57. Kincaid, ed., Buck, *King Richard the Third*, p. 183.

58. The see of Carlisle had become vacant some months before the Woodville marriage was made public, but Stillington was not appointed to that post. The first English bishopric to fall vacant *after* the announcement of the Woodville marriage was that of Bath and Wells (available from 14 January 1465).

59. Armstrong/Mancini, pp. 62–63.

60. The bishop was still at liberty on 19 January. On that date he was appointed to a commission of the peace for Southampton, *CPR 1476–1485*, p. 572. However, before Friday 6 March he had been imprisoned in the Tower of London: Gairdner, *Richard the Third*, p. 91, n. 1, citing the letter from Elizabeth Stonor, dated 6 March 1478, which states that Stillington had been imprisoned since her correspondent departed. The precise date on which Stillington entered the Tower is not recorded, but Gairdner estimates his imprisonment to date from between 13 and 20 February. Given the date of Elizabeth Stonor's letter, he can hardly have been imprisoned later than about 27 February.

61. Clarence was close to the Duchess and the Duke of Norfolk – Eleanor's sister and brother-in-law – and he might have heard about the alleged Talbot marriage from them.

62. On Tuesday 14 April 1478 Stillington was appointed to a commission of the peace for Berkshire, which implies (but does not guarantee) that by that date he was once again at liberty: *CPR 1476–1485*, p. 554.

63. Jones/Commynes, p. 397.

64. *CPR 1476–1485*, p. 102.

65. Act of Attainder against George, Duke of Clarence, January 1478, *RP*, vol. 6, pp. 193–95.

66. C.A.J. Armstrong, ed., D Mancini, *The Usurpation of Richard the Third*, Gloucester 1989, pp. 62–63; 96–97.

67. Letter from Simon Stallworthe to Sir William Stonor. J. Ashdown-Hill, *Richard III's 'Beloved Cousyn'*, p. 93, citing *Facsimiles of National Manuscripts*, part 1, Southampton 1865, item 53.

68. Secondary evidence against the Woodville marriage – including the allegations of witchcraft against Elizabeth Woodville and her mother – also featured in the list of factors enumerated in the Act.

69. The children of his brother Clarence being already debarred from the succession by Edward IV's Act of Attainder.

70. A Parliament had been summoned, but not all the members had yet arrived.

71. 'King Edward was and stoode marryed and trouth plight to oone Dame Elianor Butteler, doughter of the old Earl of Shrewesbury.'

72. The invalidity of the Woodville marriage was based upon several considerations, but what most concerns us here is the fact that it was both bigamous and secret.

73. Armstong/Mancini pp. 62–63.

74. Ashdown-Hill, 'Norfolk Requiem: the Passing of the House of Mowbray', *Ricardian* 12 (March 2001), pp. 198–217 (p. 208).

75. For details, see Ashdown-Hill, 'Lady Eleanor Talbot's other husband', and 'Lady Eleanor Talbot: new evidence; new answers; new questions'.

76. H.C. Maxwell-Lyte, ed., *The Registers of Robert Stillington, Bishop of Bath and Wells 1466–1491 and Richard Fox, Bishop of Bath and Wells 1492–1494*, Somerset Record Society, 1937, p. xiii.

77. Compare, for example, *RP*, vol. 6, p. 190; pp. 284–85; pp. 305–06.

78. The text of the 1484 act survived, however, because it was inscribed in the rolls of parliament.

79. A.N. Kincaid, ed., G. Buck, *The History of King Richard the Third*, Stroud 1979, p. 181.

80. Eleanor made legal provision to transfer all her landed property to her sister less than a month before she died.

81. Eleanor's only surviving brother, Sir Humphrey Talbot, accompanied Elizabeth, Duchess of Norfolk, to the royal wedding of Charles the Bold and Margaret of York in the Low Countries. See Beaune and d'Arbaumont, eds., *Mémoires d'Olivier de la Marche*, vol. 3, p. 111, where he is described as '*son frere, l'ung des filz de monsigneur de Talbot*'.

82. Weightman, *Margaret of York*, pp. 47–59.

83. L.T. Smith, *The Itinerary of John Leland*, parts 6 and 7, London 1907–10, p. 120.

84. Ashdown-Hill, *Eleanor*, pp. 173–74.

85. Bernard André (who wrote for the Tudors, and esteemed the claimant an impostor) said the first Yorkist pretender of Henry VII's reign impersonated Elizabeth Woodville's second son by Edward IV, Richard of Shrewsbury, Duke of York: G. Smith 'Lambert Simnel and the King from Dublin', *Ricardian* 10 (December 1996), pp. 498–536, p. 499.

86. '… there [was] never a new torche but old torches', MS BL Arundel 26, f. 30, quoted in A.F. Sutton & L. Visser-Fuchs, *The Royal Funerals of the House of York at Windsor*, London 2005, p. 73.

10 THE INFANTA AND THE NYGHT CROWE

1. 'The Nyght Crowe' was Cardinal Wolsey's term for Anne Boleyn. Probably it referred to her opportunity to caw into the king's ear at night!
2. This is a reference to Jane Seymour.
3. Those who refer to Henry's 'divorce' of Catherine of Aragon use an erroneous term.
4. Loades, *The Politics of Marriage*, p. 131.
5. For the possible allegation of bigamy in respect of Catherine Howard, see below.
6. Richmond was born in 1519, and his mother only married in 1522.
7. *Letters & Papers*, III part 2, p. 1539.
8. K. Hart, *The Mistresses of Henry VIII*, Stroud 2009, p. 137. Not surprisingly, perhaps, the king and his minions had been very anxious to ensure that this particular allegation received no public airing, and Thomas Cromwell was reportedly furious when they failed, and word of it did leak out.
9. Modern interpretations of the notes left by Henry VIII's physicians do not support the view that the king suffered from syphilis.
10. http://www.independent.co.uk/news/uk/this-britain/the-jousting-accident-that-turned-henry-viii-into-a-tyrant-1670421.html (May 2012).
11. *Inside the Body of Henry VIII*, The History Channel (consulted on the internet, April 2012).
12. A. Sutton & L. Visser-Fuchs, *The Royal Funerals of the House of York at Windsor*, London 2004, pp. 113–24.
13. Henry VIII's younger sister, Mary, Queen of France and Duchess of Suffolk, does, however, seem to have had reddish hair, based on the evidence of two surviving locks of her hair which the present writer has researched: J. Ashdown-Hill, *The Last Days of Richard III*, p. 126.
14. Loades, *The Politics of Marriage*, p. 130.
15. Catholic canons 1060; 1085.2.
16. *los reyes católicos*.
17. Loades, *The Politics of Marriage*, p. 9.
18. J Ashdown-Hill, 'The Lancastrian Claim to the Throne', *Ricardian*, vol. 13 (2003) (pp. 27–38), p. 37.
19. 'Catherine of Aragon is believed to have stayed in the village in 1501 on her way to marry Prince Arthur': http://www.charmouth.com/History.htm (April 2012). 'The Queens Arms, a famous building in the village, was built for an abbot. Catherine of Aragon used it as her residence in 1501'. http://en.wikipedia.org/wiki/Charmouth (April 2012). Forde Abbey was a Cistercian foundation, a little inland from Charmouth. The former 'Queen's Arms' has now been renamed 'The Abbot's House'. http://www.abbotshouse.co.uk/index.php?id=11 (April 2012).
20. Hart, *The Mistresses of Henry VIII*, p. 19.
21. On her wedding day Catherine was one month short of her sixteenth birthday – 16 being the age at which a marriage with a child bride could be consummated (see above). However, her husband Arthur (born 19/20 September 1486) was almost a year younger than she was. Moreover, he was probably sexually inexperienced.
22. Hart, *The Mistresses of Henry VIII*, p. 18. Later, however, Henry VIII tried to retract his statement: *Letters and Papers*, VI, p. 168.

23. Arthur had caught tuberculosis from his father.
24. See above, p. 17.
25. See above, p. 23.
26. The royal pilgrimage took place on 19 January 1511: H M Gillett, *Walsingham*, London 1946, p. 37.
27. Charles was elected emperor in 1519.
28. The relationship probably ended in 1522, when Elizabeth Blount married.
29. The mother of Mary and Anne Boleyn, Lady Elizabeth Howard, was a daughter of the second Howard Duke of Norfolk, and a descendant of Edward I (*see Family Tree 3*).
30. Historians have debated which of the Boleyn girls was the elder, but the point seems to be settled clearly by the fact that Mary's son, Lord Hunsdon, stated explicitly that Mary was older than Anne when he was petitioning Anne's daughter, Elizabeth I, for the reversion of the earldom of Ormonde. If Hunsdon had made a mistake on this point his cousin the queen would obviously have noticed.
31. It is uncertain whether Mary's son, Henry Carey, later Lord Hunsdon (born 4 March 1526), was fathered by the king or by his mother's husband. However, the king's paternity in the case of Lord Hunsdon is even more doubtful than in the case of Hunsdon's sister, Catherine.
32. Anne Boleyn's date of birth is unknown, but she was probably born in about 1500–1501.
33. Like some of the alleged deformities of King Richard III, they may have been later inventions, intended to illustrate and confirm that Anne's underlying personality was essentially evil.
34. 25 January 1533 may possibly have been the date.
35. Archbishop Warham, who had been somewhat equivocal in his policy but who, in the final analysis, had generally been in favour of the *status quo*, had died in August 1532. Cranmer, who was much more inclined to do what the king wanted, was nominated to succeed Warham in October 1532, and the papal bulls for his appointment were finally obtained in March 1533.
36. The embalmer of Catherine's body reported that all her organs were sound with the exception of the heart, which was black. This might possibly have been a secondary symptom of a melanotic carcinoma.
37. The fact that the Anglican Church now sees no impediment to marriage with a deceased sibling's widow(er) might offer a new possible interpretation of the situation, but to apply it retrospectively to the early sixteenth century would be anachronistic.

11 REVIEW OF SECRET AND BIGAMOUS MEDIEVAL ROYAL MARRIAGES

1. The *ODNB* entry on Edmund Beaufort is, however, more circumspect.

12 THE VIRGIN QUEEN

1. The known suitors of Queen Elizabeth, with the dates of their aspiration to her hand, were: 1534 the Duke of Angoulême (third son of Francis I of France); 1544 Prince Philip of Spain (King Philip II); (?)1547 Sir Thomas Seymour; 1553 Edward Courtenay (a descendant of Edward IV and the house of York); 1554 Emanuel Philibert, Duke of Savoy; 1554 Prince Frederick of Denmark; Prince Eric of Sweden; 1556 Don Carlos (son of King Philip II of Spain); 1559 King Philip II of Spain; (?)Sir William Pickering ; 1559 James Hamilton, Earl of Arran; 1559 Henry Fitzalan, Earl of Arundel; 1559 Lord Robert Dudley (later Earl of Leicester); King Eric XVI of Sweden; the Duke of Holstein; 1560 King Charles IX of France; 1560 Henry of France, Duke of Anjou; 1563 Lord Darnley; 1568 Archduke Charles of Austria; 1570 Henry of France, Duke of Anjou; 1572 Francois of France, Duke of Alençon and also later Duke of Anjou (http://www.elizabethan-era.org.uk/suitors-of-queen-elizabeth-i.htm – June 2012). Not all of these suitors were countenanced or seriously considered by Elizabeth herself, however.
2. Philip was the widowed husband of Elizabeth's dead sister – an ominous echo of the relationship of his great-aunt, Catherine of Aragon, with Prince Arthur and Henry VIII.
3. *Monsieur – tout court* – was the traditional form of address for the eldest surviving brother of a reigning king of France. The Duke of Anjou was the brother and heir of King Henri III.
4. http://en.wikipedia.org/wiki/On_Monsieur%27s_Departure (June 2012).
5. The Duke of Anjou died in June 1584.
6. http://www.elizabethan-era.org.uk/teenage-scandal-of-queen-elizabeth-i.htm (June 2012).
7. C. Paul, 'The "Prince Tudor" dilemma: hip thesis, hypothesis or old wives' tale?', *The Oxfordian*, vol. V (2002), pp. 47–69 (p. 48).
8. Paul, 'The "Prince Tudor" dilemma'.
9. Paul, *op. cit.*, pp. 48–49, 53–54.
10. Quoted in Paul, *op. cit.*, p. 56.
11. W. Camden, *The Historie of the Most Renowned and Victorious Princesse Elizabeth, Late Queene of England*, quoted in Paul, *op. cit.*, p. 57. Present writer's emphasis.
12. Both were Elizabeth's cousins on her mother's side. As the daughter of Catherine Carey, Lettice Knollys may also have been descended from Henry VIII.
13. S. Adams, I. Archer & G. W. Bernard, eds., 'A Journall of Matters of State happened from time to time within and withoute the Realme from and before the Death of King Edward the 6th until the Yere 1562', in I. Archer, ed., *Religion, Politics and Society in Sixteenth-Century England*, pp. 35–122, CUP 2003.

13 OLD ROWLEY AND MRS BARLOW

1. Historical Manuscripts Commission, *Bath MSS*, II, pp. 170–171; A. Browning, ed., *English Historical Documents, 1660–1714*, OUP 1953, pp. 119–120.
2. Since the accession to the English throne of his grandfather, James I, in 1603, the kingdoms of England, Scotland and Ireland had shared a common sovereign, but as yet there was no such institution as the United Kingdom.
3. Quoted in B. Masters, *The Mistresses of Charles II*, London 1997, pp. 9–10.

4. Masters, *Mistresses*, p. 24.

5. Officially Anne was in the Netherlands as a maid of honour to Princess Mary, the Princess Royal, elder sister of Charles [II] and James [II], wife of the Prince of Orange and mother of the future King William III.

6. C. Humphery-Smith in P. Beauclerk-Dewar & R. Powell, *Royal Bastards*, Stroud 2008, 2010, p. 264.

7. Their first child, Charles of York, Duke of Cambridge, was born on 22 October 1660 and died on 5 May 1661.

8. Quoted in Masters, *Mistresses*, pp. 11; 15.

9. Anne's father was Sir Edward Hyde, later created first Earl of Clarendon, her mother was Frances, daughter of Sir Thomas Aylesbury.

10. Lucy was descended from Edward I, and was related to Anne Boleyn and Catherine Howard – see below.

11. The use of the word 'condom' is first documented in 1706. The contraceptive is reputed to have been named after a Dr (or Colonel) Condom. This person has not been identified, but the surname (with variant spellings) was current in seventeenth-century England.

12. He is sometimes considered Charles II's eldest child, but in fact the king had earlier bastards; Masters, *Mistresses*, p. 10.

13. Which disease is not specified.

14. She was therefore of approximately the same age as Charles II, who was born on 29 May 1630.

15. T.G. Lamford, *The Defence of Lucy Walter*, Ammanford 2001, p. 5.

16. B.A. Murray, 'Lady Eleanor Butler and John Crowne's The Misery of Civil War', *Ricardian*, vol. 14 (2004), pp. 54–61.

17. Lamford, *Defence*, pp. 204–06.

18. 'Both of whom had sound political reasons for disparaging Lucy in order to discredit her son'. R. Hutton, *Charles the Second, King of England, Scotland and Ireland*, Oxford 1989, p. 25.

19. *ODNB*: R. Clifton, 'Lucy Walter'.

20. Hutton, *Charles the Second*, p. 26.

21. Masters, *Mistresses*, p. 22.

22. Masters, *Mistresses*, p. 21; Lamford, *Defence*, p. 190, citing Clarendon State Papers, vol. 2, p. 346.

23. Anne-Marie-Louise of France, Duchesse de Montpensier, only daughter and heiress of Charles' maternal uncle, Gaston, Duc d'Orléans.

24. Hutton, *Charles the Second*, p. 40.

25. Hutton, *Charles the Second*, p. 26.

26. ODNB, T. Harris, 'Scott [*formerly* Crofts], James, Duke of Monmouth and first Duke of Buccleuch (1649–1685)'.

27. Quoted in Masters, *Mistresses*, p. 14.

28. Masters, *Mistresses*, p. 16.

29. An untrustworthy pamphlet of 1683 gives Monmouth's date of birth as 9 April 1649. This appears to be the only available evidence.

30. When Monmouth became James II's rival for the throne, the latter did all in his power to discredit his nephew.

31. *ODNB*, Harris, 'Monmouth'.

32. Mercurius Politicus, 16 July 1656, published in Lamford, *Defence*, p. 192.

33. For example: 'If seventh sons do things so rare,/In you seven fathers have a share'. http://www.campin.me.uk/Dalkeith/Scotts/Scotts.htm (June 2012).

34. Beauclerk-Dewar & Powell, *Royal Bastards*, p. 36.

35. *ODNB*, Harris, 'Monmouth'.

36. *ODNB*, Harris, 'Monmouth'.

37 Masters, *Mistresses*, p. 31.

38. *ODNB*, Harris, 'Monmouth'.

39. Hutton, *Charles the Second*, p. 77.

40. Princess Mary, wife of the Prince of Orange, and mother of the future English King William III.

41. Letter dated The Hague, 9 November 1654 (*Calendar of the Clarendon State Papers*, vol. 2, p. 419); letter dated The Hague, 20 May 1655, and letter dated Hounslerdike, 21 June 1655 (Lambeth Palace Library MS 645, ff. 14, 26). Extracts published in Lamford, *Defence*, pp. 183–85.

42. 9 November 1654; Masters, *Mistresses*, p. 24.

43. Hutton, *Charles the Second*, p. 96. In many European languages the words 'wife' and 'woman' are identical. See also Masters, *Mistresses*, pp. 24–25.

44. Masters, *Mistresses*, pp. 24–25.

45. Henrietta Catherine of Orange was Princess Mary's sister-in-law. See A. Fraser, *King Charles II*, London 1979, p. 155.

46. Mercurius Politicus, p. 7108, 16 July 1656. Text published in Lamford, *Defence*, p. 192.

47. R. Fergusson, *A Letter to a Person of Honour concerning the 'Black Box'*, London 1680, p. 3.

48. Masters, *Mistresses*, p. 25.

49. Masters, *Mistresses*, p. 23.

50. Masters, *Mistresses*, p. 23.

51. Masters, *Mistresses*, p. 25. (I have been unable to trace the original source. There are letters from O'Neill to Charles in Lambeth Palace Library, but this letter is not among them.)

52. Hutton, *Charles the Second*, p. 126.

53. See, for example, Murray, *op. cit.* (2004). In fact, of course, the two cases were not entirely parallel. For instance Eleanor had actually borne no son by Edward IV – though in the seventeenth century it was thought that she might have done so.

54. Masters, *Mistresses*, p. 29.

55. Fraser, *King Charles II*, pp. 387, 483, n. 19 and illustration between pp. 400–01.

56. Hutton, *Charles the Second*, p. 188.

57. http://www.archive.org/stream/roxburgheballads05chapuoft/roxburgheballad-s05chapuoft_djvu.txt (June 2012).

58. *Mobile* = fickle people, easily swayed.

59. Fergusson, *'Black Box'*, p. 1.

60. Fergusson, *'Black Box'*, p. 8.

61. Walter Montagu Douglas Scott, 1806–1884.

62. Quoted in Masters, *Mistresses*, p. 28.

63. Charles II.

64. Queen Catherine.

65. Monmouth.

14 DR AND MRS THOMSON

1. http://www.lawpack.co.uk/cohabitation/articles/article1585.asp (May 2012).
2. She may have been created Countess of Albestroff by the Holy Roman Emperor Francis of Lorraine, husband of Maria Theresa, and father (*inter alia*) of Queen Marie Antoinette of France. Alternatively the title may have been granted by the Bishop of Metz. See H. Douglas, *Bonnie Prince Charlie in Love*, Stroud 1995, p. 177, citing L. Berry, *The Young Pretender's Mistress*.
3. Douglas, *Bonnie Prince Charlie in Love*, p. 94.
4. http://www.clanmacfarlanegenealogy.info/genealogy/TNGWebsite/getperson. php?personID=I8826&tree=CC (May 2012).
5. Catherine's appointment followed the marriage of the Prince and Princess of Wales, which took place in April 1736.
6. https://www.history.ac.uk:443/resources/office/augusta-alpha (May 2012). Walpole's letters were written on 9 August 1784 to Mann, and on 26 August 1784 to Lady Ossory.
7. Douglas, *Bonnie Prince Charlie in Love*, p. 164.
8. James' 'reign' lasted for 64 years and 108 days – more than eight months longer than the reign of Queen Victoria (who is otherwise the longest-serving British monarch to date).
9. In 1771 Louise's sister, Caroline of Stolberg-Gedern, had married Charles' cousin, Charles FitzJames Stuart, fourth Duke of Berwick.
10. A.F. Steuart, 'Last Days of Clementina Walkinshaw', *The Scottish Historical Review*, vol. XVII, no. 67, April 1920, pp. 249–51 (p. 250).
11. Douglas, *Bonnie Prince Charlie in Love*, p. 179.
12. *ODNB*, H. Douglas, 'Walkinshaw, Clementine'.
13. Douglas, *Bonnie Prince Charlie in Love*, p. 182.
14. *ODNB*, Douglas, 'Walkinshaw, Clementine'.
15. Douglas, *Bonnie Prince Charlie in Love*, p. 182.

16 QUEEN HANNAH AND PRINCESS OLIVE

1. Quoted in W J Thoms, *Hannah Lightfoot; Queen Charlotte & the Chevalier d'Eon; Dr Wilmot's Polish Princess*, London 1867, p. 25.
2. *Monthly Magazine*, April 1821, vol. li, p. 523, reprinted in Thoms, *Hannah*, p. 4.
3. *Monthly Magazine*, July 1821, vol. li, p. 532, reprinted in Thoms, *Hannah*, p. 5.
4. *Ibid.*
5. *Monthly Magazine*, October 1821, p. 197, reprinted in Thoms, *Hannah*, p. 7.
6. National Archives, RG 7_272.
7. *Monthly Magazine*, July 1821, vol. li, p. 532, reprinted in Thoms, *Hannah*, p. 6.
8. M. Macnair, *Olive Princess of Cumberland (1772–1834) a Royal Scandal*, Studley 2011, p. 16.
9. Macnair, *Olive*, pp. 14, 52.
10. Macnair, *Olive*, p. 16.
11. *Monthly Magazine*, July 1821, vol. li, p. 532, reprinted in Thoms, *Hannah*, p. 6. An alternative account described Hannah as short and very pretty (Thoms, p. 8).
12. Thoms, *Hannah*, p. 10.

13. Thoms, *Hannah*, p. 12.

14. Macnair, *Olive*, pp. 95–96, 105 and figure 4.

15. Macnair, *Olive*, p. 17, citing [Anonymous], 'An Historical Fragment relative to her late Majesty Queen Caroline', 1824.

16. Macnair, *Olive*, pp. 187–88, citing BM, Egerton MSS 1719, f.81.

17. Thoms, *Hannah*, p. 35.

18. http://yourarchives.nationalarchives.gov.uk/index.php?title=Princess_Olive_and_the_Letters_of_Junius (June 2012).

17 PRINCESS FITZ

1. Mary Anne, Walter, John, Charles, Henry, Edward and Barbara. Some modern writers refer to only six children, but seven seems the correct total, though one son – Edward – apparently died young. J. Munson, *Maria Fitzherbert the Secret Wife of George IV*, London 2001, 2002, pp. 16–17.

2. Munson, *Maria Fitzherbert*, p. 16.

3. One of Mary (Maria)'s great great grandmothers was Grace Turville, daughter of Henry Turville. Henry's relative, Francis Fortescue-Turville of Husbands Bosworth, married 'Lady' Barbara Talbot, sister of the soi-disant sixteenth Earl of Shrewsbury (J. Ashdown-Hill, 'The Bosworth Crucifix', *Transactions of the Leicestershire Archaeological & Historical Society* vol. 78 (2004), pp. 83–96.

4. Her ancestry includes members of a Car(e)y family.

5. http://archive.catholicherald.co.uk/article/5th-july-1985/7/the-fitzherrerts-five (June 2012).

6. E. Ponsonby, Earl of Bessborough, ed., *Georgiana: Extracts From the Correspondence of Georgiana, Duchess of Devonshire*, London 1955, p. 87.

7. Quoted in C. Hibbert, *George IV*, vol. 1: *Prince of Wales*, Harlow 1972, p. 51.

8. Off Park Lane, in London.

9. A. Aspinall, ed., *The Correspondence of George, Prince of Wales, 1770–1812*, 8 vols. London 1963–71, vol. 1, frontispiece. The document is now preserved in the Royal Library at Windsor.

10. The daughter of his father's sister.

11. Maria had initially planned to seek the advice of Pope Pius VI, but he had died on 29 August 1799, before the case could be put to him. Owing to the very difficult political situation in Europe, there had then been a delay until his successor was elected, in the following March.

12. S. Leslie, ed., *The Letters of Mrs Fitzherbert*, London 1940, p. 133.

13. http://archive.catholicherald.co.uk/article/5th-july-1985/7/the-fitzherrerts-five (June 2012).

14. C. Langdale, *Memoirs of Mrs Fitzherbert*, London 1856, p. 138.

18 MRS BROWN

1. H, L.F. Gale, son of a Queen's Messenger, quoted in R. Lamont-Brown, *John Brown*, Stroud 2000, 2002, p. 30.

2. Quoted in Lamont-Brown, *John Brown*, p. 48.

3. Letter from Queen Victoria to her eldest daughter, the Crown-Princess of Prussia, quoted in Lamont-Brown, *John Brown*, p. 60.
4. Lamont-Brown, *John Brown*, pp. 60–61, quoting Cullen, *Empress Brown*, p. 61.
5. Quoted in Lamont-Brown, *John Brown*, p. 60.
6. The Duchess of York & B. Stoney, *Victoria and Albert: Life at Osborne House*, London 1991, pp. 25–26.
7. *Punch*, 7 July 1866, reproduced in *New York Herald Tribune*, 3 October 1937, p. 9, http://archive.lib.msu.edu/DMC/tribune/trib10031937/trib10031937009.pdf (March 2012).
8. http://en.wikipedia.org/wiki/John_Brown_(servant) (March 2012).
9. Letter from Queen Victoria to Viscount Cranbrook, quoted in http://en.wikipedia.org/wiki/John_Brown_(servant) (March 2012).
10 http://www.famouspeople.co.uk/q/queenvictoria.html 'Widowhood' (March 2012); http://en.wikipedia.org/wiki/John_Brown_(servant) (March 2012), quoting Lamont-Brown, Raymond (2003). 'Queen Victoria's "secret marriage"', *Contemporary Review*; http://en.wikipedia.org/wiki/Queen_Victoria 'Death and Succession' (March 2012).

19 MURDERS IN WHITECHAPEL AND MYSTERIES IN MALTA

1. Letter cited in R. Callender Smith, 'The Missing Witness? George V, Competence and Compellability and the Criminal Libel Trial of Edward Frederick Mylius', 26 March 2012 (p. 2, fn. 5). Available at SSRN: http://ssrn.com/abstract=2037498 Quoted in Callender Smith, 'The Missing Witness?', p. 2
2. 'Libeller of King gets Year in Jail', *New York Times*, 2 February 1911. 'Sanctified Bigamy' as subsequently quoted in the *Evening Post*, New Zealand, 14 Poutûterangi [*March*] 1911.
3. *Ibid.*
4. *Evening Post*, New Zealand, 14 Poutûterangi [*March*] 1911.
5. *Ibid.*
6. *Ibid.*
7. Callender Smith, 'The Missing Witness?', pp. 33–34. In 1898, at the time of the ball, George [V] was not yet the Prince of Wales, since both his father and his elder brother were still alive. He was simply 'Prince George'. It was not until 1892 that his grandmother created him Duke of York.
8. http://www.maltagenealogy.com/libro%20d'oro/fiddien.html (June 2012).
9. Email from Charles Said-Vassallo, 7 October 2012.
10. I am enormously grateful to Robert Galea-Naudi for searching (albeit with only limited success) the Maltese Public Registry on my behalf for records of Laura Culme-Seymour's marriage and death, and for supplying a photograph of the grave which bears her name at Ta' Braxia (see below).
11. See Plate 32.
12. Callender Smith, 'The Missing Witness?', pp. 3, 4.
13. Callender Smith, 'The Missing Witness?', p. 5 and note 15.
14. Callender Smith, 'The Missing Witness?', p. 33.

APPENDIX 3: ORIGINAL DOCUMENTS

1. Leicestershire Record Office B. R. II/3/3: R.A. Griffiths, 'Queen Katherine de Valois and a missing statute of the realm', *Law Quarterly Review*, 93 (1977), 257–58.

2. *RP*, vol. 6, pp. 240–42.

3. http://www.british-history.ac.uk/register.aspx (May 2012).

4. *Ibid.*

5. H. Gee & W.J. Harvey, eds., *Documents Illustrative of English Church History*, London 1914, pp. 232–42.

6. G.B. Adams & H.M. Stephens, eds., *Select Documents of English Constitutional History*, New York 1914, pp. 264–67.

7. MS. Petyt 47, f. 317.

8. http://australianpolitics.com/democracy-and-politics/act-of-settlement-1701 (June 2012).

9. http://regencyredingote.wordpress.com/2008/12/19/marriage-lines-really-are-lines/ (June 2012).

10. Scotland was exempt from the provisions of this act.

11. http://www.legislation.gov.uk/apgb/Geo3/12/11/contents (June 2012).

BIBLIOGRAPHY

ORIGINAL DOCUMENTS

BL, MS Royal 14 C. vii, f. 124v
Corpus Christi College, Cambridge, Parker Library, Ms. XXXI. 121
Ipswich Record Office, HA 246/B2/498
Lambeth Palace Library MS 645, ff. 14, 26
Leicestershire Record Office B. R. II/3/3
London Lower Temple Library, MS. Petyt 47, f. 317
The National Archives, PRO C 49/16/11
Warwickshire County Record Office, L 1/79
Warwickshire County Record Office, L 1/82
Warwickshire County Record Office, L 1/85

BOOKS

Adams, G.B. & Stephens H.M., eds., *Select Documents of English Constitutional History*,
    New York 1914
Adams, N. and Donahue, C., eds., *Select Cases from the Ecclesiastical Courts of the Province
    of Canterbury, c.1200–1301*, London 1981
Anderson, D. et al., *Exploring the Middle Ages*, New York 2006
Armstrong, C.A.J., ed., Mancini D, *The Usurpation of Richard the Third*, Gloucester 1989
Ashdown-Hill, J., *Eleanor the Secret Queen*, Stroud 2009
Ashdown-Hill, J., *Mediaeval Colchester's Lost Landmarks*, Derby 2009
Ashdown-Hill, J., *Richard III's 'Beloved Cousyn': John Howard and the House of York*,
    Stroud 2009
Ashdown-Hill, J., *The Last Days of Richard III*, Stroud 2010
Aspinall, A., ed., *The Correspondence of George, Prince of Wales, 1770–1812*, 8 vols. London
    1963–71
Beauclerk-Dewar, P. and Powell, R., *Royal Bastards*, Stroud 2008, 2010

Beaune, H., & d'Arbaumont, J., *Mémoires d'Olivier de la Marche*, 4 vols., Paris 1883–88, vol. 3

Brooke, C.N.L., *The Medieval Idea of Marriage*, Oxford 1989

Browning, A., ed., *English Historical Documents, 1660–1714*, OUP 1953

Buck, G. – see Kincaid

Campbell, L.B., ed., *The Mirror for Magistrates*, New York 1960

Calendar of the Clarendon State Papers, vol. 2

Calendar of Patent Rolls 1436–1441

Calendar of Patent Rolls 1461–1467

Calendar of Patent Rolls 1476–1485

Carson, A., *Richard III: The Maligned King*, The History Press, Stroud 2008, 2012

Commynes, P. de, *Memoires* – see Jones

Cook, M., Mills, R., Trumbach, R. and Cocks, H.G., *A Gay History of Britain*, Oxford 2007

Coss, P., *The Lady in Medieval England 1000–1500*, Stroud 1998

David, S., *Prince of Pleasure*, London 1998

di Simplicio, O., *Autunno della stregoneria*, Bologna 2005

Douglas, H., *Bonnie Prince Charlie in Love*, Stroud 1995

Ellis, H., ed., Fabyan, R., *New Chronicles of England and France, 1516*, London 1811

Ellis, H., *Original Letters Illustrative of English History*, London 1827 vol. 1

Emden, A.B., *A biographical register of the University of Oxford to A.D. 1500: vol. 3. P.-Z.*, Oxford 1959

Fabyan's *Chronicle* – *see* Ellis

Fergusson, R., *A Letter to a Person of Honour concerning the 'Black Box'*, London 1680

Fraser, A., *King Charles II*, London 1979

Gairdner, J., ed., *The Historical Collections of a Citizen of London in the Fifteenth Century*, CS, new series, vol. 17, 1876

Gairdner, J., *History of the Life and Reign of Richard the Third*, Cambridge 1898

Gee, H. & Harvey, W.J., eds., *Documents Illustrative of English Church History*, London 1914

Giles, J.A., ed., *Incerti scriptoris chronicon Angliae de regnis trium regum Lancastrensium*, London 1848, part 4

Gillett, H.M, *Walsingham*, London 1946

Given-Wilson, C., ed., *The Chronicles of Adam of Usk 1377–1421*, Oxford 1997

Harris, B. J., *English Aristocratic Women, 1450–1550*, Oxford 2010

Hart, K., *The Mistresses of Henry VIII*, Stroud 2009

Hay, F.G., *Lady of the Sun: The Life and Times of Alice Perrers*, London 1966

Hibbert, C., *George IV*, vol. 1: *Prince of Wales*, Harlow 1972

Historical Manuscripts Commission, *Bath MSS*, II

Hutton, R., *Charles the Second, King of England, Scotland and Ireland*, Oxford 1989

James VI of Scotland, *Newes from Scotland*, London 1591

Jones, M., ed., De Commynes, P., *Memoires*, Harmondsworth 1972

Kendall, P.M., *Richard the Third*, London 1973

Kincaid, A. ed., Buck, G., *The History of King Richard the Third*, Stroud 1979

Lamford, T.G., *The Defence of Lucy Walter*, Ammanford 2001

Lamont-Brown, R., *John Brown*, Stroud, 2000, 2007

Langdale, C., *Memoirs of Mrs Fitzherbert ; with an Account of Her Marriage with HRH the Prince of Wales*, London 1856

Leslie, S., ed., *The letters of Mrs Fitzherbert and connected papers*, London 1940

Letters and Papers, Foreign and Domestic: Henry VIII, vols. III (part 2); VI; X

Loades, D., *The Politics of Marriage: Henry VIII and his Queens*, Stroud 1994

Lucraft, J., *Katherine Swynford the History of a Medieval Mistress*, Stroud 2006, 2010

Macnair, M., *Olive Princess of Cumberland (1772–1834) a Royal Scandal*, Studley 2011

Mancini – *see* Armstrong

Masters, B., *The Mistresses of Charles II*, London 1997

Maxwell-Lyte, H.C., ed., *The Registers of Robert Stillington, Bishop of Bath and Wells 1466–1491 and Richard Fox, Bishop of Bath and Wells 1492–1494*, Somerset Record Society 1937

Morgan, O. and Wakeman, T., *Notes on the Architecture and History of Caldicot Castle, Monmouthshire*, Newport 1854

Munson, J., *Maria Fitzherbert the Secret Wife of George IV*, London 2001, 2002

Oxford Dictionary of National Biography – *see* websites

Pedersen, F., *Marriage Disputes in Medieval England*, London 2000

Piniski, P., *The Stuarts' Last Secret, missing heirs of Bonnie Prince Charlie*, East Linton 2002

Ponsonby, E., Earl of Bessborough, ed., *Georgiana: Extracts from the Correspondence of Georgiana, Duchess of Devonshire*, London 1955

Ridley, J., *Henry VIII*, London 1984

Ridley, J., *The Love Letters of Henry VIII*, London 1988

Rotuli Parliamentorum, vol. 6

Scarisbrick, J.J., *Henry VIII*, London 1968 (1976)

Smith, L.T., *The Itinerary of John Leland*, parts 6 and 7, London 1907–10

Sury, G.G., ed., *Bayern Straubing Hennegau: la Maison de Bavière en Hainaut, XIVe – XVe s.*, Bruxelles 2010

Stone, L., *The Family, Sex and Marriage in England 1500–1800*, Harmondsworth 1979, 1990

Sutton, A., and Visser-Fuchs, L., *The Royal Funerals of the House of York at Windsor*, London 2005

Taylor, J. & Childs, W.R., eds., & Watkiss, L. trans., *The St Albans Chronicle: The Chronica Maiora of Thomas Walsingham 1376–1394*, Oxford 2002

The St Albans Chronicle – see Taylor

Thoms, W.J., *Hannah Lightfoot; Queen Charlotte & the Chevalier d'Eon; Dr Wilmot's Polish Princess*, London 1867

Tooke, J.H., *A Letter to a Friend on the Reported Marriage of the Prince of Wales*, London 1787

Wymans, G., *Inventaire analytique du chartrier de la Trésorerie des comtes de Hainaut*, Bruxelles, 1985

Walsingham, T., *The St Albans Chronicle* – see Taylor

York, the Duchess of, & Stoney, B., *Victoria and Albert: Life at Osborne House*, London 1991

ARTICLES & PAPERS

Adams, S., Archer, I. & Bernard, G.W., eds., 'A Journall of Matters of State happened from time to time within and withoute the Realme from and before the Death of King Edward the 6th until the Yere 1562', in Archer, I., ed., *Religion, Politics and Society in Sixteenth-Century England*, pp. 35–122, CUP 2003

Ashdown-Hill, J., 'The Elusive Mistress: Elizabeth Lucy and her Family', *The Ricardian*, vol. 11 (1997–99), pp. 490–505

Ashdown-Hill, J., 'The Inquisition *Post Mortem* of Eleanor Talbot, Lady Butler, 1468', *The Ricardian* vol. 12 (2000–02), pp. 563–73

Ashdown-Hill, J., 'The Lancastrian Claim to the Throne', *The Ricardian*, vol. 13 (2003), pp. 27–38

Ashdown-Hill, J., 'The Bosworth Crucifix', *Transactions of the Leicestershire Archaeological & Historical Society*, vol. 78 (2004), pp. 83–96

Ashdown-Hill, J. & Carson, A., 'The Execution of the Earl of Desmond', *The Ricardian*, vol. 15, 2005, pp. 70–93

Ashdown-Hill, J., 'Lady Eleanor Talbot: New Evidence; New Answers; New Questions', *Ricardian* vol. 16 2006, 113–32

Ashdown-Hill, J., ' "Al ful of fresshe floures whyte and reede": The Jewellery of Margaret of York and Its Meaning', *The Ricardian* vol. 17 (2007), 56–72

Bothwell, J., 'The Management of Position: Alice Perrers, Edward III and the Creation of a Landed Estate, 1362–1377', *Journal of Medieval History*, vol. 24 (1998), pp. 31–51

Callender Smith, R., 'The Missing Witness? George V, Competence and Compellability and the Criminal Libel Trial of Edward Frederick Mylius', 26 March 2012. Available at SSRN: http://ssrn.com/abstract=2037498

Griffiths, R.A., 'Queen Katherine de Valois and a missing statute of the realm', *Law Quarterly Review*, 93 (1977), 257–8.

Hampton, W.E., 'A further Account of Robert Stillington', *The Ricardian*, vol. 4 (Sept. 1976), pp. 24–27

Helmholz, R.H., 'The Sons of Edward IV: A Canonical Assessment of the Claim that they were Illegitimate', in Hammond, P.W., ed., *Richard III: Loyalty Lordship and Law*, London, 1986, pp. 91–103.

Maddern, P., 'Honour among the Pastons: gender and integrity in fifteenth-century English provincial society', *Journal of Medieval History*, 14 (1988) pp. 357–371

Mowat, A.J, 'Robert Stillington', *The Ricardian*, vol. 4 (June 1976), pp. 23–28

Murray, B.A., 'Lady Eleanor Butler and John Crowne's The Misery of Civil War', *The Ricardian*, vol. 14 (2004), pp. 54–61

ODNB – *see* Websites

Ormrod, W.M., 'Alice Perrrers and John Salisbury' – *see* http://ehr.oxfordjournals.org/content/CXXIII/501/379.full

Paul, C., 'The "Prince Tudor" dilemma: Hip Thesis, Hypothesis or Old Wives' Tale?', *The Oxfordian*, vol. V (2002), pp. 47–69

Smith, G., 'Lambert Simnel and the King from Dublin', *The Ricardian*, vol. 10 (December 1996), pp. 498–536

Steuart, A.F., 'Last Days of Clementina Walkinshaw', *The Scottish Historical Review*, vol. XVII, no. 67, April 1920, pp. 249–51

NEWSPAPERS

The Sydney Morning Herald, NSW, Wednesday 13 June 1866

The New York Times, 2 February 1911

Evening Post, New Zealand, 14 Poutūterangi [*March*] 1911

Unpublished Sources

Matteoni, F., *Blood Beliefs in Early Modern Europe*, unpublished PhD thesis, University of Hertfordshire 2009

Websites

Catholic Encyclopedia, http://www.newadvent.org/cathen/04264a.htm (consulted February 2012)

http://archive.catholicherald.co.uk/article/5th-july-1985/7/the-fitzherrerts-five (consulted June 2012) http://archive.lib.msu.edu/DMC/tribune/trib10031937/trib10031937009.pdf (consulted March 2012)

http://australianpolitics.com/democracy-and-politics/act-of-settlement-1701 (consulted June 2012)

http://blog.theukweddingshows.co.uk/wedding-industry/2008-uk-wedding-industry-statistics-43/ (consulted January 2012)

http://chschaucer.wetpaint.com/page/The+Wife+of+Bath+Translation (consulted January 2012)

http://dictionary.reference.com/browse/marriage (consulted January 2012).

http://dictionary.reference.com/browse/mistress (consulted February 2012)

http://en.wikipedia.org/wiki/Adam_FitzRoy (consulted February 2012)

http://en.wikipedia.org/wiki/Arthur_I,_Duke_of_Brittany (consulted June 2012)

http://en.wikipedia.org/wiki/Charmouth (consulted April 2012) http://en.wikipedia.org/wiki/John_Brown_(servant) (consulted March 2012)

http://en.wikipedia.org/wiki/John,_King_of_England (consulted February 2012)

http://en.wikipedia.org/wiki/Margery_Jourdemayne,_%22the_Witch_of_Eye%22 (consulted April 2012)

http://en.wikipedia.org/wiki/Marriage (consulted January 2012)

http://en.wikipedia.org/wiki/On_Monsieur%27s_Departure (consulted June 2012)

http://en.wikipedia.org/wiki/Queen_Victoria (consulted March 2012)

http://en.wikipedia.org/wiki/Richard_I_of_England (consulted January 2012)

http://en.wikipedia.org/wiki/Robert,_1st_Earl_of_Gloucester (consulted February 2012)

http://ehr.oxfordjournals.org/content/CXXIII/501/379.full (Ormrod W M, 'Alice Perrrers and John Salisbury', consulted February 2012)

http://gypsymagicspells.blogspot.com/2011/06/medieval-fish-spell-for-love.html (consulted April 2012) http://oxforddictionaries.com/definition/marriage?q=marriage (consulted January 2012).

http://oxforddictionaries.com/definition/mistress?q=mistress (consulted February 2012)

http://regencyredingote.wordpress.com/2008/12/19/marriage-lines-really-are-lines/ (consulted June 2012)

http://theroyaluniverse.com/royal-witches/ (consulted March 2012)

http://thewriteplaceatthewritetime.org/explorationoftheme.html (consulted April 2012)

http://website.lineone.net/~stephaniebidmead/ (consulted July 2012)

http://www.abbotshouse.co.uk/index.php?id=11 (consulted April 2012)

http://www.archive.org/stream/roxburgheballads05chapuoft/roxburgheballad-s05chapuoft_djvu.txt (consulted June 2012) http://www.bbc.co.uk/news/magazine-12744146 (consulted January 2012)

http://www.british-history.ac.uk/register.aspx (consulted May 2012)

http://www.campin.me.uk/Dalkeith/Scotts/Scotts.htm (consulted June 2012)

http://www.charmouth.com/History.htm (consulted April 2012)

http://www.clanmacfarlanegenealogy.info/genealogy/TNGWebsite/getperson.
php?personID=I8826&tree=CC (consulted May 2012)

http://www.elizabethan-era.org.uk/suitors-of-queen-elizabeth-i.htm (consulted June 2012)

http://www.elizabethan-era.org.uk/teenage-scandal-of-queen-elizabeth-i.htm
(consulted June 2012)

http://www.famouspeople.co.uk/q/queenvictoria.html (consulted March 2012)

http://www.geni.com/people/Ranulf-de-Blundeville-4th-Earl-of-
Chester/6000000002043244300 (consulted June 2012)

https://www.history.ac.uk:443/resources/office/augusta-alpha (consulted May 2012)

    http://www.independent.co.uk/news/uk/this-britain/the-jousting-accident-that-
turned-henry-viii-into-a-tyrant-1670421.html (consulted May 2012)

http://www.lawpack.co.uk/cohabitation/articles/article1585.asp (consulted May 2012)

http://www.legislation.gov.uk/apgb/Geo3/12/11/contents (consulted June 2012)

http://www.maltagenealogy.com/libro%20d'oro/fiddien.html (consulted June 2012)

http://www.telegraph.co.uk/news/uknews/1579006/Abbey-body-identified-as-
gay-lover-of-Edward-II.html (consulted February 2012) http://yourarchives.
nationalarchives.gov.uk/index.php?title=Princess_Olive_and_the_Letters_of_Junius
(consulted June 2012)

Oxford Dictionary of National Biography online

Clifton, R., 'Lucy Walter' (consulted June 2012)

Douglas, H., 'Walkinshaw, Clementine' (consulted June 2012)

Griffiths, R.A., 'Tudor, Owen' (consulted March 2012)

Harris, T., Scott [formerly Crofts], James, Duke of Monmouth and first Duke of
Buccleuch (1649–1685)' (consulted May 2012)

Hicks, M., 'Elizabeth, née Woodville' (consulted March 2012)

Jones, M., 'Catherine of Valois' (consulted March 2012)

Richmond, C., 'Edmund Beaufort, 1st Duke of Somerset' (consulted May 2012)

FILMS & DOCUMENTARIES

Le Retour de Martin Guerre

Inside the Body of Henry VIII, The History Channel (consulted on the internet, April 2012)

NOVELS, PLAYS, &C

Christie, A., *The Moving Finger*, London 1943, 2002

Shakespeare, W., *Henry VI*

INDEX

Controversial relationships are expressed by question marks
Monarchs are of England unless otherwise identified